Germany and the Middle East

Germany and the Middle East
From Kaiser Wilhelm II to Angela Merkel

ROLF STEININGER

berghahn
NEW YORK · OXFORD
www.berghahnbooks.com

Published in 2019 by
Berghahn Books
www.berghahnbooks.com

English-language edition
© 2019, 2026 Rolf Steininger
First paperback edition published in 2026

German-language edition
© 2015 Lau Verlag & Handel KG

Originally published in German as
Deutschland und der Nahe Osten: Von Kaiser Wilhelms Orientreise 1898 bis zur Gegenwart
in 2015

All rights reserved.
Except for the quotation of short passages
for the purposes of criticism and review, no part of this book
may be reproduced in any form or by any means, electronic or
mechanical, including photocopying, recording, or any information
storage and retrieval system now known or to be invented,
without written permission of the publisher.

Library of Congress Cataloging-in-Publication Data

A C.I.P. cataloging record is available from the Library of Congress

British Library Cataloguing in Publication Data

A catalogue record for this book is available from the British Library

EU GPSR Authorized Representative
LOGOS EUROPE, 9 rue Nicolas Poussin, 17000, LA ROCHELLE, France
Email: Contact@logoseurope.eu

ISBN 978-1-78920-038-6 hardback
ISBN 978-1-83695-384-5 paperback
ISBN 978-1-83695-385-2 epub
ISBN 978-1-78920-039-3 web pdf

https://doi.org/10.3167/9781789200386

Contents

List of Illustrations	vi
List of Abbreviations	viii
Chronology	x
Introduction to the English Edition	1
Chapter 1 Before the First World War, 1898–1914	6
Chapter 2 During the First World War	13
Chapter 3 Weimar and the Third Reich, 1918–1939	30
Chapter 4 During the Second World War	47
Chapter 5 From the Founding of the Federal Republic to the Establishment of Diplomatic Relations with Israel, 1949–1965	59
Chapter 6 From the Six-Day War to Reunification, 1967–1990	108
Chapter 7 From Reunification to the Present	150
Conclusion	158
Epilogue to the English Edition	161
Selected Bibliography	162
Index	168

Illustrations

1.1	Kaiser Wilhelm II in Damascus	8
1.2	The Jaffa Gate in 1903	9
1.3	The Wailing Wall in 1910	11
2.1	General Allenby with 'Lawrence of Arabia' and Emir Abdullah	22
3.1	British soldiers in front of the Damascus Gate	32
3.2	British soldiers in the Jewish Quarter of Jerusalem	33
3.3	Arabic pamphlet to boycott Jewish goods	35
3.4	The German colony in Haifa, 1934	37
3.5	Scene on a Haifa street	39
3.6	The Jaffa Gate	41
3.7	General strike in Jerusalem	42
3.8	British soldiers protecting Government House in Jaffa	44
4.1	Meeting between Adolf Hitler and the Grand Mufti of Jerusalem, 1941	51
5.1	Jerusalem, ca. 1949	61
5.2	Jewish celebrations in Vienna after the UN decision to divide Palestine	61
5.3	Proclamation of the new state of Israel	62
5.4	The secretary general of the Arab League proclaims a state of war	62
5.5 and 5.6	Transfer of the Herzl coffin from Vienna to Israel	63
5.7	Herzl's grave on Mount Herzl in Jerusalem	64

5.8	Protests in Jerusalem against West Germany	64
5.9	Konrad Adenauer and Nahum Goldmann	65
5.10	Gamal Abdel Nasser	79
5.11	Israeli soldiers near El Arish on their way to the Suez Canal	80
5.12	General Moshe Dayan with Brigadier-General Assaf Simhoni and Colonel Avraham Yaffe	80
5.13	From the Suez Canal back to the Negev, 1957	81
5.14	Lowering the Israeli flag, 1957	82
5.15	Theodor Heuss in Israel	86
5.16	Franz Josef Strauß and Shimon Peres	87
5.17	Ambassador Rolf Pauls	92
5.18	Rainer Barzel in Israel	96
5.19	Konrad Adenauer and David Ben-Gurion	98
6.1	Beginning of the Six-Day War, 5 June 1967	109
6.2	'Motta' Gur, paratroop commander, overlooking the Old City and Temple Mount of Jerusalem	110
6.3	Israeli paratroopers beside the Wailing Wall in East Jerusalem	111
6.4	Major-General Uzi Narkiss, Defence Minister Moshe Dayan, and Chief of Staff Yitzhak Rabin entering the Old City of Jerusalem through the Lion's Gate	113
6.5	Arab families living close to the Wailing Wall are forcibly removed from their homes	115
6.6	Israel's prime minister, Golda Meir, welcomes West German chancellor, Willy Brandt	125
6.7	Protests against Willy Brandt in Israel	126
6.8	The Yom Kippur War	128
6.9	Yitzhak Rabin in Bonn	140
6.10	Helmut Kohl in Jerusalem	144
7.1	A development project in Palestine financed by Germany	152
7.2	Angela Merkel in Jerusalem	156

Abbreviations

AA	Auswärtiges Amt (German Foreign Office)
AAPD	*Akten zur Auswärtigen Politik der Bundesrepublik Deutschland*; Edition of Documents from the AA: Institut für Zeitgeschichte, ed. on behalf of the Auswärtiges Amt (Munich: Oldenbourg, 1994–2014).
ABC	Atomic, biological, chemical weapon Bi-Zone, 1947–1949, Union of British and American Zones in Germany
AMAN	Military Intelligence Directorate (Israel)
CDU	Christlich Demokratische Union (German party)
CPSU	Communist Party of the Soviet Union
CSCE	Conference on Security and Cooperation in Europe
CSU	Christlich Soziale Union (German party)
DEFCON	Defense Condition
DM	Deutsche Mark
DP	Displaced Person
EEC	European Economic Community
EU	European Union
FAZ	*Frankfurter Allgemeine Zeitung*
FDP	Freie Demokratische Partei (German party)
FOIA	Freedom of Information Act
FRUS	*Foreign Relations of the United States*

GDR	German Democratic Republic
IDF	Israeli Defense
k.u.k.	kaiserliche und königliche Truppen (imperial and royal army)
MGZ	*Militärgeschichtliche Zeitschrift*
NATO	North Atlantic Treaty Organization
NS	National Socialist
NSAP	National Socialist Arab Party
NSDAP	Nationalsozialistische deutsche Arbeiterpartei
OKW	Oberkommando der Wehrmacht (High Command of the Wehrmacht, the German Armed Forces)
PLO	Palestine Liberation Organization
QED	quod erat demonstrandum (what was to be demonstrated)
SPD	Sozialdemokratische Partei Deutschlands (German party)
UAR	United Arab Republic: union between Syria and Egypt from 1958 to 1961. Egypt continued to be known officially as the UAR until 1972.
UN(O)	United Nations (Organization)
US	United States (of America)
VAR	Vereinigte Arabische Republik (= UAR)

Chronology

1898
11 October –
26 November
Kaiser Wilhelm II's Oriental journey; three encounters with Theodor Herzl.

1902
16 January
Work on Baghdad Railway begins.

1914–1918
First World War; an alliance between the Ottoman Empire and the German Reich; significant military involvement on the front in Palestine, Mesopotamia and Gallipoli.

1914
2 August
Secret treaty between the Ottoman Empire and the German Reich.

October
Memorandum of Max Oppenheim for 'Revolutionizing the Islamic territories of our enemies'.

12 November
The sultan calls for a Jihad (Holy War).

1914/15
Genocide of the Armenians.

1917
2 November
The Balfour Declaration: the British government supports the establishment of a 'national home' for Jews in Palestine.

9 December
General Allenby seizes Jerusalem without a fight.

1918
30 October
The Ottoman Empire surrenders.

Chronology

1921	The British approve the return of German settlers – the Templars – to Palestine.
1924 December	Reopening of the German Consulate General in Jerusalem.
1933 31 March	The Grand Mufti of Jerusalem offers his services in the fight against the Jews in Palestine.
1936–1939	Arab revolt against the British and the Jews in Palestine, led by the Grand Mufti.
1937 July	The British Peel Commission recommends the division of Palestine. The Grand Mufti again seeks contact with the German Reich and flees to Baghdad in 1939.
1940 25 July	Second Memorandum by Max Oppenheim.
1941 1 April	Pro-German coup d'état in Baghdad. German help comes too late.
1 June	British take back Baghdad; the rebels flee to Germany.
28 November	Meeting between Hitler and the Grand Mufti in Berlin.
1945 March	Founding of the Arab League.
1948 14 May	Founding of the State of Israel.
1949 23 May	Founding of the Federal Republic of Germany.
1951 13 May	Egypt is the first Arab country to declare that the state of war with Germany is ended.

1952
10 September — In Luxembourg, the signing of the reparations agreement between Israel and the Federal Republic; it was ratified by the Bundestag on 18 March 1953, despite massive Arab protests.

1956
October/November — Suez War. Adenauer supports France and travels to Paris on 6 November 1956. Beginning in 1957, huge secret arms deliveries to Israel from Bonn.

1960
14 March — Meeting between Ben Gurion and Adenauer in New York.

1964
End of year — Bonn's tank deal with Israel is exposed; East German leader Walter Ulbricht is invited to Egypt by Egyptian president Nasser.

1965
7 March — The German Federal Government announces the establishment of diplomatic relations with Israel.

12 May — Official establishment of the relationship. In response, ten Arab countries break off diplomatic relations with Bonn. In the wake of Bonn's 'Ostpolitik' and its recognition of the GDR as a second German state, there was a renewal of relations by 1972/73.

1967
5–10 June — Six-Day War. Crushing defeat of the Arabs.

1972
5 September — Attack on the Israeli Olympic team in Munich by Palestinian terrorists.

1973
6–25 October — Yom Kippur War.

1974
6 November — Five-point plan for the Middle East conflict by the EC. It becomes the basic principle of Germany's Middle East policy.

1977
20 November Historic visit of Egypt's president Sadat to Jerusalem.

1978
September 17 Camp David Agreement; criticized by German chancellor Helmut Schmidt.

1979
26 March Peace Treaty between Israel and Egypt signed in Washington.

1981
6 October Egypt's president Sadat is assassinated.

1989
9 November Fall of the Berlin Wall.

1991
17 January –
28 February Gulf War, Operation Desert Storm.

1991
3 October German reunification.

1993
13 September Signing of the 'Oslo Agreement' in Washington between Israel and the PLO.

1995
4 November Israel's prime minister Rabin assassinated.

2003
20 March The Iraq War starts.
30 April The Quartet's 'Road Map to Peace'.

2011 Withdrawal of US troops from Iraq.

2014 IS militia terrorists in Iraq and Syria. Delivery of German weapons to the Kurds.

Introduction to the English Edition

For more than one hundred years now, the conflict in the Middle East has been *the* ongoing conflict, and the Middle East *the* crisis region per se, with Germany almost always right in the middle. Germany's involvement in the Middle East began with Kaiser Wilhelm II and his support of the Zionist Theodor Herzl's establishment of a Jewish state in Palestine – an idea Sultan Abdul Hamid II opposed, Palestine being part of the Ottoman Empire. The sultan's position, however, did not affect the good relations between the Ottoman Empire and the German Empire. When the First World War broke out, Kaiser Wilhelm spoke of *jihad* – holy war – against the English, and the Middle East became a major battleground where Germany, as an ally of the Ottoman Empire, played a crucial role. Earlier, in 1898, the Kaiser had declared himself protector of 300 million Muslims. Now, however, he became in fact the protector of the Jews in Palestine, defending them from the Turks yet saying nothing against the Armenian genocide. At the end of 1917, the British assured the Zionists that they would support the establishment of a 'national home' – a state for the Jews in Palestine.

In the first few years after the First World War, Germany's role in the Middle East was minor, but that changed when Hitler rose to power in 1933. In their hatred for the Jews, the Arabs – especially Husseini, the Grand Mufti of Jerusalem – admired Hitler and forbore to conclude that Hitler's Germany was responsible for the increased Jewish immigration to Palestine and the related problems.

During the Second World War, while Nazi Germany was killing six million Jews in Europe, German foreign policy turned back to the Middle East to focus on Iraq and the Grand Mufti. In 1937 the mufti had escaped the British, first to Lebanon then to Damascus; in October 1939 he went to Baghdad, where he continued to fight the British and the Jews. In April 1941, a pro-German coup in Iraq failed due to lack of German assistance while Hitler was fixated on Operation Barbarossa, the invasion of the

Soviet Union. Britain's prime minister, Winston Churchill, stated at the time: 'Hitler certainly cast away the opportunity of taking a great prize for little cost in the Middle East'.[1] Grand Mufti Husseini fled from Baghdad to Berlin, where he was received by Hitler on 28 November 1941.

Germany went without a Middle East policy until the Federal Republic of Germany was founded in 1949. In the 1950s and early 1960s, West German money and arms helped Israel to survive, beginning in 1952 with a reparations agreement with Israel, implemented by German chancellor, Konrad Adenauer, despite opposition from the Arab states. In 1957, Bonn started supplying weapons to Israel, which led to conflict with the Arab states in 1964/65 and the most severe crisis to that time to hit the Federal Republic: the pending diplomatic recognition of the GDR by the Arab states.

Then as now, fighting in the Middle East was also in many ways about oil. The Arab states first used oil as a political weapon in the 1973 Yom Kippur War, a conflict that made the United States the decisive factor in the Middle East. Meanwhile, the Israeli settlement policy strained the German–Israeli relationship. In 1978 Chancellor Helmut Schmidt declined an invitation to visit Israel because, as he told the Israeli ambassador in Bonn, he 'would express his criticism of the settlement policy openly' (see Chapter 6). Thereafter, Bonn backed the European Economic Community's policy and was instrumental in the Venice Declaration of June 1980, in which the EEC demanded that the Palestinians receive the right to self-determination and to participate in a peace settlement.

After Germany's reunification in 1990, the situation changed. When asked to take part in the 1991 Gulf War, Germany did not send soldiers, though it contributed considerable sums of money. Germany again declined to send soldiers when the Iraq War broke out in 2003. US president George W. Bush later accused German chancellor Gerhard Schröder of betrayal.

The 100th anniversary of the outbreak of the First World War occasioned a number of relevant new publications in German about the different phases of German policy in the Middle East. The First World War and Kaiser Wilhelm II are treated by Alexander Will, Stefan M. Kreutzer Wilfried Loth/Marc Hanisch, Hansjörg Eiff and Wolfgang G. Schwanitz. Husseini and the Third Reich have been taken on by Klaus Gensicke, Jennie Lebel, Klaus-Michael Mallmann/ Martin Cüppers, and again Wolfgang G. Schwanitz. For politics in Bonn, see Markus A. Weingart, Niels Hansen, Sven Olaf Berggötz and Frederik Schumann.[2] What had been missing was a short, compact summary of Germany's role in the Middle East from Kaiser Wilhelm to the present. This story, based on the most important records and the most recent literature, was presented in my original German language edition, *Deutschland und der Nahe Osten: Von Kaiser Wilhelms*

Orientreise 1898 bis zur Gegenwart (Reinbek and Munich: Lau, 2015, 259 pages), and is now available in English.

A few words should be said about the archival materials I used. The most important records for the interwar period are the reports of the German consul generals in Jerusalem published in *Der Kampf um Palästina 1924–1939*,[3] and the reports of the Austrian consul generals published in *Berichte aus Jerusalem 1927–1938*.[4] They offer authentic insights into what was happening in Palestine, as seen and analysed by the diplomats. The reports of the Austrian consul general end in March 1938, with the German Reich's *Anschluss* of Austria. German consul general, Walter Döhle, reported to Berlin on 21 March from Jerusalem:

> On Saturday, the 12th of this month, on the morning of which the German troops crossed the Austrian border, I was asked at 7.30 in the evening, by the Austrian Consul General, to give him a swastika flag. This request was certainly met. On Sunday and Monday, the Austrian and German flags were raised on the Austrian Consulate General, on Tuesday only the German flag was raised. From the 17th of this month, no flag was raised because the Austrian office was closed. On the 18th of this month, the Austrian emblems were removed from the building.[5]

The documents for the Federal Republic of Germany are available in the series *Akten zur Auswärtigen Politik der Bundesrepublik Deutschland*.[6] One volume of documents, *Zwischen Moral und Realpolitik*, was edited by Yeshayahu Jelinek;[7] eight volumes titled *Der deutsch-israelische Dialog* were edited by Rolf Vogel;[8] I myself edited the twelve volumes *Berichte aus Israel 1946–1972*, containing the reports that Austrian diplomats in Israel sent to Vienna;[9] and two volumes covering the period 1972–1981 were published by Rudolf Agstner and me.[10] William Burr of the National Security Archive in Washington published a number of documents on the Yom Kippur War, *The October War and U.S. Policy*,[11] and the volumes of the *Foreign Relations of the United States* are particularly relevant for this war and the Yom Kippur War of 1973.[12] In addition, Henry Kissinger himself published the text of phone calls he made during the Yom Kippur War.[13]

Rolf Steininger
www.rolfsteininger.at
Innsbruck, November 2018

Notes

1. Winston Churchill, *The Second World War*, Vol. III: *The Grand Alliance* (Houghton Mifflin, 1950), 236; see also Chapter 4, 1.

2. Alexander Will, *Kein Griff nach der Weltmacht: Geheime Dienste und Propaganda im deutsch-österreichisch-türkischen Bündnis 1914–1918* (Cologne/Weimar/Vienna: Böhlau, 2012; see my review in MGZ 72, 2013); Stefan M. Kreutzer, *Dschihad für den deutschen Kaiser: Max von Oppenheim und die Neuordnung des Orients (1914–1918)* (Graz: Ares, 2012; see my review in MGZ 73, 2014); Wilfried Loth and Marc Hanisch (eds), *Erster Weltkrieg und Dschihad: Die Deutschen und die Revolutionierung des Orients* (Munich: Oldenbourg, 2014; see my review in MGZ 74, 2015); Hansjörg Eiff, 'Die jüdische Heimstätte in Palästina in der deutschen Außenpolitik 1914–1918', *Zeitschrift für Geschichtswissenschaft* 60 (2012), 3, 202–27; Hansjörg Eiff, 'Die jüdische Heimstätte in Palästina in der Außenpolitik der Weimarer Republik', *Zeitschrift für Geschichtswissenschaft* 61 (2013), 12, 1005–28; Wolfgang G. Schwanitz, *Islam in Europa, Revolten in Mittelost: Islamisten und Genozid von Wilhelm II und Enver Pascha über Hitler und al-Husaini bis Arafat, Usama Bin Laden und Ahmadinejad sowie Gespräche mit Bernard Lewis* (Berlin: trafo, 2013; see my review in MGZ 72, 2013); Sean McMeekin, *The Berlin–Baghdad Express: The Ottoman Empire and Germany's Bid for World Power, 1998–1918* (London: Penguin, 2010); Klaus Gensicke, *Der Mufti von Jerusalem und die Nationalsozialisten: Eine politische Biographie Amin el-Husseinis* (Darmstadt: Wissenschaftliche Buchgesellschaft, 2007); Jennie Lebel, *The Mufti of Jerusalem: Haj-Amin el Husseini and National-Socialism* (Belgrade: Čigoja štampa, 2007; see my review of Gensicke and Lebel in MGZ 67, 2008); Klaus-Michael Mallmann and Martin Cüppers, *Halbmond und Hakenkreuz: Das Dritte Reich, die Araber und Palästina* (Darmstadt: Wissenschaftliche Buchgesellschft, 2006); Markus A. Weingardt, *Deutsche Israel- und Nahost-Politik: Die Geschichte einer Gratwanderung seit 1949* (Frankfurt and New York: Campus, 2002); Niels Hansen, *Aus dem Schatten der Katastrophe: Die deutsch-israelischen Beziehungen in der Ära Konrad Adenauer und David Ben Gurion* (Düsseldorf: Droste, 2002); Sven Olaf Berggötz, *Nahostpolitik in der Ära Adenauer: Möglichkeiten und Grenzen 1949–1963* (Düsseldorf: Droste, 1998); Frederik Schumann, *Die deutsche Nahostpolitik 1969–1973: Die sozial-liberale Koalition zwischen Interessenpolitik und moralischer Verpflichtung* (Saarbrücken: Akademikerverlag, 2012). In English there are only two collections of essays covering the years after 1945: Wolfgang G. Schwanitz (ed.), *Germany and the Middle East, 1871–1945* (Princeton, NJ: Wiener, 2004); and Shahram Chubin (ed.), *Germany and the Middle East: Patterns and Prospects* (Continuum International: New York, 1992); and for the Third Reich: Francis Nicosia, *The Third Reich and the Palestine Question* (New Brunswick, NJ and London: Transaction Publishers, 2000). See also Rolf Steininger, *Der Nahostkonflikt* (Frankfurt am Main: Fischer Taschenbuch Verlag, 2005; new edition 2012/14). [Nahostkonflikt]

3. Rolf Steininger (ed.), *Der Kampf um Palästina 1924–1939: Berichte der deutschen Generalkonsuln in Jerusalem* (Munich: Olzog, 2007). [Palästina]

4. Rolf Steininger and Rudolf Agstner (eds), *Berichte aus Jerusalem 1924–1938: Die Berichte der österreichischen Generalkonsuln* (Munich: Olzog, 2004). [Jerusalem]

5. 'Übernahme des österreichischen Generalkonsulats'. Walter Döhle (Jerusalem) an AA, 21 March 1938. Palästina, Doc. 119.

6. Institut für Zeitgeschichte, ed. on behalf of the Auswärtiges Amt, *Akten zur Auswärtigen Politik der Bundesrepublik Deutschland* (Munich: Oldenbourg, 1994–2014). [AAPD]

7. Yeshayahu A. Jelinek (ed.), *Zwischen Moral und Realpolitik: Deutsch-israelische Beziehungen 1945–1965. Eine Dokumentensammlung* (Gerlingen: Bleicher, 1997). [Moral]

8. Rolf Vogel (ed.), *Der deutsch-israelische Dialog: Dokumentation eines erregenden Kapitels deutscher Außenpolitik*, 8 volumes (Munich: Saur, 1987).

9. Rolf Steininger (ed.), *Berichte aus Israel 1946–1972: Die Berichte der diplomatischen Vertreter Österreichs*, 12 volumes (Munich: Olzog, 2004). [Israel]; for more on this edition, see www.rolfsteininger.at/.

10. Rolf Steininger and Rudolf Agstner (eds), *Israel und der Nahostkonflikt 1972–1976* (Munich: Olzog, 2006). Rudolf Agstner and Rolf Steininger (eds), *Israel und der Nahostkonflikt 1976–1981* (Innsbruck: Innsbruck University Press, 2016).

11. William Burr (ed.), *The October War and U.S. Policy* (Washington, DC: National Security Archive, 2003). [October War]

12. Department of State (ed.), *Foreign Relations of the United States, 1964–1968: Volume XIX: Arab–Israel Crisis and War, 1967* (Washington, DC: United States Government Printing Office, 2004); *1969–1976, Volume XXV: Arab–Israel Crisis and War, 1973* (Washington, DC: United States Government Printing Office, 2011). [FRUS]

13. Henry A. Kissinger, *Crisis: The Anatomy of Two Major Policy Crises* (New York: Simon & Schuster, 2003). [Crisis]

Chapter One

BEFORE THE FIRST WORLD WAR, 1898–1914

Kaiser Wilhelm II and Theodor Herzl's "National Home" in Palestine

It all began in the nineteenth century with a phenomenon in Europe and a man from Vienna. The phenomenon was anti-Semitism; the man was Theodor Herzl.

Herzl, an assimilated Austrian Jew born in 1860, was convinced that the answer to the growing anti-Semitism in Europe was to create an independent Jewish state. In 1896, he summarized these thoughts in his programmatic, comprehensive 71-page text *The Jewish State: Proposal of a Modern Solution for the Jewish Question* (*Der Judenstaat: Versuch einer modernen Lösung der Judenfrage*). A year later, the World Zionist Congress in Basel, organized by Herzl, demanded that this Jewish state be in Palestine. As Palestine was part of the Ottoman Empire, the Zionists needed help and support to build a state there, as well as an advocate to represent their cause before Sultan Abdul Hamid II. Herzl counted on the German Reich, and particularly on Emperor Wilhelm II.[1]

From the moment he embraced Zionism, Herzl had intended to petition Wilhelm II. In June 1895, shortly before he wrote the draft for his *Judenstaat*, he asserted: 'I will go to the German Kaiser; and he will understand me because he was raised to evaluate great matters. I will tell the German Kaiser: Let us go'. Even though it was clear to Herzl that a Jewish state established with Germany's help would have to pay 'the most usurious interest', he still preferred the German path to realization of his far-reaching plans, including the founding of an aristocratic Jewish Republic in Palestine, modelled after Bismarck's Reich.

In his diary on 8 October 1898, Herzl wrote: 'To stand under the protectorate of this strong, great, moral, splendidly managed, tightly organized Germany could only have the most wholesome effects on the Jewish national character. With a single stroke', he continued, 'we would come to a perfectly ordered internal and external legal situation'. The Germans would likewise win with this alliance, because 'through Zionism it would be possible for the Jews to love this Germany again, which, in spite of it all, is still dear to our hearts!'

A year before, Wilhelm II had read a report about the first World Zionist Congress and written in the margin: 'I am very much in favour that the Jews [*die Mauschels*] go to Palestine; the sooner they move out there, the better. I will place no obstacles in their way'. On 1 December 1897, Herzl sent the Kaiser his brochure *Der Basler Kongress*. Wilhelm, who still liked the idea of a Jewish state in Palestine, wrote to his uncle Frederick I, Grand Duke of Baden, through whom the connection with Herzl had come about: 'I am convinced that settling the Holy Land with the well-funded and hardworking people of Israel will soon lead the former to unimagined prosperity and blessing'. This would lead in turn, the Kaiser reasoned, to a significant revival of Turkey's economy, which was in the best interest of the German Reich. Berlin was hopeful that the sultan would grant a concession for the construction of the Baghdad Railway. Wilhelm continued:

> Then the Turk is healthy again, meaning he gets money the natural way, without borrowing, then he is no longer ill, builds his avenues and railways himself without foreign companies and then he cannot be so easily divided. Q.e.d! Moreover, the energy, creativity and capability of the tribe Sem would be deflected onto worthier goals than draining the Christians. And many a Semite stirring up the opposition as a Social Democrat by conviction will move eastward, where more rewarding work presents itself . . . Now, I know for sure that nine-tenths of all Germans will turn away from me in horror if they should learn later on that I sympathized with the Zionists or even possibly that I would – if I was called on by them – put them under my protection!

But Wilhelm already had his retort to those nine-tenths:

> That the Jews murdered the Saviour, God knows even better than us, and he punished them accordingly. But neither the anti-Semites nor others nor I are commissioned and authorized to bully these people to adopt our manner in Majorem Dei Gloriam!

Wilhelm then recalled that one should love one's enemies, and besides:

> From the secular, realpolitik viewpoint, it must not be disregarded that the enormous power that the international Jewish capital now represents with all its danger would be an incredible achievement for Germany if the Hebrew

world would look with thanks to them?! Everywhere, Hydra raises her horrid head with the rudest, nastiest anti-Semitism, and fearfully Jews – ready to leave the countries in which they could face danger – look for a protector! Now then, those who are able to return to the Holy Land should enjoy protection and safety, and I will vouch for them with the Sultan.

Wilhelm would meet with Herzl on his trip to the Holy Land between 11 October and 26 November 1898, with stops in Constantinople, Jerusalem and Damascus; the main event was to be the Dedication of the Church of the Redeemer in Jerusalem.

Figure 1.1 Kaiser Wilhelm II with his entourage in front of a tent outside Damascus. Photo by Eric Matzon. Courtesy of Israel Government Press Office, Jerusalem.

On 13 October 1898 in Vienna, five Zionists – Theodor Herzl, Josef Seidener, Tobias Schnirer, David Wolffsohn and Max Bodenheimer – boarded the Orient Express to Constantinople. Herzl led the group. After three years, his efforts had been rewarded: he would be granted an audience with the German Kaiser, Wilhelm II, who had begun his journey to the Orient two days earlier.

Upon receiving the Zionists on 18 October in Constantinople, Wilhelm asked Herzl: 'Tell me in one word: what should I demand from the Sultan?' Herzl replied: 'A chartered company under German protection'. The Sultan had no intention of ceding or selling land to the Jews. When asked by Wilhelm, he stated: 'I cannot sell a foot of land because it is not mine but that of my people. The Jews can save their millions. Once my empire is divided, they might get Palestine for free. But only our body can be dissected. I will never agree to a vivisection.'[2] For Wilhelm, that was the red card. There would not be a German protectorate over a Jewish state in Palestine.

The Kaiser and his entourage arrived in Haifa on 24 October 1898 for the final leg of their journey, described by the English historian John Röhl.[3] As stated in the travel report, when Wilhelm II went ashore that afternoon he became the first German Kaiser since Frederick II of Hohenstaufen in 1228 to set foot on the soil of the Holy Land. As the retinue proceeded along the dusty road to Jaffa, they were joined by numerous clergy and more than five hundred additional people arriving on four steamers. The

Figure 1.2 1903: The Jaffa Gate of the Old City of Jerusalem with Turkish flags. People wave flags as a sign of adoration for the sultan. Photo by Eric Matzon. Courtesy of Israel Government Press Office, Jerusalem.

procession required no fewer than 230 tents, 120 carriages, 1,300 horses and mules, 12 cooks and 60 waiters. This huge caravan was protected by a Turkish army regiment, along with German warships that accompanied the travellers by sea, firing thunderous fusillades whenever the Kaiser's banner could be seen on the horizon.

When Wilhelm passed the Jewish settlement of Mikle Israel, he had a brief roadside encounter with Herzl before continuing to the journey's main event, the dedication of the Church of the Redeemer in Jerusalem on 31 October. And on 2 November 1898, the Kaiser received Herzl in the tent camp outside Jerusalem. 'He said neither yes nor no', Herzl wrote in his diary after the meeting, comforting himself with the thought that his efforts were not in vain: 'This brief reception will be recorded in the history of the Jews forever, and it is not impossible that it will also have historical consequences'. The official press release spoke of the Kaiser's 'benevolent interest' in all efforts 'aimed at enhancing Palestine's agriculture to ensure the best welfare of the Turkish Empire, in full respect of the sovereignty of the Sultan'.[4] Max Bodenheimer recorded his impressions:

> At first, the speech of the Kaiser had the effect of a cold shower. After further consideration, however, we thought, with regard to the critical situation, the Kaiser could not say more. Indeed, the Kaiser had said nothing of a Protectorate, but Herzl was allowed to clearly and forthrightly bring our intentions forward, and was promised that the prospect of this issue would be examined further. At this place and from the mouth of the Kaiser, this meant something.[5]

From Jerusalem the Kaiser travelled to Damascus, where, on 8 November at the grave of the legendary Sultan Saladin, he astonished the world with the following promise: 'May the Sultan and his 300 million Muslim subjects scattered across the earth, who venerate him as their Caliph, be assured that the German Kaiser will be their friend at all times (*zu allen Zeiten*)'. Despite styling himself in this way and being dubbed *Haji Wilhelm*, protector of Muslims, implying that he had made the pilgrimage to Mecca, Wilhelm made no secret of his disappointment with what he had seen in Palestine: it was 'a desolate, parched heap of stones', he wrote to his mother on the way home. Further:

> The lack of shade and water is appalling ... Jerusalem is entirely spoiled by the many, very modern suburbs ... full of Jewish settlers. There were 60,000 of these people – greasy, miserable, sluggish and degenerate – who have nothing better to do than to become equally hated by Christians and Muslims by trying to get every hard-earned penny from these neighbours. Nothing but shylocks, all of them.[6]

Prussian minister for culture, Robert Bosse, a member of the Kaiser's entourage, analysed the journey. Some fellow travellers seemed to be of

Figure 1.3 1910: At the Wailing Wall. Photo by Eric Matzon. Courtesy of Israel Government Press Office, Jerusalem.

the opinion that the German Reich would 'be on firm footing' in Palestine. To this end, Bosse said of the journey: 'How carefully our Kaiser avoided everything presenting evidence of exaggerated political aspirations or of awaking the suspicion of other nations. To this day, thank God, the foreign policy of the German Reich continues its activity on the course set by Fürst Bismarck. Specifically, in the oriental question, it is markedly a policy of peace'.[7]

Even if Wilhelm did not like Palestine or the Jews' presence there, business with the Ottoman Empire was good. Within a few years, solid ties between Berlin and Constantinople had been forged. The German Reich received the concession for the construction of the Baghdad Railway, and German and Ottoman economic relations and military cooperation grew closer. Prussian officers had been responsible for training the Ottoman army since the early 1880s, and arms sales were an important factor in Turkish–German relations. Krupp delivered five hundred field guns in 1885, Mauser and Loewe all other sorts of weapons and ammunition, such as half a million rifles in 1886. Before becoming the Ottoman minister of war in January 1914, Enver Pasha had served three years (1909–1911) as a military attaché to Berlin and developed a close relationship with Wilhelm. In December 1913, a German mission arrived in Turkey with the task of reorganizing the Ottoman army. Officers of the German military mission assumed responsibility for the command of the Turkish army under Enver's leadership.[8]

Notes

1. For Wilhelm II, his journey and his meeting with Theodor Herzl, I rely primarily on John C. G. Röhl, 'Wilhelms seltsamer Kreuzzug', *DIE ZEIT*, Nr. 42 (8 October 1998), 30–36, as well as Alex Carmel and Ejal J. Eisler, *Der Kaiser reist ins Heilige Land. Die Palästinareise Wilhelms II. Eine illustrierte Dokumentation* (Cologne: Kohlhammer, 1999); Klaus Jaschinski and Julius Waldschmidt (eds), *Des Kaisers Reise in den Orient 1898* (Berlin: Weist, 2002); and Jan Stefan Richter, *Die Orientreise Kaiser Wilhelms II. 1898. Eine Studie zur deutschen Außenpolitik* (Hamburg: Kovac, 1997). See also Raphael Patai (ed.), *The Complete Diaries of Theodor Herzl* (New York and London: Herzl Press, 1960); and my *Nahostkonflikt*, 3–9.
2. See Röhl, 'Wilhelms seltsamer Kreuzzug'.
3. Ibid., 1.
4. Ibid.
5. Max Bodenheimer and Henrietta Hannah Bodenheimer, *Die Zionisten und das kaiserliche Deutschland* (Bensberg: Schäuble, 1972), 54.
6. Röhl, 'Wilhelms seltsamer Kreuzzug'.
7. Carmel and Eisler, *Der Kaiser*, 169.
8. Cf. Sean McMeekin, *The Berlin–Baghdad Express: The Ottoman Empire and Germany's Bid for World Power 1898–1918* (London: Penguin, 2010); Elke Hartmann, *Die Reichweite des Staates: Wehrpflicht und moderne Staatlichkeit im Osmanischen Reich 1869–1910* (Paderborn: Schöningh, 2016; see my review in MGZ 76, 2017).

Chapter Two

DURING THE FIRST WORLD WAR

Kaiser Wilhelm II and Jihad

At the height of the 1914 July crisis, the Kaiser wrote in the margin of a telegram received on 30 July from Count Pourtalès, the German ambassador to St. Petersburg, that in the event that Great Britain interfered in the conflict,

> England must have the mask of Christian peaceableness torn publicly off her face. Our consuls in Turkey and India, the agents etc. must inflame the entire Muslim world to a wild uprising against this hateful, deceitful, unscrupulous nation of shopkeepers; if we were to bleed to death, then England should at least lose India.[1]

On 2 August 1914, Germany and the Ottoman Empire concluded a secret alliance. When Great Britain declared war on Germany on 4 August, the German chief of staff, Helmuth von Moltke, instructed the Foreign Office (*Auswärtiges Amt*) in the spirit of the Kaiser: 'Revolution in India and Egypt and also in the Caucasus is of the highest importance. The treaty with Turkey will make it possible for the Foreign Office to realize this idea and to excite the fanaticism of Islam'.[2]

Together with the Turks and with a call to *jihad*, the holy war, an uprising should be kindled in the Islamic world – now under Russian, British and French domination, from Morocco to India. The Turks should attack Russia immediately. One of the first German–Turkish operations was an attempt in early September to make the Suez Canal impassable by sinking a ship, thereby creating an explosive atmosphere in Egypt that eventually would lead to an uprising against the British. The operation failed. The German Admiral Staff of the imperial navy reported to the Foreign Office on 10 September 1914: 'German steamers seized, and intense surveillance by other ships caused the blockade to fail. Further attempts in Egypt unsuccessful'.³

Nevertheless, on 12 November, Sultan Mehmed V, who was also the spiritual leader of Islam, called for *jihad* against the Allies. This did not, however, meet with the expected response among Muslims. By contrast, the members of the Entente succeeded in engaging a large part of the Muslim population in their warfare. Meanwhile, the German Reich and its ally, the Austro–Hungarian Empire, saw their initial priority as finding a direct land connection to Turkey in order to arm and supply the Turkish army (which thoroughly failed on the first try, in the war against Serbia in December 1914).

After the first failure at the Suez Canal, chancellor of the German Empire Theobald von Bethmann Hollweg demanded further military action against the British in Egypt. This took the form of a strike to be executed in February 1915 by a Turkish expedition corps of sixteen thousand men. The plan was to march through the desert, cross the Suez Canal in a surprise attack and then block that route. The composition of this corps, however, was more than dubious. It was made up of 'indigenous volunteers and irregulars' who did not perform adequately and were 'insubordinate, cowardly and demanding', the German report stated. Further, the Turkish officers allegedly slept all day and had only enough energy 'to put up passive resistance' towards the Germans.⁴ The British and their units from India succeeded in crossing the canal and attacking the Turkish flanks. Although the Turks initially managed to fend off the charge, their German commander was killed. On the evening of 3 February, the German–Turkish command cancelled the operation. Not until August 1917 was a fresh assault attempted, and it also failed, exhausting the offensive power of the Turks on the Sinai front. On other fronts, though, there was heavy fighting with variable success.

At the end of October 1914, the German Max von Oppenheim laid out a blueprint for German revolutionary efforts in the Middle East in a 136-page 'Memorandum on Revolutionizing the Islamic Territories of our Enemies' (*Denkschrift zur Revolutionierung der islamischen Gebiete unserer Feinde*). The idea was crystal clear: 'In this imposed conflict with England, Islam will be one of our main weapons. The whole nature of our enemy's warfare gives us the right, and the need for our self-preservation the duty, not to leave this very important weapon unused for the ultimate goal of this conflict'. Gangs should be assembled everywhere to 'beat the English to death in the rural areas'. The last sentence of the memorandum runs as follows: 'The engagement of Islam in the present war is a terrible blow, especially for England. Let us do everything, work together with all available means, so that it is fatal'.

Who was this Max von Oppenheim (1860–1946)? A scion of the influential Cologne banking dynasty, he had at age sixteen been given a copy of *Märchen aus 1001 Nacht* (One Thousand and One Nights), a collection of oriental narratives that was to define his future. Captivated by the Orient, he moved to Cairo in 1892, rented a house in the Arab quarter, learned Arabic and, unlike the other Europeans in Cairo, fostered close contacts with locals. From Cairo he undertook expeditions to the Euphrates, Syria and Macedonia. His first attempt to enrol in the German Foreign Service failed because his name sounded 'too Semitic'. A second attempt was successful: in 1896, he was assigned to the consulate in Cairo. He quit the service in 1910, having written more than five hundred reports to the Foreign Ministry and solidified his reputation as an expert on Middle East affairs. Over the next two years he headed the excavations of Syria's 3,000-year-old Aramaic temples of Tell Halaf, which he had discovered in 1899. The artefacts unearthed there made the amateur archaeologist world famous.

When the war broke out, Oppenheim reported back to the Foreign Office, where he took on the important wartime role of establishing the *Nachrichtenstelle für den Orient* (Intelligence Bureau for the East). Based in the Foreign Office with Orientals and helpers in the Near and the Middle East, the bureau had fifteen paid employees on the staff in Berlin. It functioned as the Foreign Office's department of propaganda for the holy war, publishing an array of linguistic pamphlets and a weekly newsletter. From his office in Berlin, Oppenheim dispatched agents to bribe mullahs from Istanbul to Kabul to issue fatwas against all Europeans except Austrians, Hungarians and Germans. Oppenheim's bureau stoked the fires of jihad by concocting tales of anti-Islamic perfidies committed by Britain. German-sponsored jihadist pamphlets in French, Persian, Arabic and Urdu called on all Muslims, in language uncomfortably similar to that used by the IS and Al Qaeda today, to kill Christians. One pamphlet assured the faithful that 'the blood of the [Allied] infidels in the Islamic lands may be shed with impunity', citing the scriptural authority of the Koran as proof.

In Anglo-Saxon historiography, the verdict on Oppenheim and German Middle East policy is clear: he was 'the Kaiser's spy' – the male Mata Hari of the Orient – and Germany's Middle East strategy was a perfidious attempt to destroy the British Empire and build a German Empire in its place.[5] German historiography views it similarly, based on the famous German historian Fritz Fischer's understanding of the 1914 memorandum. Fischer saw it as further proof of Germany's 'grasping for world power', a phrase he used as the title of his much-discussed book of 1961. Obviously influenced by this interpretation, the Middle East expert Wolfgang G. Schwanitz rendered a scathing judgement of Oppenheim in 2013. Schwanitz characterized Oppenheim as the 'German father of the Holy War' and an author of justifications for the Armenian genocide, and therefore saw the memorandum as a 'diabolical plan for Jihad' with 'deadly dimensions' stretching up to today's extreme Islam: 'This German Abu Jihad included terror, boycott, mob, and political assassination'.[6]

Others see it quite differently. Stefan Kreutzer's work of 2012 concludes that Oppenheim was 'not a demagogic agitator', and 'no agitated spy of the Kaiser', but the exact opposite: merely someone who was a 'politically interested, passionate fan of the Orient'. Oppenheim's memorandum illustrated this 'liberal side, his openness towards other cultures, and his wish to assist those on the path to independence': he was not motivated by 'hate towards England or any other Entente nation. He recognized the opportunity for Germany to appear as a liberator of the oppressed Islamic nations'.[7]

Besides Max von Oppenheim, the key players in the planned uprising in the Muslim world from Morocco to India included Freiherr Colmar von der Goltz, Rudolf Nadolny, Wilhelm Waßmuß and Fritz Klein. The Prussian Freiherr Colmar von der Goltz (1843–1916) was intellectually at home in both Orient and Occident. He headed up the Ottoman General Staff from 1883 to 1895, was promoted to Field Marshal in 1911, and took over command of the 6th Turkish Army to fight the war in Mesopotamia in 1915. He was a radical enemy of the British. By the end of November 1914, the British had occupied Basra, the most important port in the Persian Gulf, intending to use it as a starting point for further military operations, but they were stopped at Kut-al-Amara in September 1915. Following plans for global war, Goltz began to flirt with the idea of an advance into India but then found himself accused of undermining the actual goals of the German war effort by fragmenting the forces. Von der Goltz remained controversial. On the one hand, his enduring influence in the Turkish officer corps had long-term impact: as is generally known, the British did not achieve decisive results until the final year of the war. On the other hand, he encouraged the Ottoman leadership – indirectly at least, through the establishment of special Kurdish cavalry units – to massacre the Armenians.

In a way, Rudolf Nadolny (1873–1953) was more successful in Persia. In late 1914, Russian troops marched into the heart of the country and surrounded Tehran. National Persian forces declared a provisional government in Kermanshah, where Nadolny worked as a chargé d'affaires. He wanted to build a miniature Persia as a launch pad for expeditions to Afghanistan and India. But his plans were hindered from the outset by problems with the Turkish ally and the German ambassador in Constantinople, and later with Secretary of State Richard von Kühlmann, who in a memoir published in 1948 called these expeditions 'a plague', adding: 'In the mind of the Germans, the Orient still retained much of the Thousand

and One Nights'. The British attack in 1917 brought Nadolny's mission to an abrupt end.⁸

Then there was Wilhelm Waßmuß (1880–1931), whom the British called the 'German Lawrence' after their Lawrence of Arabia. Late in 1914, Waßmuß led an expedition to Afghanistan to convince the emir to provoke an uprising against the British in India by invading the Punjab. But although Waßmuß had led the only successful uprising against the British occupation of Persia prior to 1918, he remained mostly unknown thereafter. Captain Fritz Klein was also successful: with the help of Arab tribes, he managed to stabilize the Turkish Mesopotamian front. His men blew up British oil lines, and in 1915 they kept Russian troops in West Persia from breaking through to Mesopotamia, thwarting the Russians' planned union with Britain.

In the end, despite the many campaigns, little remained of Germany's much-quoted 'holy war' against its enemies in the Middle East.

As for Germany's ally Austria-Hungary, it is interesting to note that at that time, Field Marshal Josef Pomiankowski personified the Habsburg Empire's military presence in the Ottoman Empire. This by no means implied cooperation with the Germans. Austria-Hungary acted as an independent, self-confident power in the Middle East, and even purposefully worked against its own ally, Germany, skilfully taking advantage of conflicts between Germans and Turks. And above all, it was active with cultural policies.⁹

Germany and the Armenian Genocide[10]

The German leaders had set high expectations for their new ally, Turkey. The Turkish army was supposed to attack Russia in the Caucasus, conquer the territory of Baku, and open the way to Persia and India. Instead, Russian troops attacked in the Caucasus in November 1914. The 3rd Ottoman Army was able to stop the Russian advance and moved on to a counteroffensive on 19 December. At first it appeared successful, making large territorial gains in Armenian territory the Russians had first occupied in 1877. The Armenians living there even supported the Turkish soldiers. But somewhat later in the course of the Russian counteroffensive, disaster struck with a devastating defeat at Sarykamysh. The Turkish troops were not equipped for either the mountain or the winter war. Nearly ninety thousand soldiers froze or starved to death, and thousands deserted. South of the Turkish–Russian front the combat devolved into trench warfare.

When Russia promised to establish an independent Armenian state, Armenian volunteer battalions entered into the fighting on the side of the Russians. In response, the Ottoman leadership deported the Armenian population and ultimately killed them; corresponding legislation was passed 27 May 1915. Copious evidence attests to what happened. On 30 June, the US consul to Harput, Leslie Davis, commented in a dispatch to Washington:

> They found another method to annihilate the Armenian race. It is nothing less than the deportation of the entire Armenian population. . . . The full implication of such a command is inconceivable, without having a clear picture about the special circumstance in this remote region. Even a massacre, as cruel as this word may sound, would be more humane in comparison. In a massacre many escape, but a wholesale deportation of this kind in this country means a longer and perhaps even more dreadful death for nearly everyone. Nevertheless, the tragedy is so terrible that one cannot contemplate it and certainly cannot live in the midst of it without being stirred to the depths of one's nature.[11]

On 16 July, Henry Morgenthau, US ambassador in Constantinople, sent the following telegram to Secretary of State Robert Lansing in Washington:

> Deportation of and excesses against peaceful Armenians is increasing, and from harrowing reports of eye witnesses it appears that a campaign of race extermination is in progress under a pretext of reprisal against rebellion. Protests as well as threats are unavailing and probably incite the Ottoman government to more drastic measures, as they are determined to disclaim responsibility for their absolute disregard of capitulations; and I believe nothing short of actual force, which obviously the United States are not in a position to exert, would adequately meet the situation. Suggest you inform belligerent nations and mission boards of this.[12]

Four weeks earlier, on 17 June, the German embassy in Constantinople had sent the following memorandum to Chancellor Bethmann Hollweg in Berlin:

> The expulsions of the Armenian population from their residences in the eastern Anatolian provinces and their resettlement to other regions are being handled ruthlessly. . . . It is evident that the banishment of the Armenians is motivated not by military concerns alone. The interior minister, Talaat Bey, recently indicated to Dr Mordtmann at the imperial embassy, in no uncertain terms, that the Porte wants to use the world war so as to deal conclusively with its internal enemies – i.e. domestic Christians – without diplomatic interference from abroad; he went on to say that such an approach was also in the interest of the Germans, being Turkey's allies, as Turkey would come out stronger for it.[13]

Johann Heinrich Mordtmann, the German consul general in Constantinople, reported: 'This can no longer be justified militarily; rather, it is about destroying the Armenians'.[14] On 4 September, this was followed by a memorandum to Bethmann Hollweg from Ambassador Count zu Hohenlohe in Constantinople:

On the 2nd of the month Talaat Bey handed over to me a German translation of several telegraphic orders that he had directed to the relevant provincial authorities in the matter of the persecution of Armenians. He intended to prove thereby that the central government was sincerely endeavoring to put an end to the transgressions against Armenians that occurred in the interior and to provide for the nourishment of the banished persons in transport. Talaat Bey had told me some days prior: la question arménienne n'existe plus [the Armenian question is no more].[15]

Ten days later, on 14 September 1915, von Hohenlohe forwarded a report from the imperial consul in Adana to Bethmann Hollweg:

The representation made to the imperial embassy by the Porte on 29 August was merely a crude deception, because ... the Porte subsequently cancelled that instruction in its entirety. Of course the authorities are complying only with the second instruction, continuing to banish without distinguishing by faith. Very likely the number of Armenians murdered by order already exceeds the number killed in the 1909 Young Turks massacres.[16]

On 7 December 1915, Ambassador Wolff-Metternich, who was on an extraordinary mission in Constantinople, followed up with another dispatch to Bethmann Hollweg:

They are claiming exigencies of war which require that inciters be punished and evading the charge that hundreds of thousands of women, children and elderly are being thrust into misery and put to death. ... Our newspapers must give voice to concerns about the persecution of Armenians and stop showering praise on the Turks. What they are doing is our work, our officers, our artillery, our money. Without our help the bloated frog will collapse in on itself. ... To succeed in the Armenian question, we must put fear in the hearts of the Turkish leadership regarding the consequences. Talaat Bey is the soul of the persecution of Armenians.[17]

At that point it was already too late: by the end of 1915, the majority of the deported Armenians had been killed. On 16 December, Bethmann Hollweg made the following annotation in the margin of that dispatch:

The proposed public dressing down of an ally in the midst of a war would be a disciplinary measure unprecedented in history. Our only goal is to keep Turkey by our side until the end of the war, regardless of whether Armenians perish in the process or not. If the war continues for much longer we will yet have great need of the Turks. I do not comprehend how Metternich can make such a proposal.[18]

Differing data put the number of victims at 800,000 to 1.5 million. Today we are very well informed about the Armenian genocide, but all Turkish governments have continued to maintain a policy of denying it. Nearly a hundred years later, on 2 June 2016, the German Bundestag almost unanimously passed a resolution calling the Armenian killings genocide. The Turkish parliament strongly condemned the resolution, 'for which historical truths relating to the events of 1915 were deliberately distorted'.[19]

The Ottoman Empire and the End of the First World War

Kaiser Wilhelm's hope that a declaration of holy war would provoke the entire Muslim world to rise up against the British was never fulfilled. Not even the sixteen thousand German and k.u.k. troops (kaiserliche und königliche Truppen) of the Asia Corps could change this. The Arabs were no longer drawn to the Ottoman Empire, especially after the British succeeded in winning them over for themselves. A bargain had been worked out between Britain's high commissioner in Cairo, Sir Henry McMahon, and the sharif of Mecca, Hussein ibn Ali. The crucial letter from McMahon to the sharif on 24 October 1915 came to light only in 1937. It stated that Britain was 'prepared to recognize and support the independence of the Arabs in all the regions within the limits demanded by the sharif' (namely Syria, Arabia and Mesopotamia) with the exception of those 'portions of Syria lying to the west of the districts of Damascus, Homs, Hama and Aleppo'. In return the Arabs would support the Allies against the Turks. This would 'result in a firm and lasting alliance, the immediate results of which will be the expulsion of the Turks from the Arab countries and the freeing of the Arab peoples from the Turkish yoke, which for so many years has pressed heavily upon them'. Eight months later, on 15 July 1916, the Arabs declared war on Turkey.[20]

At this juncture the British liaison officer Thomas Edward Lawrence, 'Lawrence of Arabia', became legendary. Hearing that name, people probably think first of the 1962 Hollywood epic by David Lean, with Peter O'Toole as Lawrence and Omar Sharif as his friend and comrade Sharif Ali. This film, which attained worldwide fame and was awarded seven Oscars, set the story in stunning desert images that produced an irrevocable myth of Lawrence: during the First World War, a British officer fighting against the Turks becomes an admired leader of the Arabs. Lawrence became the closest adviser to Emir Faisal, one of four sons of the sharif of Mecca, wore only Bedouin clothes, and spoke only Arabic. He led the Bedouins in a guerrilla war against the Turks, blew up bridges, attacked locomotives and troop transports, and interrupted important supply routes of the Turkish army by destroying railways. The highlight of 'his' desert war occurred on 6 July 1917. After a 600-kilometre march with the Bedouins through the desert, he captured the coastal city of Aqaba on the Red Sea – a feat the Turks had considered impossible.[21]

The secret British agreement with the sharif of Mecca was followed by another very problematic secret agreement with the French a few months later. Sir Mark Sykes (1873–1919), a British orientalist, and François Georges-Picot (1870–1951), formerly French consul in Beirut, had prepared to divide the Ottoman Arab provinces into areas of British and French influence. Britain would control areas roughly comprising the coastal strip between the Mediterranean and the River Jordan, Jordan, southern Iraq, and the cities of Haifa and Acre; Haifa would be connected to Baghdad by railway. France would control south-eastern Turkey, northern Iraq, Syria and Lebanon. Istanbul, the Turkish Straits and Armenia would go to Russia, while Palestine (without Haifa and Acre) would be subject to an international administration (Britain, France, Russia). This Sykes–Picot Agreement, signed in May 1916 by the British and French governments and also approved in principle by Russia, 'is still mentioned when considering the region and its present-day conflicts'.[22]

Meanwhile, the British disaster at Gallipoli in 1915 was followed by another in Mesopotamia, where a British–Indian expeditionary force suffered a major defeat in 1916. In November 1914, the British had landed in Basra under General Charles Townshend, but their advance to Baghdad turned into a fiasco. The 6th Turkish Army, under the command of Prussian General Field Marshall Freiherr von der Goltz, repelled the advance. At the end of November 1915, Townshend chose to make his stand at Kut-al-Amara – a fatal decision. On 29 April 1916, after a 147-day siege marked by the slaughter of eleven hundred horses, cholera, dysentery, scurvy and lack of water, he surrendered unconditionally. With twenty-three thousand soldiers dead or wounded, Kut-al-Amara was one of the British Army's worst defeats in the First World War. Thirteen thousand starving troops were sent on a death march of one hundred miles to Baghdad, then five hundred more to Anatolia – where they were put to work on railroad chain gangs. Few survived. Townshend, on the other hand, was treated with courtesy by the Turks and lived in comfort – some say in luxury – in Constantinople. He was released in October 1918 after the Ottoman Empire's surrender.

After the disaster of Kut-al-Amara, General Townshend was replaced by Frederick Maude. As 'friends of the Arabs', Maude's troops succeeded in conquering Baghdad on 11 March 1917. Maude courted the residents with the promise that Britain and its allies would end 'the domination of foreign tyrants [that had lasted for] 26 generations'.[23] Having conquered Baghdad, the victors went on to occupy the rest of the country. The British were mainly interested in the northern oil fields around Mosul. Meanwhile, Lawrence continued his guerrilla activities.

Not until General Edmund Allenby was appointed the new commander of the British Expeditionary Corps in Palestine in July 1917 did the actions

Figure 2.1 On 9 December 1917, British General Edmund Allenby conquers Jerusalem. Here is Allenby, four years later, with the legendary Thomas Edward Lawrence – 'Lawrence of Arabia'– (far left) and the ruler of Transjordan, Emir Abdullah (left). Photo by Eric Matzon. Courtesy of Israel Government Press Office, Jerusalem.

of the regular British forces became militarily significant. In September 1917, the Turkish Sinai front collapsed. Allenby defeated the Turks in Beersheba on 31 October, then in Gaza on 7 November. On the night of 8/9 December 1917, the Turks abandoned Jerusalem to protect the Holy City from destruction, and on 9 December the British took Jerusalem without a fight, ending the Ottomans' 673-year rule over the city. All of Rome's church bells rang – except in St Peter's Basilica. General Allenby entered the old town on 11 December. Unlike Wilhelm II, who had ridden through the Jaffa Gate on a white horse in 1898, he walked – as pilgrims had done for centuries (and as ordered by the Imperial War Cabinet in London).

Battles were fought in central Palestine from December 1917 to April 1918, and then in East Jordan from April to September 1918. With reinforcements, the German and k.u.k. troops numbered sixteen thousand, but they lost at Megiddo, the last major battle of the First World War in the Middle East. On 20 September 1918 Allenby took over the Turkish headquarters on the West Bank, even as the entire Ottoman front collapsed and the Turkish army, commanded by the German General Liman von Sanders, was vanquished. Von Sanders later justified the defeat as follows:

>]ext[In my opinion, definitive and decisive successes on the Palestinian battleground were impossible from the start, as the [British] had Egypt as a base behind them, as well as the sea as a connecting route on one flank. On the other flank, east of the Jordan, the Arab tribes fought and organized as allies, while in contrast the Turks were numerically inferior.
>
> I only possessed a cavalry of twelve hundred horses, while General Allenby had fourteen thousand well-fed horses and racing camels. Further, nowhere was it brought to account that we had only a single railway track – a completely inadequately operated line of about 1,700 kilometres to Constantinople – as the only outside connection. There were three different track gauges. That was the basis on which I was to operate.
>
> Given the limited powers of Turkey in the fourth year of the war, it seems to have been just about stalling on this front, until the big decision was made on the Western front in France. We held our front from 1 March 1918 for six and a half months under my command, against numerous British attacks. By then, the Turkish troops, who had been at the front without replacement since the spring, were torn, ragged and starving; their physical and moral strength had been exhausted, and then came the bitter end.[24]

On 30 October 1918, the Ottoman Empire and the Allies signed a ceasefire on board HMS *Agamemnon* in the harbour of Moudros on the Greek island of Limnos. The German and the k.u.k. troops were given safe passage and arrived in their homelands in January 1919.[25]

Kaiser Wilhelm II: Protector of the Jews in Palestine[26]

On 28 September 1898, Kaiser Wilhelm II personally wrote to his uncle, the Grand Duke of Baden: 'The basic idea [a national home for the Jews in Palestine] has always interested me, has even pleasantly touched me. . . . I came to the conclusion that we are dealing with a question of the most far-reaching significance'.

On his journey to the Orient in 1898, Wilhelm had met three times with the founder of political Zionism, Theodor Herzl (see Chapter 1). Although unable to get any concessions from the sultan, the Kaiser kept to his conviction and maintained his pro-Zionist and pro-Jewish stance throughout the war. For a long time it was not widely known that he was the protector of the Jews in Palestine – who at the beginning of the war numbered about 85,000: half German, half Russian – without regard to their country of origin. That pertained especially to Jews from Russia. When about two hundred of them were barred from landing in Jaffa in August 1914, the German ambassador in Constantinople, Hans Freiherr von Wangenheim, ordered the local consul, Heinrich Brode, to allow the landing, which Brode did. The rationale came from the Foreign Office in Berlin on 30 August: 'A careful treatment of the Russian Jews in Turkey seems to be in Turkey's interest, based on the impression made on the international Jewry'. On 1 November 1914, Wangenheim received the following instruction from Berlin: 'Please, if still needed, see that Jews, regardless of their nationality, are not harassed'. This was mainly directed at Jews in the United States, as the ambassador in Washington, Graf Bernstorff, had reported: 'Local Jewish circles, who are consistently pro-German, fear massacres of Jews in Turkey, for which Germany would be held indirectly responsible'.

What was true for Germany was also true for Turkey. On 3 November the Foreign Office clarified its reasoning in a message to Wangenheim: 'It cannot be denied that, especially at the present moment, it would be wise of the Porte to earn the sympathy of the international Jewish community, especially in America, with accommodating treatment of Zionism'. To be sure, this was easier said than done. Turks regarded Jewish settlements as eyesores. Russian settlers generally were under suspicion of disloyalty and espionage. Their situation became worse still after the declaration of war with Russia turned them into 'enemy aliens'. Their greatest foe was undoubtedly Turkish minister of the navy, Djemal Pasha. As top commander of the 4th Army, he was also in charge of Syria and Palestine. His goals were to rally Muslim believers against the unbelievers under the Turkish banner and to prevent independent national movements of Jews and of

Arabs. One of his first measures was therefore to forcibly deport several hundred Russian Jews from Jaffa and Tel Aviv.

German diplomacy rendered the Zionists a service that was unusual for that time by permitting their representatives in Palestine and Constantinople to use the official codes of the German embassy, as well as the courier, for two-way communication and contact with the Executive Bureau in Berlin. Thus it was the Germans and not the Turkish authorities who had insight into Zionist message exchanges. Richard Lichtheim, the long-time Constantinople-based editor of the Zionist weekly newspaper Die Welt, acted as the representative of the Zionist Organization. He maintained good relations with the German embassy and was the liaison between the organization and the US embassy in Constantinople. Arthur Ruppin, since 1908 the representative of the Zionist Organization in Palestine, later explained the utility of the codes: 'The fact that Djemal Pasha knew that the German embassy was informed from the Jewish side about his behaviour toward the Jews may have prevented him from some planned actions'.

In November 1915, the German government refined its position on Jewish aspirations in Palestine. The consuls were instructed to promote Jewish endeavours that 'serve the economic and cultural development of the Jews', particularly the 'immigration and resettlement of foreign Jews, provided that such efforts are not regarded as possible contradictions to German and Turkish interests'. Once again, the point was 'to appease public opinion in the world, [and] in particular to strengthen the American Jews in their pro-German attitude'. Nonetheless, Lichtheim remarked, with this directive 'a major European power demonstrated their willingness to support the Jewish aspirations in Palestine'. Elsewhere at this time, Turks were carrying out the Armenian genocide, which the Germans tolerated.

The United States' entry into the war in April 1917 and the closure of the US embassy in Constantinople made the Germans' protection of the Zionists even more important. This became clear as early as March 1917, when Jerusalem's Turkish governor, Ahmed Munir, acting on behalf of Djemal Pasha, ordered the deportation of all Jews from Jaffa and from various Jewish settlements, and the forcible expulsion of any who refused to be deported. The consuls of various countries protested, led by the Jaffa-based German vice-consul, Emil Schabinger. Munir's response is known:

> Mr Consul, yesterday at the government building you requested a conversation during which you declared with great tenacity and ferocity that you would mount your horse and leave if the German Israelites should leave the city. Further, you, if not killed before, would not agree to a single German Israelite leaving. You compared this action of the Ottoman government with that of the expulsion of Jews by Russia, our cruelest enemy. As you offended the hon-

our and dignity of the imperial government, I am informing you on behalf of the commander in chief of the 4th Army that you either make amends or be brought to a court martial by tomorrow noon.

Schabinger was never tried in a court martial, and the inhabitants of the villages and settlements were allowed to stay until the next harvest. However, some eleven thousand Jewish residents of Jaffa were compelled to leave the city. They went to Galilee, about a fifth of them perishing along the way.

In April 1917, Djemal Pasha ordered the deportation of the Jewish population of Jerusalem, thus sentencing about fifty thousand people to the same hunger and death inflicted on the Armenians. However, following strong objections raised by the German chief of staff of the 8th Corps of the 4th Army, Colonel Friedrich Kress von Kressenstein, Berlin intervened directly with the Turkish minister of war, Enver Pasha, who lifted Djemal's order, who, in turn in October 1917, wanted to conduct an espionage case against Palestinian Jews, a proceeding linked to clashes with citizens of Petah-Tikvah, one of the first Jewish settlements (east of Tel Aviv). Hundreds of Jews were to be forced out and sent to Damascus; people spoke of an 'attempted genocide'. The Foreign Office responded, summoning the Turkish envoy and informing Ambassador Count Bernstorff (who until April 1917 had been ambassador to Washington) on 17 October: 'It is feared that public opinion throughout the entire world could fall back into turmoil, whereby the encounter with the Kaiser's visit [Wilhelm II was in Constantinople in October] will, of course, be interpreted as evidence of our joint guilt or authorship'.

Grand Vizier Talaat Pasha responded reassuringly that, although great suffering had been inflicted on the Armenians, the Jews would not be harmed. Bernstorff wrote in his memoirs: 'Talaat was willing to promise me anything I wanted if Palestine remained Turkish after the war, but he kept repeating, at every opportunity, the words: "For your sake, I am willing to build the national home for the Jews, but I am telling you, the Arabs will kill the Jews"'.

The Germans' desire for the Jewish national home mentioned by Bernstorff must be understood in light of the Entente's efforts to gain the Zionists' support by meeting their demands for an independent state in Palestine. On 2 November, exactly sixteen days after the 17 October 1917 directive from the Foreign Office, an assurance of the British government's support for the Zionists' creation of a 'national home in Palestine' was published. Composed of only 117 words, the famous Balfour Declaration, named after the British secretary of state, James Balfour, represented an unprecedented diplomatic victory for Judaism and significantly influenced world politics, especially the history of the Middle East. Diverse reasons motivated this undertaking. The British believed that support for the Zionists might lead Russian Jews to pressure Russia to continue the war. In this regard, it was also important to win over the American Jews, who, it was hoped, had sufficient influence on President Woodrow Wilson to convince him to accept Britain's occupation of Palestine. The British may also have intended to pre-empt the Germans' promise to the Jews of Middle and Eastern Europe.[27]

Wilhelm II now wanted to respond to the British decision with something along the lines of an 'Ottoman Balfour Declaration'. In a 12 December interview between *Vossische Zeitung* correspondent Julius Becker and the grand vizier, brokered by Ambassador Bernstorff, the grand vizier declared in principle what Bernstorff later reported – namely, that Turkey was sympathetic to the repopulation and colonization of the Jews in Palestine. Talaat assured free immigration and settlement 'at the natural boundaries of the current capacity of the country', the right to free economic development, and free development of Jewish culture and self-government within the framework of existing laws. He did not, however, extend any political autonomy to the Jews. On 5 January 1918, the Foreign Office received a delegation of the Zionist Organization in Germany, headed by Otto Warburg and Arthur Hantke, and a statement was handed to them, which was published the next day:

> We acknowledge those wishes that are directed to the development of their culture, as well as the specific characteristics of the Jewish minority in those countries where Jews have a highly developed quality of life, show full understanding, and are prepared to support their concerns referring to this. With regard to the aspirations pursued by the Jewry in Palestine, in particular by the Zionists, we appreciate the statements recently issued by Grand Vizier Talaat Pasha. In particular, we appreciate the intention of the imperial Ottoman government, in accordance with the exhibited friendly action towards the Jews, to support the flourishing Jewish settlement in Palestine by granting free immigration and settlement within the limits of the country's capacity, local autonomy in accordance with state laws, and free development of their cultural identity.[28]

In this context, Wolfgang Schwanitz speaks of a German-British competition for the favour of the Jews. Under pressure from Berlin, the grand vizier submitted the 'Ottoman Balfour Declaration', whose content went as far as the Balfour Declaration. On 6 September 1918, the Ottoman Council of Ministers decreed that all bans on Jewish immigration and settlement were lifted, and the Jewish nation should be treated equally. This declaration, according to Schwanitz, 'perished together with the emperor and the Ottoman Empire. Nonetheless, Wilhelm's political course from the end of 1915 slowed the pogroms and the attempted genocide'.[29] Richard Lichtheim later described the Kaiser's contribution as follows: 'The Jewish settlement in Palestine would not have survived the war if the German government had not taken protective measures'.[30] Before emigrating to Palestine, Robert Welsch, the editor of the *Jüdische Rundschau* in Berlin, wrote from Tel Aviv in 1970 that Germany had rescued Palestine's Yishuv – the Jewish residents – at a crucial moment: 'Without Germany, a connection for the advancement after the war would not have been possible'.[31] In other words, Wilhelm II, who had declared himself the protector of Muslims in 1898, became the protector of Jews in Palestine in the First World War.

Notes

1. Cited by Marc Hanisch, 'Max Freiherr von Oppenheim und die Revolutionierung der islamischen Welt als anti-imperiale Befreiung von oben', in Loth and Hanisch, *Erster Weltkrieg*, 13.
2. Will, *Kein Griff*.
3. Ibid.
4. Ibid.
5. Donald M. McKale, '"The Kaiser's Spy": Max von Oppenheim and the Anglo-German Rivalry before and during the First World War', *European History Quarterly* 27 (1997), 199–220. See also Lionel Gossman, *The Passion of Max Oppenheim: Archaeology and Intrigue in the Middle East from Wilhelm II to Hitler* (Cambridge: Cambridge University Press, 2013).
6. Schwanitz, *Islam in Europa*, 89–91.
7. Kreutzer, *Dschihad*, 36, 42, 43, 45. In July 1940, the ever-zealous Oppenheim produced a new document, the 'Memorandum on Revolutionizing the Middle East', similar to his memorandum of 1914. He had by then become a close friend of the Grand Mufti of Jerusalem, Mohammed Amin al-Husseini, in Berlin; see also Chapter 4.
8. Cf. the essays by Bernd Lemke on Goltz, Michael Jonas and Jan Zinke on Nadolny, Stefan M. Kreutzer on Waßmuß and Veit Veltzke on Klein in Loth and Hanisch, *Erster Weltkrieg*.
9. Alexander Will, 'Der Gegenspieler im Hintergrund: Josef Pomiankowski und die antideutsche Orientpolitik Österreich-Ungarns 1914–1918', in Loth and Hanisch, *Erster Weltkrieg*, 193–214.
10. See Wolfgang Gust (ed.), *The Armenian Genocide: Evidence from the German Foreign Office Archives 1915–1916* (New York and Oxford: Berghahn Books, 2014).
11. United States Official Records on the Armenian Genocide, 1915–1918, ed. by Ara Sarafian, (Glendale, CA: Taderon Press), 40.
12. NA/RG59/867.4016/76; ibid., 55; Facsimile in http://en.wikipedia.org/wiki/file:ambassadormorgenthautelegram.jpg/. Also in Aram Simonyan, 'The Armenian Genocide and Henry Morgenthau', in www.armeniansgenocide.am/.
13. Gust, *Genocide*, 185.
14. Ibid., 291.
15. Ibid., 291.
16. Ibid., 306.
17. Ibid., 394f.
18. Ibid., 395.
19. *New York Times*, 2 June 2016; *Washington Post*, 2 June 2016; welt.de, 2 June 2016.

20. Steininger and Agstner, *Nahostkonflikt*, 9. For the McMahon letter, see Walter Laqueur and Barry Rubin (eds), *The Israel–Arab Reader: A Documentary History of the Middle East Conflict* (New York: Penguin 2001), 11–12.

21. Cf. *Lawrence von Arabien, Genese eines Mythos: Begleitband zur Sonderausstellung 'Lawrence von Arabien'* (Mainz: Zabern, 2010). Peter Thurau, *Lawrence von Arabien: Ein Mann und seine Zeit* (Munich: C.H. Beck, 2010; see my review in MGZ 70, 2011).

22. See the excellent Wikipedia article (retrieved 31 January 2017); James Barr, *A Line in the Sand: Britain, France and the Struggle in the Middle East* (New York: Simon & Schuster, 2012); David Fromkin, *A Peace to End All Peace: The Fall of the Ottoman Empire and the Creation of the Modern Middle East* (New York: Avon, 1989), 188–99.

23. See Fromkin, *Peace,* 105ff.

24. Cit. by Janus Piekalkiewicz, *Der Erste Weltkrieg* (Düsseldorf and Vienna: Econ, 1988), 578f.

25. For more on the First World War in the Middle East, see Rolf Steininger, *Der Große Krieg 1914–1918 in 92 Kapiteln* (Reinbek and Munich: Lau 2016), chapters 27, 74, 75, 77, 91; Barr, *Line*; Fromkin, *Peace*.

26. For the following I rely heavily on Hansjörg Eiff, 'Die jüdische Heimstätte in Palästina in der deutschen Außenpolitik 1914–1918', *Zeitschrift für Geschichtswissenschaft* 60 (2012), 3, 202–27. See also Egmont Zechlin, *Die deutsche Politik und die Juden im Ersten Weltkrieg* (Göttingen: Vandenhoek & Ruprecht, 1969).

27. For the Balfour Declaration, see Steininger, Nahostkonflikt, 73–78; Gudrun Krämer, *A History of Palestine: From the Ottoman Conquest to the Founding of the State of Israel* (Princeton, NJ: Princeton University Press, 2008), 148–51.

28. Jüdische *Rundschau,* 11 January 1918.

29. Schwanitz, *Islam in Europa,* 110.

30. See Eiff, 'Heimstätte'.

31. Richard Lichtheim, *Rückkehr: Erinnerungen aus der Frühzeit des deutschen Zionismus* (Stuttgart: Deutsche Verlags-Anstalt, 1970), 210.

Chapter Three

WEIMAR AND THE THIRD REICH, 1918–1939

British, Jews, Arabs and the German Consul General in Jerusalem

After Turkey was created from the ruins of the Ottoman Empire, the remainder was divided between the French (today's Syria and Lebanon) and the British. The British were the new rulers in the Middle East. They continued to control the Suez Canal, arbitrarily drew borders with the French, arbitrarily established states (Iraq, Transjordan, Syria, Lebanon) and thus lay the foundation for conflicts that continue today. Then colonial secretary Winston Churchill simply cut the area east of the river Jordan off from Palestine, called it Transjordan and gave it to King Abdullah. Churchill later praised himself for having created the emirate Transjordan with a stroke of his pen on a sunny Sunday afternoon and still having had time to paint a picture of wonderful Jerusalem.[1]

For Palestine, the Balfour Declaration was the beginning of a new phase of conflict between Arabs and Jews. In July 1922, the League of Nations transferred the administration of Palestine to Great Britain under a mandate. The corresponding text, drafted by Zionists in Paris, took the declaration literally. It became relevant under international law, binding the British government for the next twenty-five years to support the Zionists' 'establishment in Palestine of a national home for the Jewish people'.[2]

In the early postwar years, Germany did not play a role in the Middle East. At the end of the war, the British closed the German Consulate General in Jerusalem, leaving the Spanish consul to represent German interests there. In 1924 the German Consulate General was opened again under the direction of Karl Kapp (1889–1947), who had been assigned to the Spanish consul on 9 February 1923 and then made vice-consul of the re-established Consulate General on 18 December 1924; he worked there until 24 July 1926. His successor was Erich Nord (1881–1935), who was superseded by Heinrich Wolff in 1932. In July 1935, Wolff was sent into temporary retirement because his wife was Jewish. The outrage among the Jerusalem consular corps about this 'ignoble' affair (as the Austrian colleague put it) was great at that time, but it did not change the decision, so Walter Döhle (1884–1945) became the consul general in Jerusalem until 30 July 1939.

When the war ended, Britain partly expropriated non-Jewish German settlers in Palestine – about two thousand Templars[3] – and evacuated them to Egypt. The British seized their old homes but also paid good rent for them, so in 1921, when the settlers could return to their places in Jerusalem, Sarona, Wilhelma (near Jaffa) and Haifa, they had cash, 'which proved useful for them in their dealings', stated a secret 'report of a traveller from Jerusalem, who arrived on 2 February, after several months spent in Berlin', sent to the Foreign Office in Berlin in February 1921.[4] By 1925, all the property had been returned to the Templars.

In 1924, the British allowed the reopening of the German Consulate General in Jerusalem as well as the consulates in Jaffa and in Haifa. In 1926, Germany was admitted to the League of Nations as a permanent member of its Mandate Commission; hence, Germany was bound to support and promote the Palestine Mandate and Balfour Declaration. The *Jüdische Rundschau* stated: 'With regard to the Jewish national home in Palestine, the German government will follow the policy of the British in Palestine'.[5]

This was not so simple on some occasions – for example, at the annual ritual of 'Deliverance Day' staged by the British in Jerusalem to commemorate General Allenby's victorious entry into Jerusalem on 9 December 1917. A government decree had proclaimed this day a national holiday in Palestine. Every 9 December, representatives of the losers of the war – Germans, Austrians and Turks – were not only invited to the celebrations but also expected to hoist flags on the occasion. The German consul general usually left a day before the celebration started; however, he let the flags fly. His Austrian counterpart usually let the flags fly, too, because 'even' the Germans had hoisted the flags. The Turkish consul remained 'invisible, did not hoist, but did not leave either. But what does it matter?' asked the Austrian consul general, Walter Haas, in early December 1927: 'He is a former clerk from Constantinople, a man of catastrophic indolence and lack of taste, and he is intellectually and socially impossible. At night, his wife and daughter spend time with chauffeurs and servants in public dance halls. No one takes him seriously'.[6]

Figure 3.1 After the First World War, the British rule the Near East with Palestine as British mandate. British soldiers in front of the Damascus Gate of the Old City of Jerusalem. Photo by Eric Matzon. Courtesy of Israel Government Press Office, Jerusalem.

Meanwhile, clashes between Jews and Arabs became more frequent due to anti-Jewish actions instigated by the spiritual leader of the Muslims, Amin al-Husseini, whom the British had appointed 'Mufti of Palestine' in May 1921. Only twenty-eight years old at the time, Husseini was a member of a wealthy family and soon called himself 'Grand Mufti of Jerusalem', which sounded more important. When hostilities first broke out in 1929, the Grand Mufti spoke of jihad that was being waged in Jaffa, Hebron, Safed and some other places: 133 Jews and 116 Arabs were killed.

The best reports about these massacres came from German Consul General Erich Nord. On 29 August 1929 he reported to the German Foreign Office about the unrest in Jerusalem:

]ext[During the riot, the parties were equally matched in their lack of restraint. In the Arab neighbourhoods, an outright hunt for Jews took place, while in the Jewish neighbourhood, as I could observe myself, Jews armed with sticks, iron bars, and stones indiscriminately beat down every fellah in the middle of the street. These events claimed countless lives and wounded, and the police were powerless. From Friday night to Saturday, the first heavy exchange of fire took place in the city's Jewish districts in the northwest, where the Arabs, who were mainly equipped with firearms, were violently attacked. The police, who had already called for reinforcement on Friday, fended off the attacks together with the Jews, who at that point were already entirely put on the defensive, and had formed a self-protection group armed with weapons by the police, among others. The attacks cost many lives on both sides.[7]

On 14 November, Nord examined the causes and effects of the riots, and concluded:

After the Balfour Declaration had opened the gates to Palestine for the Jews, the Zionists began to settle in with no regard to the feelings of the Arabs who had been living there for generations. They took themselves for benefactors of the country, completely misjudging the real conditions. Increasingly the Arabs felt pinned against the wall. They still have little understanding of the improve-

Figure 3.2 British soldiers in the Jewish quarter of Jerusalem, with the Dome of the Rock in the background. Photo by Eric Matzon. Courtesy of Israel Government Press Office, Jerusalem.

ments that Jews brought to their agricultural and industrial activities; in their hearts, they all despise the European cultural achievements.[8]

Ten days later, he added: 'The serious situation continues, because it is notorious that Jews and Arabs are arming themselves more and more'.[9] In the circumstances, the German-Jewish representative of the *Leipziger Neuesten Nachrichten* and various social democratic papers thought that Germany should try to mediate between Jews and Arabs, an idea that Nord rejected firmly. On 21 June 1930, he wrote to the Foreign Office in Berlin:

> I consider nothing more futile, and from the German viewpoint actually more dangerous, than to intervene with German entities or even with the German government, even if only indirectly, by influencing the German-Jewish circles over the ethnic conflict, which can hardly be kept hidden from the general public. Justifiably, the British mandate would be utterly alienated by such interference of any state, which already has adequate ways to control and influence the practice of the mandatory power by England, through its representatives in the commission of the League of Nations. The purported increase in German prestige in Palestine, with the expected intransigence of both populations as well as the nature of the unbridgeable issues of reciprocal claims, would not occur but would ultimately produce a mistrust of Germany, with consequences that the Germans [*das Deutschtum*] in the country would have to bear directly.[10]

The Foreign Office shared this opinion. A memorandum dated 28 July 1930 states:

> From the German point of view, a prudent neutrality is recommended towards the English difficulties with the Arab-Zionist opposition in Palestine. In their own political interest, it is primarily the responsibility of the English government to deal with the self-generated conditions and to carry out the obligations imposed. We must confine ourselves to expressing the desire and hope that the British mandate government may succeed in politically pacifying Palestine and fulfilling the promise of promoting a Jewish national home, without thereby infringing on the Arab majority's legitimate demands to decide their political and economic future after the implementation of self-government. The British mandate policy will reveal whether promoting the establishment of a Jewish national home is compatible with these legitimate demands of the Arab majority.[11]

The situation changed after 30 January 1933, with Hitler in power. Given the special circumstances of the situation in Palestine, the new consul general, Heinrich Wolff, on 20 March 1933, found it natural 'that the news about the fate of the Jews in Germany, more than anything else, caused quite a stir amongst the Jews as well as the Arabs'.[12] A succession of corresponding measures were passed. For instance, during the Purim celebrations in Tel Aviv, Hitler was 'vilified' – presented in effigy on a horse with a lance in his hand and a board on his chest, upon which 'Death to Jews' was written in Hebrew. In front of him were two figures of bloodied Jews in a wagon, and before them stood a sign with the inscription 'Herr Hitler, Chef der deutschen Regierung' [Mr Hitler, head of the German government], and another placard reading: '*Wir aus Deutschland vertriebenen Juden wollen, dass die Pforten unseres Landes Palästina uns geöffnet werden!*' [We, the expelled Jews of Germany, demand that the gates of our country Palestine be opened to us!]. The front of the wagon bore a map of Palestine, on which the image of a lock symbolized resistance to Jewish immigration. It read: '*Die Pforten unsres Landes sind uns versperrt*' [The gates of our country are closed to us].[13] In response, the consul general lodged a protest with the mayor of Tel Aviv as well as with the British Palestine government.

Then came the possibility of a boycott of German goods, the theft of the swastika flag from the Consulate General in Jerusalem and the repeated 'defilement' (*Besudelungen*) of the door and wall of the Consulate General,[14] as well as German tourists, one of whom told the consul general with exceptional pride that 'he went to the Wailing Wall with the swastika'.[15]

It was clear to Wolff, based on the news from Germany, that the German government was about to destroy the German Jews in a way the world had never seen before. It was hardly surprising, then, that young Jews in Palestine joined together in gangs. The 'National Youth' protested German films with stink bombs and forced their removal from the programme, the 'Covenant of Daredevils' boasted of having torn down the German flag at the consulate in Jaffa, and – of all things – Wolff received a warning in the mail instructing him to write his will if he did not publish a protest against

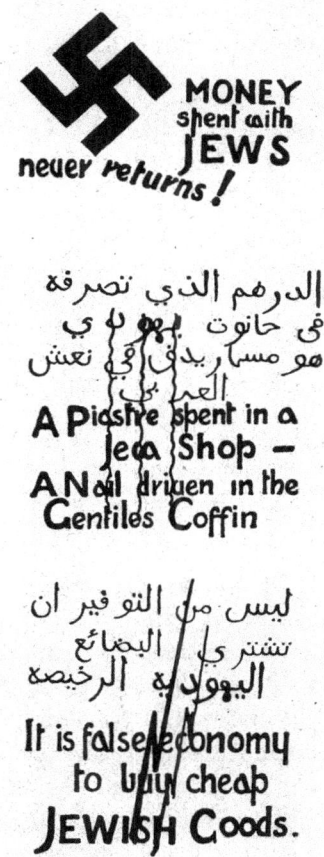

Figure 3.3 In the 1920s and especially in the 1930s, tensions between Jews and Arabs steadily increase. An Arabic pamphlet calls for a boycott of Jewish goods. Courtesy of National Archives II, College Park, Maryland.

the German government in the media within five days. Wolff described the situation at the end of 1933 as follows:

> Of course, the Jews here are most severely shocked by the horror and partial destruction of the Jews in Germany, and their reactions in the early months of last year were quite serious. These were vented with the boycott of German goods and scattered acts of violence against the Consulate General. However, it was remarkable how much faster than in other countries they proved themselves amenably inclined to tangible and economic lines of thought. The Jews here, who are responsible for the development of the National Home and the economic development of the country, are above all politicians and they realized very soon that opportunities may arise from the misfortune of Jews in Germany for Zionism and the development of Palestine. . . .
>
> The events in Germany provided Zionism with conclusive material for the right of their existence, and the shake-up of German Jews caused many inside and outside Germany to think about Zionism, the Jewish State, and the National Home, for which they once had only a pitying smile. Increased interest, deeper understanding, and an increased self-sacrifice of world Jewry for Zionist issues and objectives are the advantages that the past year brought to Zionism.[16]

Developments in Germany met with much interest from the Arab side as well, and 'a certain sense of *schadenfreude*' accompanied the heightening of tensions between the Jews and the Arabs, as Wolff reported on 20 March 1933.[17] Wolff, for his part, did not believe that the entire Arab population of Palestine was anti-Jewish; however, it was clear to him that those who considered themselves upper class and so-called intelligentsia attached great importance to emphasizing their anti-Jewish attitude: 'They cannot do enough to protest repeatedly against Jewish immigration, land sales to the Jews, Jewish capital, and whatever else they might imagine. And those that cry the loudest are they who have sold their land to the Jews and feathered their own nest. Although, not yet playing with fire, it remains to be seen where the immigration of German Jews here will lead.[18]

As early as 31 March 1933, the Grand Mufti Husseini offered his services in the fight against the Jews. Wolff reported to Berlin that same day:

> Mufti gave me detailed statements today that Muslims inside and outside of Palestine are welcoming the new regime in Germany and hoping for propagation of fascist, anti-democratic governance into other countries. Present Jewish influence on the economy and politics is harmful everywhere and needs to be opposed. In order to weaken Jews, Muslims hoped that Germany would boycott them and that the whole Muslim world would then enthusiastically join in. Mufti agreed to spread boycott among all Muslims, not only to the numerous Muslims travelling through here on pilgrimage to Mecca, but also, if necessary, by special emissaries. The anti-Jewish boycott could be easily described as a plan made in accordance with the resolution of the recently held Arab assembly in Jaffa. Mufti believes he could quickly create a boycott organization, and

Figure 3.4 1934: The German Templar colony in Haifa.
Photo by Zoltan Kluger. Courtesy of Israel Government Press Office, Jerusalem.

asks for sufficient supply of German industrial products to Palestine for local distribution by non-Jewish merchants.[19]

The admiration for Hitler's Germany spread so quickly that the desire to establish a National Socialist Arab Party (NSAP) was expressed as early as June 1933. Wolff felt it indeed commendable that the national rise of Germany found enthusiastic resonance in this part of the world, but he made it clear that the National Arab tendencies in a National Socialist party would be primarily against the local Jews and therefore against the British government, which would surely lead to a substantial change in Palestine's political situation. He considered it 'unsafe' to promote this party and risk being exposed as meddling in the affairs of the British administration in Palestine. He considered it 'highly unsafe' to make such a move, because the Jews would take it as political partisanship directed against them in favour of the Arabs.

The Foreign Office in Berlin shared these concerns 'entirely'. Moreover, it was said:

> Because of the notorious political unreliability of the Arabs, it can be assumed with certainty that with Arab indiscretion this connection would quickly become known not only in Palestine and the Middle East, but also in London and Paris. Since the war, the goal of our previous work in the countries of the Middle East was economic and cultural expansion with complete political neutrality. A change in this position, by way of our official representatives' interference in the domestic situation of these countries, would probably not only bring us economic setbacks, but also, with English and French supremacy in the Middle East, have serious repercussions for our policy in Europe.[20]

There was, in fact, no NSAP; however, this did not alter the Arabs' continuing admiration for the Nazis on rather dubious grounds, as a report of 15 January 1934 from Consul General Wolff made clear:

> The Arabs vigorously welcomed the developments in Germany, partly because the anti-Jewish orientation pleased them and partly because they envied Germany its leader all the more as they realized they lacked any leading personality. In their admiration of Germany these politically still primitive people do not get the obvious idea of making Germany responsible for the increased Jewish immigration to Palestine.[21]

There would have been reason enough for such a ploy: from 1933 up to the start of the Second World War, the Nazi regime, in cooperation with Zionists, had promoted the emigration of German Jews under the so-called Haavara Agreement (Hebrew *Haavara* = transfer), which provided that German Jews could transfer part of their assets to Palestine.[22] Nevertheless, Hitler enjoyed great popularity in the Arab world, as shown by an episode in 1936, immediately after the Arab uprising against the British broke out

Figure 3.5 1935: Scene in Haifa. Photo by Zoltan Kluger. Courtesy of Israel Government Press Office, Jerusalem.

in Palestine. The newly appointed consul general, Walter Döhle, reported that a caravan trip with colleagues from Jerusalem to Jenin had been cancelled. Döhle – who had already been greeted by an Arab with the cry 'Hoch Deutschland' (esteemed Germany) – continued the trip on his own and later reported to Berlin:

> When I stopped on the road to mount a highly visible swastika flag on the radiator of my car, in addition to the official flag attached to the flag stand, a car with Arabs came from the direction of Nablus. I spoke to the Arabs. They agreed to assist me during the passage through Jenin. The transit through Jenin went slowly, with stops about every five metres. My car was constantly surrounded by an excited crowd equipped with sticks and sabres (old German weapons). Five to six Arabs stood on the footboard of my car in a permanent parley, in which I only intervened with the Arabic words 'Konsul almani' and the German greeting 'Heil Hitler'. The response from the Arab side followed likewise with 'Heil Hitler' and applause so that the trip bore comparison to a triumphal procession. Among the Arabs, the German greeting 'Heil Hitler', symbolic of the Führer's and the Reich Chancellor's popularity, had the strongest impact on this frenzied mob.[23]

National Socialism had the same effect on the German Templars in Palestine. Local NSDAP branches had been set up there, starting in 1933, and by 1938 every third Templar was a member of the party – the highest level of party affiliation among Germans living abroad. When the war started, the British declared the Templars enemy aliens, as in 1918. Women and children could remain in their settlements, but the men were detained in Acre. When Rommel approached the Suez Canal, the British played it safe and deported the Templars to Australia.[24]

On 22 March 1937, in a comprehensive 17-page memorandum, Consul General Döhle considered further German policies with regard to Palestine. Because Döhle's statements about the Arabs were in many ways valid for the coming years, they are quoted here at length:

> On every level, the Palestinian Arabs show great affection for the new Germany and its leader, a support that is worth all the more as it is based on purely idealistic concepts. The German name has, since pre-war times, had a good ring to it, and the visits of the Prussian crown prince in 1869 and the visit of the German Kaiser in 1898 are still mentioned in conversations with the Arabs. The performance of the German troops during the war in Palestine has likewise contributed to strengthened German prestige. The efficiency and the good understanding that the German colonists [the Templars], established towards the Arabs and maintained for decades, has strengthened Germany's reputation [das Ansehen des Deutschtums].

However, what is decisive for the affection that now exists towards Germany among the Arabs is the admiration which our Führer enjoys. Especially at times of unrest, there have been more opportunities to determine how deep this liking extends. If you made yourself known as a German when threatened by an Arab crowd, this was generally a free pass for unobstructed passage. If you identified yourself with the German greeting 'Heil Hitler', the attitude changed suddenly into admiration and the Germans received an ovation, in which the Arabs responded vigorously to the German greeting. The enthusiasm for our Führer and the new Germany is probably so widespread because the Palestinian Arabs, in their struggle for their existence, have longed for an Arab 'Führer' and because they felt united with the Germans in the struggle against the Jews. It must be our

Figure 3.6 Jaffa Gate of the Old City of Jerusalem. Photo by Eric Matzon. Courtesy of Israel Government Press Office, Jerusalem.

endeavour to preserve and maintain the existing Arab sympathy for the new Germany and its leader. For this, it is not so much a very active Arab policy that is necessary, but rather an avoidance of obviously promoting the development of the Jewish National Home.²⁵

On 7 July 1937, the British submitted the so-called 'Three State Plan' (also called the 'Three Partition Plan') of the Peel Commission, named after the Chairman William Robert Wellesley, Earl Peel: Palestine would be divided into an Arab state, a Jewish state, and a corridor from Jerusalem and Bethlehem to Jaffa along with the enclaves Nazareth and Tiberias, which would remain under British control.²⁶ Döhle did not think much of the plan. He wrote to Berlin on 7 July: 'This type of partition would mean a death blow for the Germans [*das Deutschtum*] in Palestine, because, in the long run, the existence of German settlements is impossible in the Jewish state'. Döhle added further objections:

> The English interests are fully respected. Creating a new mandate for those 'holy places' would give England a very nice moral justification for remaining in the country; and by the contractual agreements with the Jewish and Arab states, England's influence in the area would remain safeguarded, not only politically but also militarily; and the costs would be limited to an amount that should not exceed what England has paid so far. That is why the plan is an ideal 'English' solution.²⁷

Figure 3.7 In April 1936, the newly formed Arab High Committee calls for a general strike 'until national victory'. It is a rebellion against the Jews and the British, and becomes the 'Holy War' for the 'Holy Land'. Here Arabs reading slogans hung on the Al-Aqsa mosque in the Old City of Jerusalem. Photo by Eric Matzon. Courtesy of Israel Government Press Office, Jerusalem.

On 15 July 1937, one week after the plan was announced and two days before the British undertook to arrest him, the Grand Mufti met with Döhle and left no doubt that the Palestinian Arabs as well as the rest of the Arab and Muslim world had rejected the plan. Döhle reported to Berlin:

> In their fight against Jews and pro-Jewish policies, the Arabs hoped for support of those great powers whose interests were in alignment with Britain, France and Turkey on one hand, and Italy and Germany on the other. The Grand Mufti emphasized the appeal New Germany held for the Arabs, and expressed hope that Germany would face the Arabs' struggle as a friend and be willing to support them. . . . More precisely, he expressed his wish that Germany would be prepared to take a stand against the Jews and the plan to create the Jewish State, whether in the press or otherwise. . . . The Grand Mufti then expressed his intention to send a confidant to Germany incognito to discuss German and Arab Muslim interests, which he considered to be the same.[28]

Although the confidant arrived in Berlin, he was not received at the Foreign Office. In November 1937, the Grand Mufti tried again, sending another delegate to Berlin. In return for German support for the Arab uprising, the Grand Mufti offered:

1. Promotion of trade relations.
2. Pro-German propaganda and the spread of an 'appealing atmosphere' for the Reich, especially with regard to a possible war.
3. The spread of National Socialism in the Arab world.
4. Promotion of the anti-communist movement.
5. Support for an anti-Jewish economic boycott led by Germany.
6. Terrorist acts in mandate territories and colonies controlled by France.
7. Continuation of the fight against establishment of a Jewish state in Palestine.
8. Propagation of German culture in the Arab world.
9. Exclusive takeover by German capital and 'intellectual forces' once the Arab liberation movement succeeded.[29]

To the German ambassador in Baghdad, Fritz Grobba, it was made clearer. The Palestinian freedom fighters hoped 'for German aid and are of the opinion that Germany, which sends them its Jews, must also send them weapons to fight them'.[30] Again, the Grand Mufti received a rather disappointing response: not wanting to provoke the British in Palestine, Berlin maintained its stance. As Grobba pointed out: 'We wish to live in good relations with England and therefore, despite all liking for the Arabs, cannot support an uprising directed against England'. A probable additional factor was the general attitude towards the Arabs. In late 1933 Consul General Wolff once described it as follows: 'Regarding the attitude of the Arabs, one can only say, it is always the same. The mash must be kept at a boil and stirred to the right and then again to the left, and then they call it politics'. He also mentioned something Lawrence of Arabia had said about the Arabs: 'I do not know how one can take the Arabs seriously at all. I know them well. It is not worth the effort'.[31]

And yet there were numerous testimonies of friendship shown by the Arabs towards Germany. Grobba analysed this phenomenon in December 1937. He saw its origins in the Ottoman era, going back to Kaiser Wilhelm II's Arab-friendly remarks during his travels in the Orient in 1898, and to the German–Turkish alliance during the war. Added to that was the Arabs' realization that Germany was the only great European power that was both strong enough to help the Arabs achieve their national goals and unlikely to pursue its own intentions in Arab territory.

Seeing the Führer as having restored national unity and liberty to the German people, the Arabs came to consider him a role model. Even today, Hitler is generally admired in the Arab world. Meanwhile, the Arabs' confidence in Germany was expressed above all in their repeated requests for German aid; furthermore, they regarded Germany as their only real ally in their struggle against the establishment of a Jewish state.

Nevertheless, for some Arabs Germany's reluctance led to doubts. At the beginning of 1938 Döhle sent an alarming article from a local Arab newspaper that questioned the oft-cited German–Arab friendship: 'What has Germany done to earn a reputation as a friend of the Arabs? . . . The German anti-Jewish policies brought on a strong influx of German-Jewish

Figure 3.8 British soldiers with steel helmets secure the Government House in Jaffa. Photo by Zoltan Kluger. Courtesy of Israel Government Press Office, Jerusalem.

emigrants to Palestine: this was the 'good thing' that Germany brought to the Arabs'.[32] This ultimately remained a lone voice; basically, nothing about the Arabs' attitude had changed, as the following action makes clear.

In 1938, two years after the Arabs first rose up against the British and Jews in Palestine, the self-proclaimed religious fighter Abu Durra, leader of the uprising movement in the northern district of Palestine, appealed directly to Adolf Hitler as the 'great leader of Germany, who created everlasting honour and glory for his nation', to inform him of the 'atrocities and cruelties' of the British military government. In a letter to Hitler dated 23 December 1938, he added: 'This unjust government perpetrated every barbarity and committed every cruelty. It blew up numerous villages, arrested thousands of peaceful residents and seriously abused them. It hanged men, robbed possessions, destroyed their houses and dwellings; it also tried to question their honour. Shame on this government and shame on their alleged justice and civilization!' Then Abu Durra wrote about the Jews:

> We will tell them what you, the leader of Germany, said about the Jews during a conflict: he, who in the midst of bullets and shells, takes the cigarette from his brother does not deserve to enjoy it at a time of peace. The Jew, who was stingy towards you with cigarettes during the war, can in no way be useful to Germany. I would not like to make you, great German leader, acquainted with the Jews. You know them and their history, and knew them even before we met them.

Abu Durra ended by expressing the following wish: 'That you, who with one word makes Europe tremble, bring our cause to all of Europe'.[33]

Notes

1. Cf. Steininger, *Nahostkonflikt*, 12–14.

2. Terms of the British Mandate are in Laqueur and Rubin, *Israel–Arab Reader*, 26–30, here 30.

3. The Temple Society (*Tempelgesellschaft*) was a German Protestant sect that was expelled from the Lutheran Church and settled in Palestine in the late nineteenth century. Members referred to themselves as Templars.

4. 'Geheim. Bericht eines Reisenden aus Jerusalem, der am 2. Februar nach mehrmonatigem Aufenthalt in Berlin eingetroffen ist'. XX to AA (Berlin), 9 February 1921. *Palästina*, Doc. 1.

5. Cf. Hansjörg Eiff, 'Die jüdische Heimstätte in Palästina in der Außenpolitik der Weimarer Republik', *Zeitschrift für Geschichtswissenschaft* 61 (2013), 12, 1005–28.

6. 'Deliverance Day am 9. Dezember 1927'. Walter Haas (Jerusalem) to Bundeskanzleramt/Auswärtige Angelegenheiten (Vienna), 18 December 1927. *Jerusalem*, Doc. 13.

7. 'Schwere Unruhen in Palästina'. Walter Hess (Jerusalem) to AA, 29 August 1929. *Palästina*, Doc. 16; see also Doc. 14 (27 August 1929), Doc. 15 (28 August 1929), Doc. 17 (12 September 1929).

8. 'Ursachen und Nachwirkungen der Palästinaunruhen'. Erich Nord (Jerusalem) to AA, 14 November 1929. Ibid., Doc. 22.

9. 'Fortdauernd ernste Lage in Palästina'. Erich Nord (Jerusalem) to AA, 25 November 1929. Ibid., Doc. 24.

10. 'Deutsche Objektivität im Palästinakonflikt'. Erich Nord (Jerusalem) to AA, 21 June 1930. Ibid., Doc. 34.

11. Cited in Eiff, 'Weimarer Republik', 1024.

12. 'Stellung der hiesigen Bevölkerung zu den judenfeindlichen Geschehnissen in Deutschland und zur Hakenkreuzfahne'. Heinrich Wolff (Jerusalem) to AA, 20 March 1933. *Palästina*, Doc. 59.

13. Ibid., Doc. 60 (25 March 1933: 'Verunglimpfung der Person des Herrn Reichskanzlers beim Purim Faschings- Fest in Tel Aviv'), Doc. 67 (8 May 1933), Doc. 71 (18 May 1933), Doc. 72 (23 May 1933), Doc. 75 (24 June 1933).

14. 'Wiederholte Besudelungen der Tür und Mauer des Generalkonsulats'. Heinrich Wolff (Jerusalem) to AA, 24 February 1934. Ibid., Doc. 90.

15. 'Bevorstehender Besuch deutscher Touristen in Palästina'. Heinrich Wolff (Jerusalem) to AA, 9 March 1934. Ibid., Doc. 91.

16. 'Politische Übersicht über das Jahr 1933'. Heinrich Wolff (Jerusalem) to AA, 15 January 1934. Ibid., Doc. 88.

17. 'Stellung der hiesigen Bevölkerung zu den judenfeindlichen Geschehnissen in Deutschland und zur Hakenkreuzfahne'. Heinrich Wolff (Jerusalem) to AA, 20 March 1933. Ibid., Doc. 59.

18. 'Arabische Einstellung zur Lage der Juden in Deutschland'. Heinrich Wolff (Jerusalem) to AA, 20 April 1933. Ibid., Doc. 65.

19. Heinrich Wolff (Jerusalem) to AA, 31 March 1933. Ibid., Doc. 62.

20. 'Beabsichtigte Gründung einer Nationalsozialistischen Arabischen Partei'. Heinrich Wolff (Jerusalem) to AA, 27 June 1933. Ibid., Doc. 76.

21. 'Politische Übersicht über das Jahr 1933'. Heinrich Wolff (Jerusalem) to AA, 15 January 1934. Ibid., Doc. 88.

22. For the Havaara Agreement, see Nicosia, *Third Reich*, 29–49.

23. 'Zwischenfall in Dschenin'. Walter Döhle (Jerusalem) to AA, 28 April 1936. *Palästina*, Doc. 99.

24. Cf. Ralf Balke, *Hakenkreuz im Heiligen Land: Die NSDAP-Landesgruppe Palästina* (Erfurt: Sutton, 2001). Several Templars returned to Palestine after 1945, but after the founding of Israel in 1948 there was no room for them and they had to leave the country. Some went back to Germany, others to Australia. They were generously compensated by the State of Israel; in the Luxembourg Agreement of 1952 (see Chapter 5), 54 million Deutschmarks were earmarked for them.

25. 'Prüfung der Frage, ob unsere Palästina gegenüber bisher verfolgte Richtlinie beibehalten werden kann oder ob sie eine Änderung erfahren muß'. Walter Döhle (Jerusalem) to AA, 22 March 1937. 17 pages; facsimile in *Palästina*, 426–43.

26. For details, see Krämer, *Palestine*, 278–84.

27. 'Dreiteilung Palästinas und ihre Folgen für die deutschen Kolonisten'. Walter Döhle (Jerusalem) to AA, *Palästina*, Doc. 110.

28. 'Großmufti und Dreiländerplan'. Ibid., Doc. 113.

29. *Akten zur Deutschen Auswärtigen Politik*, Series D, Bd. 5, Nr. 576, 654f.

30. Gensicke, *Mufti*, 37.

31. 'Fortschritt in Palästina und Stillstand in Transjordanien. Arabische Uneinigkeit. Die landlosen Arbeiter und ihre Ansiedlung'. Heinrich Wolff (Jerusalem) to AA, 25 March 1933. Ibid., Doc. 78 ['Von der Haltung der Araber kann man wohl nur sagen, es ist immer dasselbe. Der Brei muss am Kochen erhalten und mal rechts- und dann wieder mal linksherum gerührt werden, und das nennen sie dann Politik treiben'].

32. Cited in Alexander Schölch, 'Das Dritte Reich, die zionistische Bewegung und der Palästina-Konflikt', *Vierteljahrshefte für Zeitgeschichte* 30 (1982), 661.

33. Original and translation sent by Walter Döhle (Jerusalem) to AA. *Palästina*, Doc. 136.

Chapter Four

DURING THE SECOND WORLD WAR

Hitler and Iraq: A Wasted Opportunity?

Most Arabs admired Hitler as the Führer of Greater Germany and applauded his anti-Jewish policy. In 1939, in the first few months of the war, shops in Syrian towns frequently displayed posters with Arabic sayings such as 'In Heaven, God is your ruler; on earth, Hitler'. In the streets of Aleppo, Homs and Damascus, a popular anti-French and anti-British verse in a local dialect said: 'No more "Monsieur", no more "Mister". God in Heaven, Hitler on earth!'[1]

A little later, German politics again came to focus on the Middle East, primarily Iraq. Iraq was artificially produced after the First World War by Britain's colonial secretary, Winston Churchill, who had the astounding idea of joining two completely separate oilfields, Kirkuk and Mosul, by forcing Sunnis, Shiites and Kurds – three religious groups with hardly anything in common – together into one state. Iraq was thus created to serve the political, strategic and economic interests of Great Britain. The British made Faisal the king of Iraq in 1921, yet the British high commissioner was still the highest authority in the country and remained so even after Iraq became formally independent in 1932. Whereas the Iraqi army leadership honoured this arrangement in the following years, the lower ranks became increasingly excited about Nazi Germany and Fascist Italy, with whose help they hoped to build a truly independent Iraq.[2]

Germany warmly welcomed these affections. The German ambassador in Baghdad, Fritz Grobba, had been encouraging them since 1932. His organized cultural-political activities and extensive dissemination of propaganda culminated in the thesis of the traditional German–Arab friendship and shared hostility to Britain. Young followers even formed a paramilitary organization modelled after the Hitler Youth. Early in the war, on 6 September 1939, Prime Minister Nuri al-Said, who was Britain's man, broke off diplomatic relations with Germany, but the pro-German faction in Iraq became stronger nonetheless after the initial German victories. Al-Said resigned in March 1940 but stayed on as foreign minister in the new cabinet of Prime Minister Rashid Ali al-Gailani, whom the British had pressured to step aside for the compromise candidate Taha al-Hashimi. However, the pro-German faction was unwilling to accept this and had the support of the Grand Mufti of Jerusalem, Amin al-Husseini, who in 1939 had come from Damascus to Baghdad, where he had continued his fight against the British and the Jews as a declared admirer of Hitler. In February 1941, he sent his secretary and friend Ottman Kamal Haddads to Hitler with a letter, in which he proposed the following:

> The Arab people should stand together with the Axis powers and contribute to the well-deserved elimination of the Anglo-Jewish coalition. British policy in Palestine is aimed at creating obstacles to the unity and independence of Arab countries, forcing them into direct confrontation with all Jews, those dangerous enemies, whose secret weapons are finance, corruption and intrigue, and who, incidentally, stand alongside the British bayonets. But all along, the Arab people have had only the warmest sentiments for Germany and the Axis. No propaganda in the world could change this truth.[3]

They asked for weapons and financial support, and for a declaration of independence of a future great Arab empire.[4]

On 11 March 1941, an answer was composed by State Secretary Ernst von Weizsäcker at the Foreign Office, who was authorized to communicate the following in Hitler's name to the Grand Mufti:

> Germany, which has never had Arab territories in its possession, has no territorial objectives in the Arab region. It is of the opinion that the Arabs, an ancient civilized people, have proven their suitability for administrative activity and, along with military virtues are, for all intents and purposes, able to govern themselves. Germany, therefore, recognizes the complete independence of the Arab states, or, where it has not been reached, the right to obtain it. Germany is willing to cooperate closely with the Arabs, to support them militarily as well as financially, and to supply war materiel.[5]

On 1 April 1941, the Iraqi army organized a coup d'état under the Axis-friendly ex-prime minister, Rashid Ali al-Gailani. The British embassy in Baghdad, like all other key positions, was occupied, and al-Gailani was appointed as the new prime minister. Berlin recognized the pro-German government and advised it 'to take up armed resistance against England' with the assurance that 'Italy and Germany will prepare support with weapons and ammunition'.[6] Thirty days of shock ensued in Iraq and the Middle East as Rommel pushed forward in North Africa, Crete was conquered and the Italians bombed Haifa. The British suspected that German troops would land in Syria and then advance through Iraq and Iran into India. Iraq should have been the initial spark of the Arab uprising in the region.

With the Germans' help, the Iraqis wanted to shake off the 'English yoke' and free themselves from London's power. The Grand Mufti called for jihad. British prime minister Winston Churchill recognized the danger and reinforced the British troops in Basra in order to establish a permanent military base there. The British–Iraqi war began on 2 May, when the Iraqis attacked their Habbaniya airbase in Baghdad.

Fritz Grobba (1886–1973) was one of the foremost Middle East experts on the German side at the time. In 1923 the Foreign Office had made him a consul and sent him to establish diplomatic representation in Kabul, where he was a chargé d'affaires from 1924 to 1926; and from 1932 until the severance of diplomatic relations with Iraq on 6 September 1939, he was the German ambassador in Baghdad. In early March 1941, he submitted a secret 'outline of the Arab issue'. Point 4 was about 'the importance of Iraqi oil for warfare in the Middle East'; a map titled 'The Crude Oil in the Middle East' (*Das Erdöl Vorderasiens*) featured oil facilities, oil wells, pipelines, and so forth.[7] Indeed, oil may have been the main factor in Hitler's decision to focus on the Middle East. On 5 March, Hitler designated Iraq as the main source of fuel to the Axis powers in 'operations between the Mediterranean and the Persian Gulf'. In a memorandum to Hitler on 27 April, Foreign Minister Ribbentrop stated it was 'quite likely that the British will, by all means, try to establish themselves in Iraq, against the will of the Iraqi government and army, for the purpose of gaining control of the Mosul oil'.[8]

On 6 May 1941, Hitler set up the 'Special Force Junck', named after fighter pilot Colonel Werner Junck, to secretly undertake to ignite a jihad against the British – exactly what Kaiser Wilhelm II had wanted during the First World War.[9] Next, Foreign Minister Ribbentrop mobilized Grobba, who flew from Aleppo to Mosul under the alias 'Frank Gehrke' and arrived in Baghdad on 11 May. Meanwhile, in Vichy-ruled Syria, the German diplomat Rudolf Rahn organized fifty wagonloads of arms and accompanied the train to Mosul. However, the entire operation was under an unlucky star: several things went wrong from the outset. Major Axel von Blomberg, son of Field Marshal Werner von Blomberg, was to coordinate the activities with the insurgents. On 12 May 1941, he was on approach to land in Baghdad, but his aircraft was not yet registered there and the Iraqis mistakenly fired. Although the pilot managed to land safely, a bullet struck Blomberg in the neck, killing him instantly. (Also on board was legation secretary Günther Pawelke, who worked at the Baghdad embassy for Grobba and later as ambassador in Cairo from 1952 to 1954; see Chapter 5.)[10]

Not until 23 May 1941 did Hitler decide to support the coup d'état without reservation. In Directive No. 30, 'Middle East', he stated: 'In the Middle East, the Arab liberation movement is our natural ally against England. In this context, the rise of Iraq is of particular importance. . . . I have decided, therefore, to propel the development of the Middle East forward, by supporting Iraq'. Air Force General Hellmuth Felmy was appointed as central authority for all Arab affairs concerning the Wehrmacht, under the code name Special Staff F. The members of the military mission were to be classified as volunteers (like the Condor Legion during the Spanish Civil War) and wear a tropical uniform with Iraqi badges; they were responsible for navigating the German planes. Throughout the process, the Foreign Office was to steer the propaganda thus: 'An Axis victory will liberate the countries in the Middle East from the English yoke and thereby allow free exercise of their right of self-determination. Those who love freedom, join the front line against England'.[11]

But it was already too late. The German airmen's situation was disastrous; they lacked everything. Reinforcements could not be sent because 'Operation Barbarossa', the German invasion of the Soviet Union, was going to start on 22 June. On 1 June, the British recaptured Baghdad, where pro-German Iraqis had killed 179 Jews in a pogrom. Most of the rebels fled via Tehran and Italy to Berlin, where they lived until the end of the war. Al-Gailani, who had been sentenced to death in absentia in Baghdad, was initially also in Tehran, where the German Mission was instructed to explain Germany's position to him: 'For our policies in the Arab world, it is of great importance not to give the impression that we drop our friends as the result of one failure'.[12] Churchill wrote in his memoirs: 'Hitler certainly cast away the opportunity of taking a great prize for little cost in the Middle East'.[13] Fritz Grobba, in a memoir published in 1967, complained that 'German prestige will suffer from this for a long time'.[14]

On 11 June 1941, Hitler and the High Command of the Wehrmacht (OKW) issued Directive No. 32, 'Preparations for the period after "Barbarossa"', which read (in part):

> [Exploitation of the Arab Freedom Movement.
> The situation of the English in the Middle East will be rendered more precarious, in the event of major German operations, if more British forces are tied down at the right moment by civil commotion or revolt. All military, political and propaganda measures must, to this end, be closely coordinated during the preparatory period. As central agency abroad, I nominate Special Staff F, which is to take part in all plans and actions in the Arab area, and whose headquarters are to be in the area of the Commander of the Armed Forces South East. The most competent available experts and agents will be made available to it. The Chief of the High Command of the Armed Forces will specify the duties of

During the Second World War

Special Staff F, in agreement with the foreign minister where political questions are involved.[15]

Grand Mufti Husseini in Berlin

The Grand Mufti escaped disaster in Baghdad by fleeing via Italy to Berlin, where he arrived on 6 November 1941 and demanded 'a larger Jewish residence'. He stayed in Berlin until the end of the war. Not long before that, Abdalla Frangi, a representative of the Fatah in Germany, had said that the mufti had been 'allowed to stay in Berlin, but was being completely ignored by the Germans'.[16] We know now that the exact opposite was true. The mufti pursued two goals: the extermination of Jews – and thus no 'national home' for the Jews in Palestine; and the independence of the Arabs. Hatred of Jews connected the mufti to the Nazis, especially the head of the SS, Heinrich Himmler. In principle the National Socialists regarded Arabs too as 'racial enemies', but this changed in the course of the worsening war situation. Hitler received the Grand Mufti on 28 November 1941, when,

Figure 4.1 28 November 1941: Meeting between Adolf Hitler and the Grand Mufti of Jerusalem, Husseini, in Berlin. © ullstein bild – Heinrich Hoffmann.

according to Wolfgang G. Schwanitz, they 'finalized the genocide pact for the extermination of the Jews'.[17]

This thesis is highly controversial, given the dubiousness of the notion that Hitler needed the mufti in order to exterminate the Jews. Foreign Minister Ribbentrop and Fritz Grobba were present during the meeting. The official protocol states:

> The Grand Mufti began by thanking the Führer for the great honour he had bestowed by receiving him. He wished to seize the opportunity to convey to the Führer of the Greater German Reich, admired by the entire Arab world, his thanks for the sympathy that the Führer had always shown for the Arab and especially the Palestinian cause, and to which he had given clear expression in his public speeches. The Arab countries were firmly convinced that Germany would win the war and that the Arab cause would then prosper. The Arabs were Germany's natural friends because they had the same enemies as Germany, namely the English, the Jews and the Communists. Therefore they were prepared to cooperate with Germany with all their hearts and stood ready to participate in the war, not only negatively by the commission of acts of sabotage and the instigation of revolutions, but also positively by the formation of an Arab Legion. . . .
>
> Of Germany's victory the Arab world was firmly convinced, not only because the Reich possessed a large army, brave soldiers, and military leaders of genius, but also because the Almighty could never award the victory to an unjust cause. In this struggle, the Arabs were striving for the independence and unity of Palestine, Syria and Iraq.
>
> The mufti then mentioned the letter he had received from Germany on 8 April 1941, which stated that Germany was holding no Arab territories and understood and recognized the aspirations to independence and freedom of the Arabs, just as it supported the elimination of the Jewish national home.
>
> A public declaration in this sense would be very useful for its propagandistic effect on the Arab peoples at this moment. It would rouse the Arabs from their momentary lethargy and give them new courage. . . .
>
> But if they were not inspired with such a hope by a declaration of this sort, it could be expected that the English would gain from it.
>
> The Führer replied that Germany's fundamental attitude on these questions, as the mufti himself had already stated, was clear. Germany stood for uncompromising war against the Jews. That naturally included active opposition to the Jewish national home in Palestine, which was nothing other than a centre, in the form of a state, for the exercise of destructive influence by Jewish interests. Germany was also aware that the assertion that the Jews were carrying out the functions of economic pioneers in Palestine was a lie. The work there was done only by the Arabs, not by the Jews. Germany was resolved, step by step, to ask one European nation after another to solve its Jewish problem, and at the proper time to direct a similar appeal to non-European nations as well. . . .
>
> Germany was now engaged in very severe battles to force the gateway to the northern Caucasus region. The difficulties were mainly with regard to maintaining the supply, which was most difficult as a result of the destruction of railroads and highways as well as the oncoming winter. . . .

The Führer then made the following statement to the mufti, enjoining him to take it to the uttermost depths of his heart:
1. He (the Führer) would carry on the battle to the total destruction of the Judeo-Communist empire in Europe.
2. At some moment, which was impossible to set exactly today but which in any event was not distant, the German armies would in the course of this struggle reach the southern exit from Caucasia.
3. As soon as this had happened, the Führer would on his own give the Arab world the assurance that its hour of liberation had arrived. Germany's objective would then be solely the destruction of the Jewish element residing in the Arab sphere under the protection of British power. In that hour the mufti would be the most authoritative spokesman for the Arab world. It would then be his task to launch the Arab operations, which he would have secretly prepared. When that time had come, Germany could also be indifferent to the French reaction to such a declaration.

Once Germany had forced open the road to Iran and Iraq through Rostov, it would also be the beginning of the end of the Britain's global empire. He (the Führer) hoped that in the coming year it would be possible for Germany to thrust open the Caucasian gate to the Middle East. For the good of their common cause, it would be better for the Arab proclamation to be put off for a few more months than for Germany to create difficulties for herself without being able thereby to help the Arabs.

He (the Führer) fully appreciated the eagerness of the Arabs for a public declaration of the sort requested by the Grand Mufti. But he would beg him to consider that he (the Führer) himself had been the chief of state of the German Reich for five long years during which he was unable to make to his own homeland the announcement of its liberation. He had to wait for that until the announcement could be made, on the basis of a situation brought about by the force of arms, that the Anschluss had been carried out. The moment that Germany's tank divisions and air squadrons had made their appearance south of the Caucasus, the public appeal requested by the Grand Mufti could go out to the Arab world.

The Grand Mufti replied that it was his view that everything would come to pass just as the Führer had indicated. He was fully reassured and satisfied by the words that he had heard from the chief of the German state. He asked, however, whether it would not be possible, secretly at least, to enter into an agreement with Germany of the kind he had just outlined for the Führer.

The Führer replied that he had just now given the Grand Mufti precisely that confidential declaration.

The Grand Mufti thanked him for it and stated in conclusion that he was taking his leave from the Führer in full confidence and with reiterated thanks for the interest shown in the Arab cause.[18]

Hitler's public declaration in favour of the Arabs, as requested by Husseini, never happened; nor did anything come of the agreed-upon destruction of the 'national home' for the Jews. On the contrary, six years later almost exactly to the day, on 29 November 1947, the United Nations General Assembly decided on the partition of Palestine into an Arab state and a Jewish state, with Jerusalem to be an internationalized city. Five months later, on 14 May 1948 – fifty years and nine months since Theodor Herzl's organization of the First Zionist in Basel in 1897 – the new State of Israel came to into being.

In his memoirs, Grobba summarized Germany's Middle East policy during the war as one of wasted opportunities.[19]

On 28 April 1942, the German government promised Husseini and al-Gailani that Germany and Italy would assist the Arabs' fight for freedom and recognize the independence of the involved states.[20] However, this did not change Hitler's restrained, cautious attitude towards the Arabs' struggle. He was still against making a statement at that time, for in his view everything depended on the military development. Hitler made his position clear in a conversation with Benito Mussolini at Klessheim Palace near Salzburg on 29 April 1942:

> Such a declaration could only be effectively supported militarily when the Axis troops are south of the Caucasus. An insurrection of the Arabs could then be useful militarily and could then be supported militarily. If, on the other hand, the declaration were given to the Arabs now, there would be two possibilities. One was that the Arabs would not take note of it. In that case, such a declaration would be worthless to the Axis. Indeed, it would even be harmful, as the opposition would conclude that the Axis lacked influence in these areas. The other possibility is that the Arabs could take note of this declaration and start an insurrection, which, under the present circumstances, would be defeated by the British, who would capture the most active Axis-friendly Arabs, and thereby cause considerable damage to the interests of the Axis in the Middle East. Such developments could only be prevented when the Axis troops were south of the Caucasus. He (the Führer), however, had great concern that a proclamation at the present moment could not be supported by Axis troops.[21]

On 14 May 1943, Ribbentrop, Air Force General Felmy and Grobba discussed 'the political preparation of the German advance to the Arab countries'. According to the corresponding notes, they thought that the Arab people still had a hostile attitude towards England. Supporting this view were the ever-repeating assassination attempts on British officers; the attacks on British military transports, railway bridges, and so on; the flooding of the Rashid military camp near Baghdad to circumvent the surrender of weapons as demanded by England, and the execution of three of al-Gailani's followers. Martyrs were created as a result, and a blood feud emerged. With regard to the German propaganda it was stated:

> The atmosphere is further influenced by German propaganda, mainly through radio and leaflets. This propaganda is also for the station in Athens, controlled by the Arab Higher Committee in the Foreign Office. The Grand Mufti and

Gailani are satisfied by these assurances, and supposedly weigh in actively with propaganda on radio broadcasts.

The highlight of the propaganda would be that they both appeal to the Arab people to revolt against the English. 'The time shall be determined by us, probably after taking Tbilisi'.[22]

Subsequently, the focus was on the tasks of Special Staff F. It had established a German-Arabic teaching department in Súnion, near Athens, and was training approximately 130 Arab students from Germany and Syria to volunteer as military unit leaders and perform special tasks. They were also to build the framework of the newly formed Iraqi-Arab army. It is well known that it never came to that.

In February 1943, Hitler ordered the formation of a Muslim SS division in Croatia. For the mufti, this was a great moment: Muslims became *Muselgermanen* whom the mufti eagerly recruited.[23] And when it came to hatred of the Jews, no one could outdo him. He became the 'Goebbels of the Arabs', using the German shortwave station Radio Zeesen in Berlin, with relay stations in Bari, to air anti-Jewish broadcasts in the Middle East. In these he repeatedly urged the Arabs: 'Kill the Jews wherever you find them, out of love of God'.[24] On 13 May 1943, the mufti asked Ribbentrop 'to do the utmost to prevent the emigration of Jews from Bulgaria, Romania and Hungary'.[25]

2 November 1943 – the anniversary of the Balfour Declaration – was a very important date in the mufti's activities. Radio Berlin broadcast the meeting he called in Berlin to oppose the declaration. On this occasion he read out two telegrams, the first from Himmler:

> The National Socialist Movement of Greater Germany has, since its beginning, inscribed upon its flag the fight against world Jewry. It has, therefore, followed with particular sympathy the struggle of the freedom-loving Arabians, especially in Palestine, against the Jewish interlopers. The recognition of this enemy and of the common struggle against him form the firm foundation of the natural alliance that exists between National Socialist Greater Germany and the freedom-loving Muslims of the whole world. In this spirit I am sending you on the anniversary of the infamous Balfour Declaration my hearty greetings and wishes for the successful pursuit of your struggle until the certain final victory.

The second telegram was from Ribbentrop:

> I am sending my greetings to Your Eminence and to the participants of the meeting held today in the Reich capital under your chairmanship. Germany is linked to the Arab nation by old ties of friendship, and today we are united more than ever before. The elimination of the so-called Jewish national home and the liberation of all Arab countries from the oppression and exploitation of the Western powers is an unchangeable part of the Great German Reich policy.

Let the hour not be far off when the Arab nation will be able to build its future and find unity in full independence.[26]

On 30 September 1944, Husseini asked: 'Is it not in our power to destroy the Jews, to obliterate those of whom there are only eleven million?' Before the war, there were seventeen million Jews. Did the mufti know that the Nazis had killed six million? He had intervened several times to prevent the emigration of Jewish children, especially from Bulgaria, Romania and Hungary, countries that were under German influence.[27] He had interceded with local foreign ministers as well as with Ribbentrop. He had propagated the 'resettlement' of children to Poland, where they would be 'under active surveillance'.[28] In 1943 the Red Cross proposed the release of five thousand Jewish children in exchange for twenty thousand German prisoners. The mufti prevented this: through Heinrich Himmler's personal intervention, he arranged for the children's deportation to concentration camps, where they were murdered. Several times he had called for Jerusalem and Tel Aviv to be bombed.[29]

The mufti received 90,000 Reichsmarks per month from the Foreign Office and had the use of an aryanized villa in Berlin-Zehlendorf, along with five other residences. When he was not at his villa, he resided in a suite at the Adlon Hotel. On 7 May 1945, he fled to Bern via Austria and was then extradited to France. In May 1946 he returned to Cairo, where al-Gailani was already living. There, Husseini took a leading position in the Palestine Higher Executive, propagating an uncompromising anti-Jewish policy. He was still considered the leader of the Palestinians, and was therefore responsible for further development in Palestine. His work can be described as: spreading Nazism in the Muslim Brotherhood and cooperating with its fighters to prevent a Jewish state; inciting the Arab population during the British mandate; rejecting the 1947 UN partition resolution to establish Israel; inciting an Arab attack on Israel in May 1948; and organizing the assassination of Jordan's King Abdullah I in 1951 after Abdullah appointed someone else as Grand Mufti. The Grand Mufti of Jerusalem Amin al-Husseini, whose nefarious activities in Berlin during the war long remained largely unknown, ranks among the worst anti-Semites and is one of the most controversial figures of the twentieth century. He died in Lebanon in 1974 at the age of seventy-seven. One of the mourners was his distant relative Yasser Arafat.[30]

Notes

1. Cited by Stefan Wild, 'National Socialism in the Arab Near East between 1933 and 1939', in *A Backgrounder of the Nazi Activities in North Africa and the Middle East during the Era of the Holocaust*, ed. by the International Sephardic Leadership Council (New York: Sephardic Council, 2006) (www.sephardiccouncil.org).
2. Cf. Henner Fürtig, *Kleine Geschichte des Irak* (Munich: C.H. Beck, 2004), 35–37; Fritz Grobba, *Männer und Mächte im Orient: 25 Jahre diplomatischer Tätigkeit im Orient* (Göttingen: Musterschmidt, 1967), 176–204.
3. Grobba, *Männer*, 319.
4. For Husseini's letter of 20 January 1941, see ibid., 319–22. For Husseini's proposed text of a political declaration, see Lebel, *Mufti*, 84.
5. See Gensicke, *Mufti*, 44ff.
6. Grobba, *Männer*, 218.
7. Politisches Archiv des Auswärtigen Amts, Berlin, BA 61123. Facsimile in Anand Toprani, 'Oil and Grand Strategy: Great Britain and Germany, 1918–1941', PhD dissertation, Georgetown University, Washington DC, 2012, 480 (www.repositorylibrary.georgetown.edu).
8. Herbert Michaelis and Ernst Schraepler (eds), *Ursachen und Folgen*, Vol. XVI: *Das Dritte Reich* (Berlin: Wendler, n.d.), 532.
9. Earlier, on 25 July 1940, the same Max Oppenheim known from the First World War had spoken up again. He recommended blocking the Suez Canal, cutting off the Royal Navy's oil supply through the pipeline in Haifa as well, and fomenting revolution in India. Oppenheim envisioned Fritz Grobba in the particularly important role of controlling the Arab nationalists. In sum, this was more or less a reprint of Oppenheim's first memorandum of October 1914; see Chapter 2.
10. By the end of the war, Fritz Grobba had become a senior public prosecutor. In 1946 the Soviets convicted him of 'espionage' and sentenced him to ten years' imprisonment. He returned from the Soviet Union in 1955 and later wrote his memoirs, in which he offered an alternative portrayal of Blomberg's death. According to Grobba, Blomberg was killed when their plane became involved in a dogfight with a British aircraft. Pawelke, however, contradicted this version. See Grobba, *Männer*, 233–35.
11. *Ursachen und Folgen*, Vol. XVI, 533ff.
12. Ibid., 539.
13. Winston Churchill, *The Second World War*, Vol. III: *The Grand Alliance* (London: Houghton Mifflin, 1950), 236.
14. For Grobba's standpoint, see Grobba, *Männer*, 220–48.
15. H.R. Trevor-Roper (ed.), *Blitzkrieg to Defeat: Hitler's War Directives, 1939–1945* (New York: Holt, Rinehart and Winston, 1964), 80–81.
16. Cf. Gensicke, *Mufti*, 159.
17. Cf. Schwanitz, *Islam*, 150–68.
18. 'Record of the Conversation between the Führer and the Grand Mufti of Jerusalem on November 28, 1941, in the Presence of Reich Foreign Minister [Ribbentrop] and Minister Grobba in Berlin'. Laqueur and Rubin, *The Israel–Arab Reader*, 51–55. Deutsche Fassung: *Aufzeichnung des Gesandten Schmidt über die Unterredung zwischen Adolf Hitler und dem Großmufti von Jerusalem, Hadji Mohammed Amin el Husseini, am 28. November 1941*, in Ursachen und Folgen, Vol. XVIII, *Das Dritte Reich*, 137–40.
19. Grobba, *Männer*, 317.
20. Ursachen and Folgen, Vol. XVIII, *Das Dritte Reich*, 141, note 5.
21. Ibid., 154.
22. Ibid., 141–43.
23. Gensicke, *Mufti*, 115.
24. Ibid., 103.

25. Ibid.
26. Both telegrams cited in: Lebel, *Mufti*, 163f.
27. Gensicke, *Mufti*, 251.
28. Ibid., 108.
29. Ibid., 141. For concentration camps, see e.g. the 45-minute award-winning documentary by Heribert Schwan and Rolf Steininger, *'Ihr habt es gewusst!' Die Konzentrationslager Buchenwald und Dachau nach der Befreiung* ['You knew about it!' The concentration camps Buchenwald and Dachau after liberation], based on US Army colour material and shown on German TV in 1995; a copy is on loan at the Yad Vashem in Jerusalem.
30. Gensicke, *Mufti*, 162.

Chapter Five

FROM THE FOUNDING OF THE FEDERAL REPUBLIC TO THE ESTABLISHMENT OF DIPLOMATIC RELATIONS WITH ISRAEL, 1949–1965

Chancellor Konrad Adenauer and Reparations

In the first years after the war there was no German Middle East policy. Germany had nothing to do with Palestine and the establishment of Israel in 1948, except in that Egypt and other Arab states became 'safe havens' for ex-Nazi leaders, and Israel would not have come to exist without the Jews of the displaced persons (DP) camps. But with the founding of the Federal Republic in 1949, this 'new' Germany became a member of the 'Western Club' and took on an important role in the Cold War. Its Middle East policy was focused on four points:

1. Germany's historical responsibility for the Holocaust and consequent obligations towards Israel.
2. The interests of the European partners and the United States in the region.
3. The interests of the Arab states.
4. The claim to sole representation of Germany (with regard to the East German GDR).

This policy originated in 1951 in a memorandum of the newly established Foreign Office, which stated: 'It must not be overlooked that, because we have no relations with Israel, the Federal Republic has given a favourable starting position in the Arab world'.[1] A year later the Foreign Office pointed out that 'we must also keep an eye on those in the Middle East who are our friends',[2] meaning the Arabs with whom Germany had traditionally maintained good relations.

As was so often the case after the Second World War, the economy determined the political developments. Otto Wolff, president of the German Chamber of Industry and Commerce, noted a few years later: 'First comes trade, then the flag'.[3] The Middle East was no exception. For example, under a trade and payments agreement reached in late 1948 between Egypt and the so-called Bi-Zone (the British and the American zones in Germany), West Germany's volume of trade with Egypt had reached parity with France's by the end of 1949. And on 13 May 1951, Egypt became the first Arab country to officially declare that the state of war with Germany had ended.

On 15 May 1948 – the first day of the new state of Israel – the armies of Egypt, Jordan, Syria, Lebanon and Iraq invaded Israel. Secretary general of the Arab League, Abdul Rahman Azzam, declared: 'This will be a war of extermination and a momentous massacre, which will be spoken of like the Mongolian massacre and the Crusades'. Ahmed Shukeiry, an aide to the well-known Husseini, described the invasion as 'the elimination of the Jewish state'.[4] As early as late May, British foreign minister Ernest Bevin was convinced that the Jewish state would not last: 'The Zionist dream has come to an end', he told the Austrian ambassador Heinrich Schmid.[5] He was mistaken, as were many others.

About 600,000 Jews lived in Israel when it was founded in May 1948. When Israel defeated the Arab states in the 1948/49 War of Independence, more than 700,000 Palestinians fled or were expelled. The Arabs termed what happened then *al-nakba*, the catastrophe. Only a ceasefire was reached between the Israelis and the Arabs – nothing more, no peace treaty. The Arabs still wished for Israel's destruction. Recognizing that the state of Israel needed more people in order to survive, Israel's Ben-Gurion government declared the objective of motivating as many Jews as possible to come to Israel, despite the lack of infrastructure. This pertained not only to the Jews in the Arab states of Iraq, Egypt, Yemen, Morocco and Tunisia, but also in Turkey and Iran, where they were threatened and seen as potential allies of Israel. This led to spectacular Israeli Air Force operations in 1949. 'Operation Magic Carpet' flew 55,000 Jews from Yemen to Israel, and 'Operation Ezra and Nehemiah' – popularly known as 'Operation Ali Baba' – flew 113,000 Jews from Iraq. Jews coming from Turkey, Iran and the Arab states numbered approximately 350,000 – as many as the Holocaust survivors in Israel. Israel's doubling of its population within three years led to major problems, among them the impending famine the country was facing by the end of 1950.[6]

Figure 5.1 Jerusalem, ca. 1949. Photo by Dr Rudolf Agstner, Vienna.

Figure 5.2 Carrying a portrait of Theodor Herzl, Jews of Vienna celebrate the UN decision of 29 November 1947 to divide Palestine into two states: one for the Jews, one for the Arabs. Courtesy of National Archives II, College Park, Maryland.

Figure 5.3 On the afternoon of 14 May 1948, a few hours before the termination of the British mandate, and under the portrait of Theodor Herzl in the city museum of Tel Aviv, David Ben-Gurion proclaims the establishment of the State of Israel. Photo by Zoltan Kluger. Courtesy of Israel Government Press Office, Jerusalem.

Figure 5.4 15 May 1948: At a press conference in Cairo, the secretary general of the Arab League, Abdul Rahman Azzam Pasha, proclaims a state of war between the Arab states and Israel: 'This will be a war of extermination and a momentous massacre, which will be spoken of like the Mongolian massacres and the Crusades'.
Courtesy of National Archives II, College Park, Maryland.

Figures 5.5 and 5.6 In August 1949, Theodor Herzl's last wish is carried out: he is to be buried in the Promised Land. Herzl's coffin is brought from Vienna to Israel on the first international flight of the new Israeli airline El Al. An honour guard of government ministers awaits his coffin at Lod airport. Photos by David Eldan and Sam Diamond.
Courtesy of Israel Government Press Office, Jerusalem.

Figure 5.7 Herzl's grave on 'Mount Herzl' in Jerusalem, named after Theodor Herzl, the founder of political Zionism and the 'founding father' of Israel. Photo by Moshe Pridan. Courtesy of Israel Government Press Office, Jerusalem.

Figure 5.8 Political protest led by the leader of the nationalist Heruth party, Menachem Begin, precedes the 1952 restitution agreement with West Germany. Begin accuses Prime Minister David Ben-Gurion of selling the memory of the six million victims for profit: 'Our honour is not for sale, our blood will not be redeemed by goods. Let us wipe out the shame'. Photo by Hans Pinn. Courtesy of Israel Government Press Office, Jerusalem.

It was under these circumstances that Israel – which regarded itself as the legitimate heir of the exterminated Jews – first made claims for compensation from Germany. In a memorandum of March 1951 to the four occupying powers in Germany – the United States, Great Britain, France and the Soviet Union – Israel demanded 1 billion US dollars from West Germany and 500 million US dollars from East Germany to compensate Jewish people's material losses and to integrate Holocaust victims into Israeli society. The three Western Powers advised the Israeli government to speak directly with Bonn. Not until March 1952 did the Soviet Union respond, by stipulating that a peace treaty with Germany must be concluded before reparation negotiations could begin.[7] West German chancellor Konrad Adenauer, on the other hand, agreed to enter into discussion and also to deliver the required statement before the Bundestag, which he addressed on 27 September 1951:

> Unspeakable crimes have been committed in the name of the German people, calling for moral and material indemnity. . . . The Federal Government is prepared, jointly with representatives of Jewry and the State of Israel, to bring about a solution to the material indemnity problem, thus easing the way to the spiritual settlement of infinite suffering.[8]

Soon after, West German minister of justice, Thomas Dehler, was involved in an incident in Düsseldorf on 15 December 1951, when, as a

Figure 5.9 Konrad Adenauer visits Israel in May 1966. The former German chancellor with Nahum Goldmann, president of the Jewish World Congress, whom he had met in 1951 in London, where he promised restitution. Photo by Fritz Cohen. Courtesy of Israel Government Press Office, Jerusalem.

guest of the Association of Jewish Lawyers in Germany and West Berlin, he stated that it was thus far the Allied policy, 'under the influence of the Jew Morgenthau',[9] that was responsible for the delay in reparations. His assertion provoked protests and displeasure from German Jews. The press affirmed Dehler's claim, and his calming explanations succeeded in lessening the bad impression his speech had made – a bad impression that, incidentally, was created not just by the completely incongruous reference to Morgenthau, but also by Dehler's remark that everything the Germans had done to the Jews had happened to the Germans as well. The prominent journalist Walter Dirks seized upon this statement, writing with biting mockery in the *Frankfurter Neue Presse*: 'We had to wear a brown swastika on our suits, all had to take the name Wilhelm, and six million Germans were annihilated in American camps!' Students at the University of Göttingen collected money for the purchase of olive tree seedlings to be planted in Israel. This 'olive tree donation' made a favourable impression on the Jewry (*die Judenschaft*).[10]

A decisive moment in further indemnity efforts was a secret meeting between Adenauer and Nahum Goldmann in London on 6 December 1951, at which Goldmann presented the Jewish demands. Goldmann was the co-chairman of the Jewish Agency and president of the World Jewish Congress. On his initiative, the Conference on Jewish Material Claims Against Germany – the Claims Conference – had been set up in October 1951, one month after Adenauer's speech in the Bundestag. At the end of this secret meeting, Adenauer signed a letter acknowledging Germany's responsibility for Nazi crimes and confirming that the German government would do everything possible to compensate the Jewish people for the injustices committed. The basis for negotiations would be the Israeli demand from March 1951.[11]

In Israel, Menachem Begin (1913–1992), the leader of the right-wing Heruth Party, opposed negotiations with Germany, organizing mass protests under the slogan: 'Our honour cannot be bought. Our loss of blood cannot be remedied by anything. Let us wipe out the shame'. Karl Hartl (1909–1979), who from 1950 to 1955 was Austria's first diplomat in Israel, considered Begin a 'fascist'.[12] Prime Minister Ben-Gurion (1886–1973) confronted his political opponents with such conviction – 'Let not the murderers of our people be also their heirs!'[13] – that even the General Zionist party secretly counted on help from Germany. Despite the population's widespread reluctance to negotiate with Germany, Israelis expected material benefits as well as cash relief. Hence, the nationalist Heruth's fanatical appeal only drew some one thousand people onto the streets of Tel Aviv. 'They wandered around without great enthusiasm for an hour-and-a-half', Hartl observed.[14]

Formal German–Israeli negotiations began in Wassemar, a suburb of The Hague, on 21 March 1952. The Israelis, unwilling to set foot on German soil, appeared pointedly 'strong', as was reported in Tel Aviv: they declined to offer the customary handshake to the German delegation leader Franz Böhm, known for his unblemished anti-Nazi record; and took care to avoid using German, speaking English instead.[15] The Israeli negotiators also rejected the terms 'restitution' and 'reparations', proposing *Shilumim* in their place. *Shilumin* in the Bible means payment or retribution.

The talks proved difficult. In the end, Protocol No. 1 established that goods and services worth a sum of 3 billion Deutschmarks would be delivered to Israel over fourteen years, while Protocol No. 2 obligated the West German government to provide the Claims Conference with 450 million Deutschmarks for the relief, rehabilitation and resettlement of Jewish victims of Nazi persecution, according to the urgency of their need as determined by the conference.[16] Four days before the signing of the agreement, Adenauer summed up what it was all basically about for the members of the CDU party's central committee:

> I hope that the Cabinet will not give me a hard time. Doing so would mean a foreign policy disaster of the first order. This would not only be a political catastrophe, but it would also impair – to a very large extent – our entire endeavour to secure foreign loans again. Let us be clear about the fact that the power of Jewry in the economic field remains exceptionally strong. Therefore, and the expression may appear exaggerated, this reconciliation with the Jewry is an absolute necessity for the Federal Republic, not only morally and politically, but also economically.[17]

The agreement was signed on 10 September 1952 in a secret ceremony at Luxembourg's City Hall and is thus known as the Treaty of Luxembourg. German government press secretary Felix von Eckardt told the press that the German government would be

> deeply regretful, should the restitution for the Jewish people be misunderstood in the Arab world. There has always been a true and clear friendship between Germany and the Arabs. The German government is determined to continue and expand these friendly relations with great care. The motives that led the German government to finalize the contract, can, therefore, never be found by inventing any unfriendly manner whatsoever towards the Arab states. Rather, they lie solely in a true sense of moral responsibility for the enormous suffering that was inflicted on the Jewish people by the Nazi regime. The government feels confident that the Arab world will understand and agree with the motives . . . and that this agreement is in no way directed against our Arab friends.[18]

The Arab friends saw it quite differently, as will be shown.

The agreement was a compromise. Financially, it was just barely manageable for Germany (the federal budget for 1953 was 27 billion Deutschmarks).[19] Among mainstream Germans, the agreement was anything but popular. The more newspapers and party leaders tried to explain it as a natural consequence of the German people's moral guilt, the less the agreement was 'emotionally acceptable for the majority of the people', as Josef Schöner, Austria's ambassador in Bonn, put it. Schöner continued: 'Many times I have heard sharp accusations from ordinary people that one is "uselessly throwing money after the Jews without their changing their hostile attitude towards everything German". Instead one should increase retirement benefits or build apartments for our own people, etc.'[20] Israel, by contrast, saw the agreement as 'outright salvation', in Goldmann's words.[21] At a press conference in Paris, Israel's foreign minister, Sharett, described the treaty as an 'event of the greatest moral and economic significance, which will occupy a unique place in the annals of international relations'.[22]

Quite a few people took a more critical stance. Karl Hartl spoke of 'blood money' (*Blutgeld*).[23] On 23 June 1952, there was an assassination attempt on Israel's Austrian-born transport minister, David Z. Pinkas, the leader of the religious Mizrachi Party that gave Ben-Gurion a majority in the Knesset. In early October, a bomb attack on Sharett's office won sympathy from Hartl:

> All things considered – and I'm trying to put myself in the role of a Jew whose father and mother were killed in a concentration camp – for me it would, in this case, also somehow seem difficult and unworthy to receive payment in the form of a toilet (*Wasserklosett*) from Düsseldorf, as compensation for my murdered parents. Bomb assassinations, and especially unsuccessful bomb assassination attempts, make the position of those who had to sign the contract easier.

Moreover, Hartl assumed that Israel, given its difficult situation, would have to re-export German reparation goods, which was not permitted under the agreement. Bonn would not pass up the chance to suspend the deliveries or even stop them entirely, if Israel was clearly the one violating the agreement: 'On top of this, I can probably assume that the Jews who were murdered by the Nazis are rotting at a faster and faster pace and will disappear, as admonished ghosts. Wine gets better with age; corpses get worse'. He viewed the 'Israeli illusions' regarding the German reparations as exaggerated: the Israelis had 'tried too late, to their detriment, to replace the moral guilt of Germany with hard cash'.[24]

After the Wassemar negotiations began, the Arab League twice sent notes of protest to the German Foreign Office: first on 21 July 1952, then again on 19 August. They argued as follows:

1. The Israeli government could not be considered representative of the Jews wronged by the Nazi regime in Europe.

2. At the time of the Nazi government, Israel did not exist.
3. By providing payments and supplies to the State of Israel without legal title, the German government would not only subsidize the enemy of the Arab states, which was at war with Israel, but also fail to uphold neutrality.
4. The German government was contributing to the threat to the security and existence of the Arab states.
5. Israel was not in a position to absorb the reparation goods and would therefore re-export them in breach of the contract.
6. This development would strain the friendly relations between Germany and the Arab states.

On 6 September 1952, Hasso von Etzdorf of the Foreign Office noted: 'In fact, it must be expected that the German–Israeli agreement will trigger undesirable political and economic reactions in the Arab world'. Thus Germany had much to lose, should the Arab countries disrupt or sever their mutual economic ties. Foreign trade between West Germany and the Arab countries had grown rapidly in the postwar period. In 1951, total exports amounted to approximately 200 million Deutschmarks. German exports to Egypt and Syria in particular had risen markedly since the pre-war period. To support his argument, Etzdorf listed the following points:

1. The German people are heavily burdened by the crimes committed in their name by the Nazi regime and cannot expect a free path to the future without restitution.
2. Germany cannot reduce its obligations by pointing out that other nations have a comparable complicity to address. Rather, it is all the more firmly convinced that reparations are a path that could lead to the resolution of refugee misery in other nations.
3. The injustices Nazi Germany committed against the Jews cannot be placed on equal footing with what the State of Israel has done to the Arabs. The displaced Arabs are refugees, whereas Nazi Germany killed millions of Jews.
4. Of the total reparations to Israel, hard commodities make up only 17–22 per cent, and only about 7 per cent are goods in short supply; the rest are mostly consumer goods whose resale is prohibited by the agreement.

Moreover, Etzdorf recalled, the members of the Arab League 'are not united in all matters' when doing business. It was therefore doubtful that a boycott of German goods by all Arab countries would be rigorously carried out: Arab countries needed scarce goods from Germany and would have to keep the German market open to sell their own products. Moreover, the then current depression in the cotton market would weigh especially heavily on Egypt, Germany's most important trading partner in the region. Etzdorf stated very convincingly: 'The sympathies of the Arabs towards Germany are ultimately not shaken that quickly, because the argument that Germany never showed political aspirations towards Arabs will never lose its effect. However, we should not miss any opportunity to emphasize these sympathies'. He then proposed the following: compliance with the Lebanese Red Cross's request for a significant donation; a generous contribution of donations to assist Arab refugees; and a goodwill mission to be sent to the Arab States 'to explain our actions and convince them of our ongoing friendship'.[25]

Ten days later, though, Etzdorf changed his mind and recommended against sending the goodwill mission, for the following reasons:

1. It could cloud the positive impression that the Israeli agreement has produced worldwide, especially among the Jews.
2. There is a risk that the Western powers – particularly the British and French – would regard our Middle Eastern policy with suspicion. British and French propaganda would exaggerate the objectives of the mission.
3. The mission might run risks in different capitals. There is a danger that the mufti [Husseini] and the ultra-national elements will provoke demonstrations. Because we have no diplomatic representation there, we cannot adequately prepare for the visit.
4. Relationships and circumstances in individual Arab countries are so different that the task can hardly be done by one and the same mission, as the delegates would have to apply a different tactic in each place.
5. We have no reason to create the impression that we must make amends by sending a goodwill mission to the Arab states, appearing as if we had something to repair and thereby appealing to the compassion of the Arab governments.
6. In fact, we have nothing to offer.
7. There is a risk that Arabs who played a role during the war in Germany, e.g. the mufti, would turn up intending to play a major role again – against our will.

At the same time, he recommended that the Federal Republic send diplomatic representatives to the Arab capitals soon, to 'explain our position through newspaper articles in the Arab world and to invoke the old

German–Arab friendship as well as the cultural and economic relations'. Should the Arab League send a mission to Germany, 'it should be treated with particular friendship and handled honourably'.[26] Three days later it was clear that the situation was getting ever more complicated and that newspaper articles would no longer suffice. The signing of the agreement 'hit Cairo like a bombshell', as Robert Friedlinger-Pranter, Austria's ambassador in Cairo, reported to Foreign Minister Karl Gruber in Vienna.[27]

At a press conference on 19 September, the Arab League's deputy secretary general, Ahmed el-Shukeri, further clarified the position of the Arab states:

> The agreement has triggered dismay and indignation in the Arab world and has an extremely worrisome aspect: it saddens us to see how, under this agreement, German factories and companies will deliver goods that will repair Israel and significantly strengthen its economic and military potential and, as a result, further the conquest of the neighbouring countries, which is the clearly outlined Zionist intention. Israel's economy is by no means an economy that serves only peaceful purposes, but is part of the known Zionist goals of future conquests and political domination of the neighbouring countries.

Therefore, the Arab League had decided to send a delegation to Germany 'to do everything possible to prevent this agreement from taking effect as well as to create a favourable atmosphere for closer cooperation between Germany and the Arab countries'. Shukeri continued:

> Israel has no right to seek retribution. In the entirety of international law, we do not know of any precedent in which a state is assigned rights before it exists. Israel, which was created by armed violence through offensives and injustice, continues to pursue Zionist goals that lead to the domination of Arab countries, that prevent their national rebirth, and that exploit their natural resources and wealth. The Arabs hope that Germany will recognize how vitally important this agreement is for them.[28]

The Arab press initially reacted with a storm of indignation. The Cairo newspapers took the position that the agreement would encourage Israel to attack Egypt. The Egyptian government was urged to take major steps to prevent its ratification, such as severing diplomatic relations and boycotting German goods.[29]

In Bonn, Etzdorf realized that the agreement had 'caused some alarm in the Arab world' and that the 'driving force behind the protest' emanated from certain Arab nationalist circles led by al-Husseini, the former Grand Mufti of Jerusalem, who 'had repeatedly created unrest in the Middle East'. Etzdorf advised against harsh rejection of the Arabs' arguments, recommending instead that it be pointed out that although the German government had given them careful consideration, it was also obliged to consider certain aspects that 'might be difficult for our Arab friends to understand', namely:

1. The German people are heavily burdened by the crimes committed in their name by the Nazi regime and cannot believe (*kann nicht glauben*) in a free path to the future without restitution. The agreement may point the way to the resolution of other nations' refugee hardships, a goal to which we hope to have made an exemplary contribution.
2. The National Socialist government was responsible not only for the displacement of hundreds of thousands of Jews, but also for the deliberate extermination of several millions. This fact brings the German people into a situation that cannot be grasped by normal standards; legal objections are inadequate.

Then Etzdorf unambiguously stated:

> There is no doubt that the German Bundestag will ratify the agreement. Germany has always proven to be a friend of the Arabs. It has never pursued political aspirations in the Arab states. We are even more convinced of the sustainability of the friendship between Germany and the Arabs, which has remained untarnished, even after the collapse of the German Reich in 1945. That encourages us even now to expect understanding and insight from our friends. The German government asks its Arab friends not to heed to simple insinuations that German goods should be boycotted. . . . The German government considers such communications mere fakery that cannot shake the firmly grounded German–Arab friendship.[30]

The Arab reactions to this did not reflect agreement. Permission to open a West German industrial exhibition in Cairo in December 1952 was withdrawn. Saudi Arabia and Yemen made it clear that there would be no diplomatic relations. At the UN, the Arab League proposed two measures in opposition to the agreement: one to require the UN to confiscate any German payments to Israel, and a second to declare the Federal Republic an aggressor nation, should the agreement be ratified.[31]

Bonn listened carefully and decided its first counteraction would be to accelerate the process of staffing its offices in Arab countries. Ambassador Hansjoachim von der Esch, on holiday in Sweden with his Swedish wife, was put on a special plane and rushed to Syria. The representative at the United Nations, Hans Riesser, was instructed to present the UN with a donation of $100,000 for the Arab refugees. Günther Pawelke, who was hastily dispatched as the new ambassador to Cairo, later complained to his Austrian colleague that without this agreement he would have entered Cairo as 'a little king', but now he was looked upon as 'a criminal'.[32]

Before Pawelke had left for Cairo, State Secretary Walter Hallstein had directed him 'to convince Egypt not to join the Arab League delegation'. If that could not be prevented, Pawelke was to ensure that, 'at least, no member of the Egyptian military should participate in the delegation'. But it was already too late: immediately after his arrival in Cairo, Pawelke was received by Foreign Minister Ahmed Farrag Tajeh, who informed him that the delegation had already arrived in Frankfurt and that the government had appointed an Egyptian representative: a member of the embassy in Rome who should already be in Germany. Farrag did not disclose that this 'member' was Ahmet Hassan, the military attaché of the Egyptian embassy in Rome and the head of the delegation. Several times, Farrag referred to the agreement as a 'stab in the back of the Arab world' (*ein Dolchstoß in den Rücken der arabischen Welt*). The new and noticeably strengthened Egypt would 'fight to the bitter end' against the ratification. Egypt considered itself the leading country of the Arab world, and 'any softening would be interpreted by all Arabs as betrayal of the common cause'.[33]

Meanwhile, the Arab delegation caused quite a headache for the Bonn officials, who did not know on whose behalf the delegation spoke – the Arab League's, or the individual countries'. Moreover, the delegates did not present any credentials, yet insistently tried to influence German decision makers, mentioning the 'good old days' of the Grand Alliance between Hitler and Husseini. The Grand Mufti had written a personal letter to Adenauer. This series of diplomatic irregularities, and probably also the presence of an Egyptian military officer, resulted in Hallstein's very ill humour while talking to the delegation. This became particularly evident in their third conversation on 28 October, when Hallstein, in rare dramatic form and completely undiplomatically, told the delegates they should leave the country after two days: 'If and when you want to stay a day or two more and see a few people, we don't want to be petty'.[34]

This prompted the next outcry in Cairo. The Egyptian prime minister and strong man, General Mohammed Naguib, informed Ambassador Pawelke with 'extreme agitation' that limiting the stay of the delegation would hurt Egypt and himself personally, as head of the army. Pawelke inferred that the circumstances were pushing Naguib to consider extreme measures, such as severing diplomatic ties between Germany and Egypt. In the middle of the night, Pawelke was again summoned to the general, who emphatically declared that after the events in Bonn, the Egyptian government was 'less than ever in a position to implicitly accept the ratification of the agreement'. The ambassador had the impression that Naguib was extremely upset and would have taken drastic measures, had it not been for a consultant who restrained him. Pawelke reported to Bonn that if the German government insisted on sending the delegation away, he would not 'succeed in preventing the general and his advisers from ending the relationship with Germany'. He therefore urged against calling on the delegation to depart.[35]

The delegation stayed three more days. A memorandum it left at the Foreign Office before its exit again made clear the sentiments of the Arab League, namely, that 'the Arabs harboured no anti-Semitic tendencies' and that Arab governments' attitudes towards Israel were 'exclusively determined by the instinct of self-preservation'; that Israel was not entitled to any payments because it was 'not the legal successor of the persecuted Jews'; and that German subsidies to Israel would not be accepted (*seien abzulehnen*) because they 'will disturb the balance in the Middle East'.[36]

Incidentally, Karl Hartl argued similarly. In November 1953, he wrote to Austria's vice-president, Adolf Schärf, in Vienna: 'I am for justice, but the shirt of an unemployed Austrian is of more interest to me than the Israeli mortars that are pounding the Arab villages to pieces. At least 45 per cent of the budget of the State of Israel is spent on the military for mortars or aeroplanes. All the money we concede to the Jewish negotiators in Vienna goes to Israel. But we owe Israel nothing – not one Groschen!'[37] Foreign Office first secretary, Alexander Böker, noted on 4 November, that the German government was obviously in trouble. He had several concerns about Germany's foreign policy. First, it could occasion considerable setbacks in trade. At the same time, a serious and long-term cooling of German–Arab relations in the context of a critical world situation could result in diminished Western influence in the already unstable Middle East. Were this to happen, the Soviet Union might seize the opportunity to penetrate the Middle East and exploit the tense economic and political relations between the Arab world and the West. Domestically, Böker feared that parliamentary support for the Israel agreement would crumble on the side of the governing coalition, leaving the ratification without the desired overwhelming majority vote. He was also worried about business circles: fear of significant losses in the Middle East might push them into right-wing and anti-Semitic associations. Furthermore, implementation of the Israel agreement could prompt Arabs to resort to extortionate tactics that would make doing business more difficult for individual companies.

Although it seemed increasingly necessary to adopt a more flexible attitude towards the Arabs, it was also apparent that the agreement 'as such represented an irrefutable fact and that the reputation in the world of the German government and the German people would not permit a non-ratification or non-implementation of the agreement'. Böker then took up an idea that Hallstein had mentioned in a conversation with the Arab delegation, namely to explore ways of engaging the UN after it had consulted with Israel.³⁸ Three days later, the urgency of the issue was clear. As Pawelke reported, Naguib stressed to him that the Arab League 'would leave nothing undone to try to unify the entire Islamic world to oppose Germany and join Arab countermeasures'. Meanwhile, the general also wanted to help to ease the tensions. On the same day, Egypt's Foreign Ministry secretary general, Abdul Pasha, submitted a document requesting that the German government wait to put the agreement before Parliament until the matter had been discussed with the Arab states. Pasha described the situation within the Arab League as 'maximally strained' and, stressing the 'extreme seriousness of the situation', repeatedly asked Pawelke not to sugarcoat his report to the German government.³⁹

On 21 November, Pawelke flew to Bonn to consult with Adenauer and key Foreign Office personnel. Adenauer wanted to respond to Pawelke's suggestions for giving the Arab countries a chance 'to save face'. Pawelke thought General Naguib would be satisfied if the UN were engaged, whereas Herbert Blankenhorn, close confidant of Adenauer and the head of the Political Department in the Foreign Office, found this a dubious prospect. Adenauer then specified that the UN would deal only 'in accordance with the Israeli government'.⁴⁰ The Israelis, upon being informed of the proposal, were 'very worried' and expressed 'major concerns' to the Foreign Office: in the UN, Israel would be forced to take a stand against the inclusion of these points; then it would be necessary to recapitulate the history of the agreement and 'thus also drag the entire, very embarrassing past back into the light'.⁴¹

At that time, the German government was interested only in helping the moderate Arab elements, in order to get the boycott threat out of the way. An instruction to Ambassador Pawelke on 9 December indicated that the instrument for accomplishing this was money. In so far as deliveries to Israel strengthened the economy of the Jewish state, the German government was ready to offer compensation to the Arab states. As for Egypt, the German government was considering support for Egypt's efforts to modernize its economy, as well as other economic undertakings of the Egyptian government.⁴²

The Foreign Office no longer saw any reason to dramatize the situation: 'Previous Arab sanctions of this kind have failed due to lack of solidarity'.⁴³ It was as simple as that. Adenauer refused to postpone the ratification: 'We could not give in without losing face', and besides, 'more consideration should be given to America than to the Arab states'. The chancellor was quite optimistic that the Arab states 'could be convinced' through special perks.⁴⁴ In plain text, that meant credit commitments of 400 million Deutschmarks – including in connection with the planned project of Cairo's Aswan Dam.

By November 1952, Austria's ambassador in Cairo, Friedinger-Pranter, an expert in Middle East affairs, had characterized the whole thing as a 'tempest in a teapot' precipitated by Egypt, primarily in order to achieve economic goals. Egypt, Friedinger-Pranter suggested, had probably made 'all the noise' to obtain favourable payment terms and persuade Germany to accept larger quantities of cotton:

> Certainly, the matter was strongly exaggerated here. In the Orient, it is typical to find a scapegoat for existing grievances. Then, under the Wafd [the party that won independence from Britain], the Englishmen were evil. Now, the Jews or the states that supported Israeli's aspirations were blamed and made responsible for the misfortune that befell the Arabs. . . . Egypt is, of course, economically, financially and strategically dependent on the West. The overemphasis of its national issues is always only a tool in the hands of the local politicians.[45]

The German Bundestag ratified the agreement on 18 March 1953. Three weeks later Chancellor Adenauer made his first trip to the United States, where he was received by President Dwight D. Eisenhower in the White House on 7 April. The visit was a great success – not least because of this agreement. In the spring of 1964, when Adenauer dictated the first draft of his memoirs, he interpreted the agreement as follows:

> Israeli Agreement 1952 – Atonement with the Jews. An inner obligation to make recompense, as far as that is possible. The Israeli Agreement of decisive importance for the image of Germany in the world. If the Israeli Agreement had not been concluded, the visit to the United States would not have gone off so successfully.[46]

Karl Hartl put it more bluntly: 'Germany had to be made socially acceptable to 5 million American Jews'.[47]

Egypt, for its part, was yet to recognize that it already held an important card in the form of the German Democratic Republic (GDR). On 9 February 1953, a GDR delegation arrived in Cairo to sign a trade agreement. There were now two kinds of Germans in Egypt, represented by West German ambassador Günther Pawelke (as of October 1952) and GDR trade representative Kurt Enkelmann (as of February 1953). Some Egyptians needed time to get used to this duality – especially the Egyptian Post Office, whose messengers consistently confused the two German sides: Soviet invitations to East Germans were delivered unread to the West German embassy, and Egyptian cancellations to attend East German receptions were also sent to the West German embassy. By contrast, East and West Germans – amazingly enough, in that era – met at sports clubs and cafes, or at the Swiss-German bookshop Lehnert and Landrock, where Bavarian and Saxon dialects alike were unmistakable.[48]

Tanks for Israel

Once the Luxembourg agreement was ratified, the discussion turned to establishing diplomatic relations between the Federal Republic and Israel. Bonn had offered this in 1952, but Jerusalem declined. Now Israel was the pressing party, and Bonn declined. The Foreign Office explained the decision by repeatedly pointing to the Arab states that had threatened to recognize the GDR in the event that diplomatic relations were established between Bonn and Jerusalem. The Hallstein Doctrine hung over West Germany's Middle East policy like a sword of Damocles.

What did the Hallstein Doctrine imply? The establishment of diplomatic relations between Bonn and Moscow following Adenauer's visit to Moscow in September 1955 was declared a special case by the Federal Government, since the Soviet Union, as a victorious power together with the three Western powers, was still responsible for Germany as a whole. The doctrine – named after Bonn's state secretary in the Foreign Office, Walter Hallstein – was an open warning: any state's establishment of diplomatic relations with the GDR would be regarded as 'an unfriendly act directed against the vital interests of the German people' that would prompt the Federal Government to react by severing diplomatic relations with that state. This doctrine became the blueprint for West German foreign policy for the next decade. The deal with the Arab states was that they did not recognize East Germany, and West Germany in turn did not recognize Israel.

After talks with Foreign Minister Heinrich von Brentano and Walter Hallstein, on 13 February 1956 Nahum Goldmann informed Israeli foreign minister, Moshe Sharett, of the German position: 'Some top German politicians, particularly in the Foreign Office, are not very keen to establish diplomatic relations with us. They fear that Egypt and other Arab states would in that case recognize East Germany. It is clear that the Foreign Office, influenced by the German embassies in the Arab countries, recommends postponing the matter'.[49] From 3 to 7 April 1956, fifteen German ambassadors attended a conference in Istanbul, chaired by Walter Hallstein, precisely to discuss this issue. The outcome was a recommendation not to establish diplomatic relations with Israel. Hallstein explained: 'For reasons of self-respect, we cannot admit that our decision on this issue depends on the Arab states. With such an admission, we would lose face. According to the members of the Middle East missions, this would have disastrous consequences, especially there'.[50]

Was that a statement from pro-Arab, anti-Israel German diplomats in the Foreign Office? In a diary entry of 12 February 1960, Herbert Blankenhorn, one of Adenauer's closest advisers, wrote of a 'pro-Arab tendency in the Foreign Office'.[51] The Israeli historian Yeshayahu Jelinek, born in

Czechoslovakia in 1933, revived this argument in the late 1990s, delivering a damning indictment of the responsible German diplomats:

> They grew up in other times and they were not merely in Jews' perception but deep in their hearts racists and colonialists. During the crucial meeting in Istanbul in the spring of 1956, they repeatedly spoke about the 'Orientals' in a derogatory way. Also, the Jews were still judged by old stereotypes. The present text claims that the decisions regarding diplomatic relations were based on irrational, uncritical thinking. Intellectually, the Foreign Office dealt with natives and colonies, despite boasting that Germany had no colonial tradition in the Middle East.[52]

The German historian Sven Olaf Berggötz followed up on Jelinek's accusations in his dissertation, and concluded in 1998 that one cannot help but 'qualify it to some degree'.[53] When the Foreign Office was re-established in 1951, eleven diplomats with Middle East experience were reappointed to posts with responsibility for the Middle East. Brentano mentions the 'not-to-be-underestimated influence of the Middle East Department under General Consul Voigt', who headed the department from 1953 to 1962. In 1994, Yohanan Meroz, Israel's ambassador in Bonn from 1974 to 1981, called Hermann Voigt 'a worn-out Ribbentrop diplomat' whose qualifications consisted of 'having been the last consul of the Third Reich in Jerusalem'.[54] This allegation is often repeated, but it is false: Voigt was never consul in Jerusalem. In his excellent book on German–Israeli relations under Adenauer and Ben-Gurion, published in 2002, Germany's ambassador to Israel from 1981 to 1985, Niels Hansen, mentions a few facts about Voigt: Voigt was born in the Templar colony of Sarona, attended school in Haifa, and worked in the Foreign Service as of 1915, spending four years in Constantinople. In 1944 he took a forced leave of absence, and on 15 January 1945 he was forced to retire. Although he was regarded as an 'Arab', he made every effort to maintain a balance.[55]

According to Hansen, only five of the eleven Foreign Office diplomats identified by Berggötz were relevant to making decisions with regard to the Arab countries.[56] If the diplomats 'entertained prejudices against Israel, these prejudices are not apparent in the files', Berggötz stated.[57] Alexander Böker, as head of Subsection B in the Political Department I of the Foreign Office, at one point referred to the payments to Israel as 'tribute payments' (*Tributzahlungen*) – a debatable designation.[58] In any case, Bonn advanced another argument to explain its reluctance to establish diplomatic relations with Israel, as Hallstein emphasized in a meeting at the Foreign Office in 1957:

> In most Arab countries we are seen as representatives of the entire West. If our policy runs the risk of significantly deteriorating the position of the West – and

this question must surely be affirmed – we must not carry out the decision. We could then ultimately play into the hands of the Soviets and strengthen anti-Western forces in the Middle East.[59]

In 1954, Egypt's charismatic Gamal Abdel Nasser overthrew General Naguib and became Egypt's prime minister. Seeing himself as the leader of the Arab world, Nasser aligned his politics more and more with Moscow, and in September 1955 an agreement was signed for the supply of Soviet arms to Egypt. In less than a year, the Soviets had delivered two hundred MiG jet fighters, one hundred tanks and six submarines. Nasser nationalized the Suez Canal Company in July 1956, and the Suez War broke out in late October when Israel, Great Britain and France attacked Egypt. An extraordinary coalition between the United States and the Soviet Union forced Great Britain and France to withdraw from Egypt.[60] Israel did not withdraw. Adenauer rejected the US–Soviet action, and on 6 November he ostentatiously travelled to Paris in support of humiliated France.

Under pressure from the United States, Israel finally withdrew from Sinai in spring 1957. Weapons (including nuclear technology) for Israel now came from France, and on a large scale from the Federal Republic.

Figure 5.10 Gamal Abdel Nasser, Egypt's strong man. He considers himself the leader of all Arabs and Moslems and is the enemy of Israel, France and Great Britain.
Courtesy of National Archives II, College Park, Maryland.

Figure 5.11 On 29 October 1956, Israel attacks Egypt. Israeli soldiers near El Arish on their way to the Suez Canal. Photo by Moshe Pridan. Courtesy of Israel Government Press Office, Jerusalem.

Figure 5.12 General Moshe Dayan (centre) proclaims the end of the Sinai campaign, with Brigadier-General Assaf Simhoni (left) and Colonel Avraham Yaffe (right). Photo by Hans Pinn. Courtesy of Israel Government Press Office, Jerusalem.

Figure 5.13 Early 1957: From the Suez Canal back to the Negev; a picture of Nasser also goes to Israel with the returning troops. Photo by Moshe Pridan. Courtesy of Israel Government Press Office, Jerusalem.

The chief actors here – German defence minister, Franz Josef Strauß, and secretary general of the Israeli Ministry of Defence, Shimon Peres – first met in December 1957 in Strauß's home in Rott am Inn in Bavaria. Strauß made good on his promise to help by secretly procuring equipment and weapons from the depots of the Bundeswehr, the German army. Strauß later wrote in his memoirs that subsequently, 'as a diversion, in some cases a theft report was filed with the police. Helicopters and aeroplanes were flown without insignia to France and shipped from Marseilles to Israel'.[61]

In early March 1960, Israel requested submarines, air defence missiles, air-to-air missiles, and surface-to-surface missiles. Strauß was inclined to accede, but the decision was Adenauer's. That same month, Adenauer met with Israeli prime minister, Ben-Gurion, in New York and promised financial support to Israel (covered later in this chapter), agreeing also to additional arms supplies. In June 1962, Peres presented Bonn with the following wish list: six speedboats, three submarines, thirty-six howitzers, twenty-four helicopters, twelve Noratlas transport aircraft, fifteen tanks, fifty-four anti-aircraft guns, and Cobra missiles, with a total value of 240 million Deutschmarks. Opposition arose from the Foreign Ministry: 'I won't take any responsibility for that', Foreign Minister Gerhard Schröder warned, while State Secretary Karl Carstens declared himself 'absolutely against it'. Nonetheless, the delivery was carried out in an operation categorized as 'technical assistance' and assigned the code name *'Frank./Kol.'*,

Figure 5.14 March 1957: Lowering the Israeli flag (in Sharm el Sheik).
UN troops taking over the Israeli positions in the Sinai.
Photo by Hans Pinn. Courtesy of Israel Government Press Office, Jerusalem.

short for *Frankreich* (France) and *Kolonie* (colony). Only some of the weapons were made in Germany; the rest were purchased and their origins obscured (*unterschiedlich getarnt*) before being transported to Israel. Everything transpired under the utmost secrecy, known only to a very small group of German politicians in Bonn.[62]

A new, critical phase in German–Israeli relations began in mid-1964, when the United States asked Bonn to supply Israel with heavy war material, in particular 150 American M48A1 tanks from the Bundeswehr. The deal was approved during Chancellor Ludwig Erhard's June 1964 visit to Washington. On 13 June, US secretary of defense, Robert McNamara, spoke to the chancellor, emphasizing that the deal must remain secret. Erhard met later that day with President Lyndon B. Johnson, who addressed the matter. Erhard advised caution, stating that 'the support for Israel should be granted not too loudly, not too much, and not too fast'. The deal was so secret that no documents were created of the talks held with the Israelis at the Defence Ministry in Bonn. Later, with some frustration, Foreign Office state secretary Karl Carstens remarked to Ministry of Defence state secretary Karl Gumbel that something must have been discussed, because 'the tanks did not reach an Israeli ship in Rotterdam on their own'. Not until 23 February 1965 did Gumbel explain how things had happened: they had agreed to supply twenty tanks per month. However, as this was a 'tricky' matter, he had asked that it not be discussed in the Cabinet.[63] The plan was to ship the tanks with the built-in weapons from Rotterdam to Genoa, with the Italian Ministry of Defence as the addressee. In Genoa, the weapons were to be dismantled and later returned to Germany, while the tanks were to be refitted with new weapons and equipment from the United States and finally shipped to Israel. However, this process did not apply for the first forty tanks, which were not unloaded in Genoa but transported directly to Israel. The next twenty were loaded on a ship in January 1965 and held in Italy for refitting.

When asked by the Free Democratic Party (FDP) chairman Erich Mende 'why the Americans themselves did not deliver', Chancellor Erhard answered: 'They wanted to give us the chance to make a gesture proving our solidarity with the Israelis. We especially, who have so much behind us (*Gerade wir, die wir ja allerhand hinter uns haben*), should do our part to help to strengthen the security of the Israeli people with a delivery from our arsenal, at our expense'.[64] The United States wanted to stay behind the scenes – understandably from its perspective, since the Americans had just delivered weapons to the Jordanian army. With Germany's help, the military balance in the Middle East remained, so to speak, free of direct US involvement.

But in late 1964 and early 1965, information about the tank deal was leaked, creating a huge scandal. The Egyptian president, Gamal Abdel Nasser, reacted by inviting the GDR state council chairman Walter Ulbricht for a state visit to Egypt. All Bonn's efforts to prevent the visit failed. At a meeting on 3 January 1965, Schröder told Erhard that Israel had 'in a way blackmailed' the Federal Republic.[65] The Federal Government then decided to end tank deliveries and replace them with cash payments.

Almost simultaneously, leaders of large Jewish organizations in the United States orchestrated three interventions with Ambassador Karl Heinrich Knappstein in Washington to express their 'great concern' about the government's decision not to deliver any more tanks. Knappstein dismissed the men politely, explaining that 'one of the main objectives of German foreign policy, namely the sole right of representation (*das Alleinvertretungsrecht*) is on the line, and all other considerations must be subordinate to this goal'.[66] Carstens instructed Knappstein to ask the State Department for help in this matter and convince the Americans 'to act quickly towards Israel'.[67] As Erhard put it, 'the US got us into this mess and they should help us out again'.[68]

When the State Department refused to comment, Knappstein went to undersecretary of state for political affairs, Averell Harriman, to remind the United States of its moral obligation and to stress that the Federal Republic was 'faced with perhaps the worst foreign policy crisis since its founding'. Harriman replied that Bonn's request came at an extremely inopportune moment, and to comply would present the United States with a major problem.[69] On 13 February, US assistant secretary of state, William Tyler, told Knappstein that the US government did 'not see itself in a position to fulfil the wish of the Federal Government to offer diplomatic support'. Knappstein concluded that this decision was 'final'. In his view, 'domestic pressures' also played a role: a 'rising number of incoming telegrams' conveyed 'that the representatives of stakeholder organizations presented themselves yesterday here at the State Department. They discussed the possibility of a nationwide campaign against us due to the termination of the arms sales'.[70]

At almost the same time, US businesses began to boycott German products. On 17 February, Knappstein reported that textile companies in New York had begun to cancel orders from the Federal Republic; other companies intended to stop importing Pfaff sewing machines. The embassy registered 'concerned enquiries from importers' who had received 'cancellations of orders, with some in substantial amounts'. The Foreign Office in Bonn noted that the Americans were 'using us as an excuse because, with consideration of the Arab world, they wanted to avoid openly looking like an arms supplier to the Israeli army'.[71]

On 18 February, Knappstein met with Secretary of State Dean Rusk, from whom he 'received more positive feedback' than before. The ambassador pointed out that the Germans had since realized that arms sales to Israel depended largely on America's initiative. It was feared that the US attitude towards such a vital question for Germany could lead to serious discontent among the German public: 'More is at stake than just the German–Israeli relations', as the boycott in the United States led by Jewish business and protest actions together could produce reactions in Germany that 'would be regrettable not only for Israel but also for the United States', Knappstein cautioned. Rusk assured him that his government would help: 'We are partners in the same foxhole,' and 'we will not let you in the foxhole'.[72]

On 22 February in Bonn, US ambassador George McGhee spoke first to Schröder, then to Erhard. He told Schröder that the US ambassador in Cairo had addressed the Egyptian government. The Egyptians did not want to risk severance of ties with the Federal Republic and would not treat Ulbricht as a head of state. Schröder brought up the mood in the Federal Republic: the whole affair could have very unpleasant consequences for mutual trust with the United States. As a large part of the public saw it, the Americans had put the Germans in a very difficult situation. Internally, government spokesman Karl-Günther von Hase repeated what Knappstein had told Harriman, namely that it was 'the worst crisis in the Federal Republic's existence'.[73] And now the Americans were either unwilling or unable to help the Federal Republic! Ultimately, the matter could 'grow into a serious burden on the German–American relationship'.[74] In McGhee's meeting with Erhard the chancellor emphasized that it was important 'to maintain a common front', thereby pointing to the Jewish boycott in the United States and the press reports:

> This is unpleasant; there is a lot at stake here (*das ist miserabel; hier steht viel auf dem Spiel*). The invitation to Ulbricht is a general attack on Germany's exclusive mandate policy, to which the Western powers have committed. Losing control in the Middle East would unsettle not only German policy, but also trust in the United States, leading to the inevitable question of what an American guarantee is worth.

McGhee disclosed that the United States had warned Egypt not to elevate the status of East Germany. In addition, the embassy staff had been instructed to refrain from taking part in official events related to Ulbricht's visit. Erhard seemed satisfied.[75]

Two days earlier, on 20 February, Schröder had warned in a meeting with the chancellor that nothing should happen before, during or immediately after Ulbricht's visit 'that could blow the weak fuses currently keep-

Figure 5.15 On 8 May 1960, Theodor Heuss (right), West German president from 1949 to 1959, meets with Ben-Gurion (left) in Jerusalem; Ben-Gurion's secretary, the Vienna-born Teddy Kollek (who later becomes mayor of Jerusalem); and the head of the so-called Israel mission in Cologne, Felix Shinnar (next to Heuss). Photo by David Gurfinkel. Courtesy of Israel Government Press Office, Jerusalem.

ing Egypt from recognizing the zone [the GDR]'. At the same meeting, FDP minister of economic cooperation, Walter Scheel, fearing that Egypt might block German ships' passage through the Suez Canal, had stressed that he was not willing to publicly back the entire set of issues unless each additional shipment was stopped: 'Not one more screw should be sent'.[76]

With regard to Ulbricht's visit, ministers heatedly debated whether Germany should break off diplomatic relations with Egypt or whether suspension of economic aid would be enough. In a dramatic meeting on 4 March, Schröder indicated that the Americans would feel very sorry about it should Bonn sever diplomatic relations. The discussion was not concluded, but Horst Osterheld, head of the Foreign Office Bureau at the Federal Chancellery, noted later that a slight majority would have voted for the break-off.[77]

Then the Americans intervened forcefully. On 5 March, Erhard received the ambassadors of the three Western powers. Osterheld recorded the following: 'This time McGhee acted disrespectfully towards the chancellor, almost like a politruk. Seydoux [the French ambassador] expressed to me that no Russian could so sharply command Ulbricht, as McGhee had just done'. UK ambassador, Frank Roberts, took the same line as McGhee, 'but significantly more skilfully'.[78]

Figure 15.16 May 1963: The former West German minister of defence, Franz Josef Strauß, with Israel's deputy minister of defence, Shimon Peres, in Peres's office in Jerusalem. They had first met in December 1957, beginning a close military cooperation between Israel and West Germany. Photo by Moshe Pridan. Courtesy of Israel Government Press Office, Jerusalem.

The Americans decidedly opposed severing relations with Cairo. McGhee spoke in a 'very tough and urgent' way:

> It is often easier to sever relations than to resume them. If you do it, Egypt will recognize East Germany and then other Arab countries would follow suit. You would play right into the Communists' hands. Germany has enjoyed popularity in the Middle East. The Americans have little influence. The West needs German influence there.[79]

Following the discussion, the Cabinet met again. Osterheld noted:

> Had it come to a vote, it probably stood twelve to eight against Erhard, i.e. against severance of the relations. The slight majority was against it – partly because they feared that other Arab states would break with us and East Germany would fill that void, and partly, or perhaps predominantly, because of the pressure from the Allies, with McGhee at the head.[80]

Diplomatic relations with Egypt were not severed. The Israelis received only forty tanks.[81] The twenty tanks left in Italy were returned to Germany. Then the United States delivered 110 tanks of a more modern type. In the end, Chancellor Erhard faced a single task with regard to Israel – establishing diplomatic relations, which ultimately was carried out by the chancellor's confidant Kurt Birrenbach.

The Establishment of Diplomatic Relations with Israel

On 7 March 1965, an Israeli El Al plane at Zurich airport waited more than four hours for a passenger from Cologne: the CDU Bundestag member Kurt Birrenbach. Having taken on its expected passenger, the plane landed at 11 p.m. at Israel's Lod Airport (since 1973 Ben Gurion Airport), where a secret-service-like action transpired. A black limousine drove up to the aircraft. Birrenbach's name was blacked out on the passenger list. He was led into the airport building by an Israeli colonel and two officials of the Bonn Ministry of Defence. There, to his astonishment, he heard an announcement that 'a Mr Birrenbach' should please go to the El Al information desk. Since he was in fact on a secret mission, he did not comply.

Birrenbach had the delicate assignment of explaining to the Israelis that Bonn would now provide financial compensation instead of more weapons. In March and again in April, Birrenbach flew to Israel to lay the groundwork for formal diplomatic relations with Israel. The older he grew, the more he considered this mission to be the culmination of his political career. In Israel, he could negotiate as a foreign minister, thus assuming a role he had always wanted to play.[82]

Birrenbach was virtually predestined for this mission. In 1933, as a 26-year-old junior lawyer, he joined the Nazi Party, but three years later he left it and suffered the consequences: no job as a civil servant, no lawyer's licence. A relationship with a half-Jewish woman was his actual destiny. When his application for a marriage license was rejected, he opted to emigrate. He and his fiancée managed to secure passage aboard the last ship to leave Germany in May 1939. The first stop was Uruguay, where they married. Then they spent thirteen years in Argentina. In 1952, Birrenbach returned to Germany, where he was a deputy general manager of the Steel Union, the successor to United Steelworks (*Vereinigte Stahlwerke*). Two years later, he became chairman of the board of Thyssen AG for Investments, a position from which he was able to enter politics. The key figure in Birrenbach's rise was Robert Pferdmenges, banker and chairman of August Thyssen-Hütte, and above all a close confidant of Chancellor Adenauer. In 1955, Pferdmenges recommended Birrenbach to Foreign Minister Heinrich von Brentano and to Heinrich Krone, chairman of the CDU/CSU parliamentary caucus.

In 1957 Birrenbach was elected to the Bundestag. He was active on the Foreign Affairs Committee, where he remained until 1976. He had wanted to be foreign minister from the beginning – as he admitted in later years – but never got the position, despite CDU chancellors considering him for the office four times. He loved his independence too much; he was not a 'real' politician, especially not a party politician; and he was unmoved by 'old boy' networks or pressure along party lines. In 1977, former chancellor Kurt Georg Kiesinger, who knew Birrenbach best, once referred to him as 'The Adviser' (*Der Ratgeber*).

Birrenbach's advisory activity was not always easy. Adenauer rejected his advice on two crucial occasions – the Berlin crisis in 1961 and Great Britain's application to join the European Economic Community (EEC) in 1963. After the Berlin Wall was built in 1961, Birrenbach campaigned for understanding with the Americans about their plans to negotiate with the Soviets. These plans could only be at the expense of the Federal Republic and could not move forward with Adenauer, who was willing to risk confrontation with the Americans over this issue. Birrenbach was not even invited to participate in preparations for the chancellor's visit to Washington in November 1961.[83]

The second occasion involved a similar situation a year later, in December 1962. Birrenbach wrote Adenauer a very cutting letter 'full of indignation and despair', as Birrenbach put it. He urged the chancellor to assure France's president, Charles de Gaulle, that Great Britain's EEC membership was of vital interest for Germany.[84] The answer came in classic Adenauer brevity: 'I judge the whole European situation differently from the way you do. I am willing to talk to you about it when the occasion arises'. It never arose. Birrenbach did not enter the Palais Schaumburg, site of Adenauer's office, during the rest of Adenauer's chancellorship.[85]

That changed under Chancellor Ludwig Erhard, who valued him more – perhaps because Birrenbach, like Erhard himself, was not much of a 'politician'. It was Erhard's choosing him for the Israel mission that made the deputy famous among the public. Birrenbach's negotiations in Jerusalem were tough, yet the last meeting on 11 April 1965 was 'particularly friendly'. From the outset, Birrenbach was focused on one issue, namely, 'the three major Western allies' vital concern that the Federal Republic should not be eliminated as a mitigating factor or as an economic potential from the critical zone of the Middle East'. At the 11 April meeting, Israeli prime minister, Levi Eshkol, indicated that 'Israel was also concerned that the Federal Republic continue to be present in the Middle East'.[86] The director general of Israeli Ministry of Foreign Affairs, Arieh Levavi, stated for the record:

> I want to assure you that we consider it in our national interest that in the new phase – which we will begin in the near future – the Federal Republic be associated with as little disturbance as possible in the Arab world. It is not only in your national interest, but also ours. We are seriously concerned that these Arab threats be waged only temporarily, if at all; that is also why we welcome, not only with sympathy but also with vital interest, your efforts to dampen the reaction of the Arab world [so that it is kept] to a minimum. Furthermore, there is no difference in our views.[87]

On 7 March 1965, the same day that Birrenbach first flew to Israel, Bonn announced its willingness to establish diplomatic relations with Israel. On 8 March, UAR president Nasser responded with harsh rhetoric. With its treacherous policy, he asserted, the Federal Republic had revealed itself as the worst of the imperialist powers. Nasser would expose the West German imperialists in Africa to the whole world and fight them everywhere. He had 'never seen such a shameless people as the West Germans anywhere in the world'. The reaction to Bonn's announcement would be determined by a joint decision of all Arab states.[88] On 12 May 1965 the Federal Republic and Israel officially announced their establishment of diplomatic relations. As a reaction, all Arab states – except Morocco, Libya and Tunisia – broke off diplomatic relations with the Federal Republic (Iraq on the same day; the UAR, Jordan, Saudi Arabia and Syria on 13 May; Algeria, Lebanon and Yemen on 14 May; and the Sudan on 16 May. In addition, Kuwait backed out of an agreement on the exchange of ambassadors). The foreign ministers of the Arab League met in Cairo on 14/15 March, where a proposal to collectively recognize the GDR was advanced. Massive opposition from Saudi Arabia prevented this, leaving it ultimately up to the individual states.[89]

Bonn viewed its damages in the Arab world as bad enough, but less than feared. Neither consular, nor economic, nor cultural relations had ended. Further, none of the ten Arab states recognized the GDR, which was the decisive factor. On 15 May, Austria's ambassador to Cairo, Gordian Gudenus, reported to Foreign Minister Bruno Kreisky in Vienna that the Egyptian newspaper *Al Ahram* had published a long, 'surely official article' stating openly why the UAR had not recognized the GDR: the issue had led to disunity among the Arabs, and another push would only complicate the situation; by recognizing the GDR, Cairo would only waste all its ammunition. Gudenus further reported that Cairo was displeased with the situation it had been forced into: 'In Egyptian business circles there is open criticism'.[90]

Henceforth, Bonn's policy had two aims: first, to keep the Arab states from recognizing the GDR; and second, to restore their relationships with West Germany. At the peak of the crisis, ministerial director Franz Krapf, head of Political Division II in the Foreign Office, prepared a memorandum for discussions with Jewish leaders in the United States. This document, more than any other, clearly summarized the objectives of Bonn's future Middle East policy:

> Our Middle East policy must not be seen as an isolated policy. It also cannot be understood from an isolated viewpoint of only Israel or only the Arab countries. Rather, our Middle East policy is but one part of our policy of reunification, seen against the background of the East–West relationship.

The reunification of Germany in peace and freedom is the main goal of our policy. The claim to sole representation of the German people is part of our reunification policy. The communist regime in East Germany's Soviet Zone [i.e. the GDR] is trying to bring this into dispute. As one of its key approaches it has targeted several Arab states, in particular the UAR. Therefore, it must be part of our policy to prevent the Soviet Zone from breaking through in those countries. The UAR has a key position in this regard.

In our efforts regarding the Arab states, the traditionally good relations between Germans and Arabs have benefited us so far. Ulbricht is ruthlessly trying to exploit these traditional relationships. Meanwhile, our relations with the Arab states are also influenced by our relationship with Israel. In recent years, this issue has repeatedly put our Middle East policy in a bind.

Our stance in the UAR is about fundamental German interests. If we are manoeuvred out of the UAR, we will lose our position not only in other Arab countries, but also most likely in a larger number of African and Asian countries. . . . Our position in the Arab countries, however, has implications not just for our own reunification policy, but also for the position of the free world in these countries vis-à-vis communism. Our traditionally good relations with the Arab states make our position stronger than that of most Western countries. To give up this position would only benefit communism.[91]

On 19 August 1965, Ambassador Rolf Pauls (1915–2002), a former officer of the German Wehrmacht, handed over his credentials in Jerusalem, and on 20 August his colleague Asher Ben Natan (1921–2014), a former agent of the Israeli Secret Service, did the same in Bonn.

Back at the end of 1953, while discussing who might succeed the Austrian diplomat Karl Hartl in Israel, Hartl had given the socialist deputy chancellor Adolf Schärf some advice: it should not be some fool from the western Austrian province Vorarlberg, nor a Catholic, nor a Jew who 'would be considered a traitor by a diverse group of Zionists'. His successor should not be anyone 'who had anything to do with the Nazis', or anyone who had ever been an officer in the Wehrmacht, so as not to give the particularly unpleasant 'press hacks' in Israel a 'genuine target'. His successor should be a younger comrade who was as free of anti-Semitism as possible. When asked why, Hartl answered: 'He'll become an anti-Semite here anyway'.[92]

Bonn lacked such advice, although Israel's foreign minister, Golda Meir, had clearly expressed her opinion: 'The Germans should at least send an ambassador who did not participate in the war'.[93] Bonn sent Rolf Pauls, not a 'younger comrade'. Born in 1915, Pauls was a highly decorated officer of the German Wehrmacht (Knight's Cross), who had lost his left arm during the war. With his appointment, Bonn sought to demonstrate a new normality and to emphasize the distinction between soldiers and Nazis. In Jerusalem, not everyone saw it that way. Golda Meir was 'absolutely against' him,[94] and the chief of protocol refused to either meet him at the airport or participate in the subsequent ceremony. The first demonstrators, at the airport, held posters reading 'We want a German-free Israel'. Their numbers grew in Jerusalem, where thousands demonstrated with banners that said 'six million times no'. Pauls reported to Bonn:

> During the final approach in the president's car, the last kilometres were plagued by deafening screams from several thousand demonstrators marching with placards on both sides of the street. The uproar reached its first climax when the German national anthem was played. In an interview, President Zalman Shazar and Golda Meir explained, among other things, the deep feelings that underlie the demonstrations. . . .
>
> The talk lasted longer than the allotted time because in the meantime the police had apparently temporarily lost control of the demonstrators outside the official residence. Without the intervention of mounted police and a superb secret service shielding the car, my departure would have ended in chaos. The president's car in which I rode was damaged by stones and by hurled clubs with posters attached. In the embassy staff car that followed, a window was broken. Several police officers and demonstrators were injured, and some protestors arrested.[95]

The German embassy, right in the middle of Tel Aviv, had to be secured with a fence twelve feet high (later reduced to five feet). Years later Shimon Peres (1923–2016), who – having served as foreign minister, prime minister, and president – was one of Israel's most prominent politicians, called Pauls a 'highly successful diplomat who earned the respect of both

Figure 5.17 On 12 May 1965, West Germany and Israel establish diplomatic relations. The first German ambassador is Rolf Pauls, a former officer of the German Wehrmacht, here on his way to present his credentials to Israel's President Zalman Shazar in Jerusalem. Photo by Moshe Pridan. Courtesy of Israel Government Press Office, Jerusalem.

Israel and his own people'.⁹⁶ In her memoirs, Golda Meir (1898–1978) called Pauls, who later became ambassador in Washington, the 'most reliable and best friend of Israel'.⁹⁷ However, this did not keep him from sending some very critical reports to Bonn. When they became available in 2005, many people whom Pauls had 'favourably impressed', such as the long-term editor of the *Jerusalem Post*, the Vienna-born Ari Rath, were a little 'shocked'.⁹⁸ Pauls' reports, however, are anodyne compared to the reports his Austrian colleague Karl Hartl sent during the early 1950s. Hartl regarded Israel as a 'premature birth and perhaps a miscarriage',⁹⁹ a thing that had been given the name Israel, an 'artificial state' with a border that 'sweats blood', that 'lives off of the money of American Jews', that 'allowed blood to be compensated with money (from Germany)' – all in all, a 'small, very poor country'.¹⁰⁰ If it would cease to exist that would probably lead to serious problems, but not to war.¹⁰¹ Israel was, 'whether it wants it or not, nothing but a spatter of the Europe Hitler destroyed, which remained glued to the coasts of Asia Minor'. In Hartl's opinion it had to be considered proven by April 1954 'that the grafting of Europe onto the ancient Near East branch was unsuccessful – this scion never got the sap from the roots and, without outside aid, it will wither'.¹⁰² Hartl, a staunch supporter of Austria's claim to be 'the first victim of Hitlerite aggression' (as the Allies had said in the famous Moscow Declaration of 1943),¹⁰³ considered Israeli nationalism little different from German nationalism. In Israel there was 'the ugliest and most primitive limitation of believing [Jews] to be the chosen people, and God's mercy to the world – first and foremost to the Arabs – if instead of one and a half million Israelis there were 80 or 200 million. . . . The Jews are not even so kosher when they believe they have the chance to do so'.¹⁰⁴

Interpreting a high-ranking Israeli Foreign Ministry official's reflections on a recent border clash, Hartl described the Israelis as reformulating the old law of the desert, so to speak, with respect to the Arabs: 'No longer a tooth for a tooth, but a whole set of teeth for a tooth'.¹⁰⁵ In Hartl's opinion, the Israelis' attitude towards the Arabs was like that of American settlers towards Indians or of Australian farmers towards 'Australoids' (*Australneger*) in the early nineteenth century. Hartl spoke of the 'undeniable chauvinism of the people who view the Arabs as people of a second and third grade'.¹⁰⁶

These are just some of the least offensive of Hartl's statements; statements from a man who was a socialist, an anti-Nazi, married to a Viennese Jew, who had started his services in Israel with best intentions in January 1950, and then, two years later – an anti-Semite! In August 1954, he wrote to a colleague in Vienna: 'You don't know how healthy anti-Semitism is: it has kept me alive here the last two years'.¹⁰⁷

Asher Ben Natan's presentation of credentials in Bonn was less dramatic than that of Pauls in Jerusalem. The Hessian SPD minister president, Georg August Zinn, represented President Heinrich Lübke. Contrary to diplomatic norms, CDU foreign minister Gerhard Schröder was absent; in his place was Walter Scheel, the minister of economic cooperation. Ben Natan later reported: 'The Bonn population, which was used to such ceremonies, hardly took notice. The media, on the other hand, recognized this as a historic event, and also devoted attention to my person', not least because the ambassador bore a striking resemblance to the popular German actor Curd Jürgens.[108]

Ben Natan had been born in Vienna, attended the Hebrew school there, and early on became active in the Zionist movement. After the *Anschluss* of Austria in 1938, he fled through Yugoslavia to Italy and from there emigrated to Palestine. In 1945, he was back in Vienna, and from Salzburg he led the famous refugee organization *Bricha*.[109] Later, he held a leading position in the Israeli Secret Service. Before his appointment as ambassador to Bonn he had been in Paris, organizing arms purchases in France. In late 1965, Ben Natan complained to his Austrian counterpart in Bonn, Josef Schöner, that he had it much harder in Bonn than Pauls did in Israel. Schöner recorded what Ben Natan had told him:]/t[

> He must constantly demand and request something from the Germans. There are still so many outstanding problems, broken promises, unfinished commitments, and contracts, that he constantly had to become unpleasant with German authorities. Certainly, people in the Foreign Office were demonstratively friendly, but when money was involved (and lots of money was involved), when deliveries and loans were involved, it was very difficult to fulfil Israeli wishes. In addition, during all negotiations at the conference table, there were eleven invisible members 'sitting there': the representatives of the Arab states that broke off relations with Bonn. . . . This makes his work considerably more difficult.

Then Ben Natan made a few personal remarks. Schöner reported:

> He realized that every German he met treated him with 'obtrusive' kindness and courtesy. It amused him time and again when every second German learned who he was and thought it necessary to assert, within five minutes, the fact that he had had Jewish friends before the war and helped them as best he could and at his own risk. He categorically ignored such assertions, which did not prevent them from possibly being discussed a second time. Apparently the still latent bad conscience in Germany led to an attitude that one Austrian author had called 'Radau-Philo-Semitisms', which might or might not unexpectedly change to its opposite. Ben Natan saw this attitude as 'schizophrenic'.[110]

'Normal' relations between Germany and Israel did not exist. Israeli politicians repeatedly pointed out to Germans that historically Germany had a special duty towards Israel and was responsible for its security and welfare.

On 15 November 1965, Golda Meir told Rainer Barzel, chairman of the CDU/CSU parliamentary caucus: 'We can work together without disguising the past; however, we will never be even. Jewry and Israel lack not only the six million murdered, but also all their descendants'.[111] Ben Natan was correct on at least one point: during this phase of negotiations with Israel, in which Bonn's possible resumption of diplomatic relations with 'Islamic states' was at stake, the presence of their 'invisible representatives' was felt around the negotiation table. Moreover, a man who had been in charge of arms purchases in France was now ambassador in Bonn, which made the Arabs suspicious of the entire situation. Bonn's secret arms deals with Israel were not forgotten.

As for future relations with Israel, particularly economic aid from Bonn, the negotiations proved very difficult from the start, especially because of a precondition set by Israel: fulfilment of a promise Adenauer was supposed to have made to Ben-Gurion in March 1960 at a private meeting in Adenauer's suite in New York's Waldorf Astoria Hotel. Ben-Gurion had requested 500 million US dollars (2 billion Deutschmarks) for development in the Negev. The chancellor had responded only: 'We will help you' – nothing more. A West German spokesman later denied that the 500 million US dollars had been promised, yet the Israelis insisted that Germany was to pay it under the so-called 'Operation Business Friend' (*Aktion Geschäftsfreund*).[112] In October 1965, State Secretary Rolf Lahr bluntly told Ben Natan: 'With normal relations our cooperation must return to normal. Therefore, our economic aid to Israel should be part of our overall development policy'. Ben Natan responded: 'Obviously an extreme problem is emerging; the main question ultimately is how much you pay'.[113]

Israel demanded continued annual payments of 150 million Deutschmarks until the 2 billion DM were reached, and 200 million DM a year for the following five years on top of that. Prime Minister Golda Meir told Pauls: 'Germany may grant development aid to many countries. Historically, it bears a special responsibility towards Israel and is primarily responsible for its security and prosperity'.[114] Rolf Lahr spoke of extremely difficult negotiations, describing Israel's demands as being of 'untenable magnitude' (*untragbare Größenordnung*).[115] Considering budget problems and the 'invisible' Arabs in the background, Germany was prepared to pay 'only' 75 million Deutschmarks in addition to the 75 million already paid – and not until January 1966. In 1966, the economic aid would continue on the same scale as before: 150 million Deutschmarks annually. The offer basically adapted Operation Business Friend to the new 'normal' situation – that is, to 'legalizing' the payments. All this took place at a time when the Israelis assumed that continuation of the operation was a done deal and hoped for more assistance.[116]

Two opposing reactions to this offer were advanced in the Israeli Cabinet: (1) increase the demands, or (2) decline to engage in negotiations at all due to the insufficient offer. Regarding the second option, Ambassador Pauls feared the worst-case scenario:

> The Israelis would expose our payment of 650 million Deutschmarks (see indiscretion on arms deliveries [the leak about the tanks in 1964]; the secret service connections between the Israelis and the Arabs allow them to launch everything without leaving a trace). Then we will have the Arab pack at our necks (*die arabische Meute am Hals*) – worse than if we were to provide the Israelis with greater economic aid now – and we will have a deep crisis in German–Israeli relations, despite the help we have provided them for years. The Jews will unchain all the dogs from Jerusalem to London to New York.[117]

A few days earlier, Golda Meir had informed Rainer Barzel that if the Germans refused to see that they owed Israel economic aid for the sake of its very existence, she was 'inclined to instruct Ben Natan to stop talking altogether and forgo everything'.[118] The Cabinet decided to continue negotiations only if Bonn declared itself willing to carry out Operation Business Friend until the sum of 2 billion Deutschmarks had been fully paid, while the amount going beyond this would be subject to further negotia-

Figure 5.18 In November 1965, six months after the establishment of diplomatic relations between Germany and Israel, Rainer Barzel, the chairman of the CDU/CSU parliamentary caucus, visits Israel. Photo by Moshe Pridan. Courtesy of Israel Government Press Office, Jerusalem.

tions. State Secretary Lahr saw this approach as coming down to 'coercing a concession, which we always denied, to give the Adenauer/Ben-Gurion talks the status of an official agreement. . . . We are willing to discuss everything with the Israelis, but not under pressure'.[119] Bonn held to its offer of 150 million Deutschmarks.

Israel's policy up to this point led Ambassador Pauls to a fundamental evaluation in January 1966. He saw Israel's policy towards Germany as inconsistent:

> They desire to take benefits as well as profit from Germany, but at the same time try to overlook Germany's existence as much as possible. Should the result of the imminent negotiations be impressive enough to make it impossible for Israel to mobilize the Jews of the world – especially in New York – against Germany, that would suffice. We cannot garner the goodwill of the influential sector of the Israeli population in the foreseeable future. Therefore, their dissatisfaction should not distress us. The coverage of Germany in the Israeli press is almost entirely lacking in standards.

Initially, Pauls saw the basic task of German diplomacy towards Israel as

> making Israelis aware that reparations and foreign policy are two different things. Reparations draw the view backwards. Israel must understand that given the establishment of diplomatic relations and our continuing support, we are no longer willing to tolerate their unqualified obstructions in vital questions about our borders, our security policy, and our reunification policy.

Then he became explicit (this is what shocked Ari Rath; see above):

> We should make clear to the Israelis that we see through their constant plea about our moral obligation: they say morality, but mean filling their coffers (*dass sie Moral sagen, aber Kasse meinen*), and are not willing to partially exonerate us for our effort. An Israeli told me a while ago: 'We are a small country, but compared to Germany we are a great power'. I replied: 'Don't overplay your hand'.[120]

On 3 March 1966, Rolf Lahr stated: '150 million Deutschmarks will certainly be a major disappointment for Israel, and probably cause a crisis in the negotiations'. This could be avoided with more money, but 'we do not have that money, especially since we must always keep in mind that the Arab states will inevitably depict aid to Israel as a certain prejudice in favour of them. We must stick to the 150 million Deutschmarks'.[121]

In the end, Bonn added another 10 million Deutschmarks, and the German–Israeli Economic Aid Agreement was signed on 12 May 1966. On this occasion, government press secretary Karl-Günther von Hase explained that this money, as part of the global policy on economic cooperation, was linked to projects, as was the case in many other countries.

He expressed hope that it would soon be possible to normalize the German–Arab relationship: 'The German government attaches great value to restoration of the traditional friendship'.[122] Clearly, this also meant that diplomatic relations would adhere to the Hallstein Doctrine – in other words, there would be no diplomatic recognition of the GDR by the Arab states. Prior to 1966, only Yugoslavia and Cuba had diplomatic relations with the GDR. On 27 January 1966, State Secretary Karl Carstens spoke of the 'remarkable – one must say, "astonishing"' – success of Bonn's policy with regard to the GDR, but cautioned, with particular reference to the UAR and Syria, that 'we must not, however, close our eyes to the fact that the process of eroding this policy will progress, irreversibly'.[123]

The GDR had officially maintained a commercial representation in Cairo since 1955, and a branch office was opened in Alexandria the following year. In December 1957, a GDR representative with the title 'Ambassador' began his service in Cairo. The Consulate General of the GDR, with a staff of 130 higher officials and employees – compared to only 20 at the West German embassy – was established on 14 September 1959. Alexander Böker at the Foreign Office told Egyptian foreign minister Mahmoud Fawzi in October 1964 that the 'Soviet Occupation Zone' [i.e. the GDR] had managed to 'establish itself in an extraordinary way' in Cairo, and pursued activities that were highly detrimental to West German interests, not

Figure 5.19 May 1966: the 96-year-old former West German chancellor, Konrad Adenauer, visits Israel. Here with 80-year-old Ben-Gurion in Ben-Gurion's Kibbutz Sde Boker in the Negev (with Ben-Gurion's wife Paula and German ambassador Rolf Pauls). Photo by Fritz Cohen. Courtesy of Israel Government Press Office, Jerusalem.

only within the UAR but also throughout the Arabian and African world. Fawzi was obviously not very comfortable discussing this topic.[124]

In 1964, the GDR's 'Cairo model' served as the blueprint for arranging for GDR representation in Zanzibar. A German–Arab Society had been founded in East Berlin in 1958, and in 1959 GDR prime minister Otto Grotewohl visited six countries in the region. During the 'tank crisis' of February/March 1965, the UAR welcomed Walter Ulbricht with the fanfare reserved for a head of state. From 9 to 16 March 1966, GDR foreign minister Otto Winzer visited the UAR, where he met President Nasser, among others, and further talks took place outside the conference room between members of the Arab League and the foreign ministers of Algeria and Iraq. In Cairo, West German legation councillor Helmut Redies concluded that Winzer's visit had been 'extremely detrimental' to the interests of the Federal Republic. He reported to Bonn: 'The talks that Winzer held with Arab personalities gave him an opportunity to make many false allegations about our policies – especially towards Israel and the Arab states'.[125]

At the Arab League meeting in March 1966, Syria and the UAR proposed to recognize the GDR and establish diplomatic relations. Morocco and Sudan intervened, and the issue was postponed until the next summit, in Algiers in September. However, on 22 July 1966 President Nasser declared that the UAR would not participate in the September summit, as 'reactionary elements' had conspired with the 'imperialists' against Arab nationalism. As a result, the conference was postponed indefinitely.[126]

Bonn soon came to regard Syria as the 'most dangerous point', as Alexander Böker said on 19 August 1966.[127] The danger of Syria developing diplomatic relations with the GDR was evident. Legation councillor Gerhard Pfeiffer, head of the German task force at the French embassy in Damascus, reported from the Syrian capital that the German–Israeli relationship – especially the economic aid negotiations – was being monitored 'carefully, critically and suspiciously', and continued:

> The difficult situation since the cease of diplomatic relations in May 1965 has been exploited by the GDR for their own purposes without hesitation. During the last twelve months, the Zone [GDR] has literally showered Syria with delegation and friendship trips, giving the public a picture of German–Syrian friendship in which their word 'German' stands for the GDR. Thus the ground for the establishment of diplomatic relations is well prepared.[128]

Israel continued to play the decisive role – and still posed a problem. Foreign Minister Gerhard Schröder warned Chancellor Erhard on 10 May 1966 that any increase in the financial benefits for Israel might be 'the straw that breaks the Arabian camel's back, so to speak'.[129]

In Syria, and even in Iraq, the threat of diplomatic relations with the GDR loomed. Foreign Office ministerial director Hermann Meyer-Lindenberg remarked on 1 June 1966:

> Given the current situation, such an action by Syria could create a dangerous situation for us in the UAR, Iraq, Algeria and Yemen. Already, the Syrian government has informed us informally that it is now going to implement its decision, made last year, to close our consulate in Aleppo. . . . Currently, the Federal Government does not have any means of pressure or enticement of any kind whatsoever to appeal directly to Damascus not to recognize the Soviet Zone.[130]

On 10 June, Gerhard Pfeiffer pointed out that Syria's behaviour towards the GDR depended on the USSR: 'It is thus clear that the establishment of diplomatic relations with the Zone is no problem for the ruling politicians. The recognition can be announced any day. Regarding the Arab world, only foreign policy and tactical considerations play a role in selecting a point in time – and what the Soviets want. They don't care what we think'.[131]

On 1 July 1966, the GDR and Iraq signed a cultural cooperation agreement in Baghdad. GDR foreign minister Winzer granted the Yemeni consul general the exequatur on 29 July. On 19 August, Alexander Böker warned: 'Time is working against us. The restoration of our presence in the Middle East is becoming an urgent issue for our foreign policy'.[132]

What was to be done? The resumption of diplomatic relations was blocked, not only by Syria but foremost by the UAR. Nasser wanted to be sure Bonn would follow through with the decisive resumption talks and meet his financial demands. Yet for political and economic reasons, Bonn was neither willing nor able to go this route. Politically, it would mean accepting Cairo's Soviet-supported and GDR-friendly policy – with unpredictable consequences for the exclusive mandate policy in the non-aligned world. Economically, Bonn also would have to reckon with several hundred million Deutschmarks in claims, which not only exceeded its current possibilities but also could result in further financial blackmail.

In contrast, a prudent policy was set out to help governments better disposed towards Bonn – such as those in Sudan, Jordan, Libya and Saudi Arabia – to collectively resume relations with Bonn. These governments had repeatedly pointed out that such a resumption would not be possible without a gesture from Bonn that would compensate for its support for Israel and save them from an unacceptable loss of face.

Böker now proposed additional German support for Palestinian refugees, who posed a problem for all Arab states.[133] At a meeting on 7 September 1966, the Cabinet deferred a corresponding proposal from the Foreign

Office until a meeting on 13 October, at which foreign minister Schröder reiterated that resumption of diplomatic relations with the ten Arab states was one of the 'most urgent tasks of German foreign policy'. The Cabinet declined, however, first because of the difficult financial situation, and second because of a 'political dislike' (*politische Abneigung*) of the proposal. Its main arguments were that the Arabs kept the refugee problem alive artificially, doing nothing to ease the lot of the refugees; that this action – additional support for Palestinian refugees – would greatly anger Israel; and that the Arabs were ungrateful and there was not the slightest guarantee that they would honour the action with the resumption of relations.[134]

On 26 January 1967, SPD foreign minister Willy Brandt noted that the Federal Cabinet had agreed to provide 'special aid to Palestine refugees', but only after diplomatic relations with the Arab states were actually resumed.[135] This approach succeeded only with Jordan. Bonn feared that Jordan's resumption of diplomatic relations on 24 February 1967 would spur new attacks on King Hussein by the radical Arab states, especially Syria and the UAR. To bolster support for the king, refugee aid would be paid. Bonn had hoped the public announcement of this arrangement would make other Arab states more inclined to follow Jordan, but it did not work. As Secretary General Hassouna of the Arab League stressed in April, the league would not decide in Bonn's favour unless Bonn changed its policy towards Israel.[136]

Although the UAR continued to play an extremely important role, Egypt's foreign policy met with rejection from the Western powers, especially the United States and Great Britain. Moreover, Egypt's acceptance of GDR policy justified the assumption that Cairo would only agree to restoration of diplomatic relations with Bonn if an ambassador from East Berlin could be accredited in Cairo.

By early May 1967, the UAR's diplomatic recognition of the GDR was imminent. State Secretary Lahr noted on 6 May:

> How we will ultimately react, should there actually be diplomatic relations between Cairo and East Berlin, depends to no small degree on whether such a step by Cairo remains isolated or whether it will trigger a more or less far-reaching chain reaction. . . . In the long run, it cannot be in our interest to eliminate ourselves from the Middle East. At least for a time, however, we will probably be able to do without relations with the UAR. Considering Egypt's dismal economic situation, our economic interest is very low. The future of the Nasser regime is uncertain. Problems will differ depending on whether and to what extent other Arab countries will follow Nasser's example. For the time being, therefore, further development remains to be seen.[137]

Economic aid for Israel was still on the agenda. On 2 June 1967, Lahr proposed 160 million Deutschmarks, prompting Böker's interesting comment on 5 June: 'How long will these tribute payments (*Tributzahlungen*) continue? This can only bring disaster in the long run – certainly no improvement in German–Israeli relations or our position in the Middle East'.[138] On that same day, a new war began in the Middle East.

Notes

1. 'Israel und seine Beziehungen zur Bundesrepublik'. Memorandum by Rudolf Steg, AA, 8 January 1951. *AAPD 1951*, Doc. 5.
2. Niels Hansen, *Aus dem Schatten der Katastrophe: Die deutsch-israelischen Beziehungen in der Ära Konrad Adenauer und David Ben Gurion* (Düsseldorf: Droste, 2002), 291.
3. Sven Olaf Berggötz, *Nahostpolitik in der Ära Adenauer: Möglichkeiten und Grenzen 1949–1963* (Düsseldorf: Droste, 1998), 49.
4. Azzam and Shukeiry, cited in: Benny Morris, *Righteous Victims: A History of the Zionist–Arab Conflict, 1881–2001* (New York: Vintage Books, 2001), 219; see also David Barnett and Efraim Karsh, 'Azzam's Genocidal Threat', *The Middle East Quarterly* (Fall 2011), 85–88.
5. 'Palästina'. Heinrich Schmid (London) to Karl Gruber (Vienna), 27 May 1948. *Israel 1946–1949*, Doc. 50.
6. 'Politische und ökonomische "Malaise" in Israel'. Karl Hartl (Tel Aviv) to Karl Gruber (Vienna), 22 October 1951. *Israel 1950–1951*, Doc. 103.
7. On 10 March 1952, Stalin startled Western leaders by proposing the creation of a reunited, unoccupied, neutral and 'democratic' German state. For the story of the so-called 'Stalin Note', see Rolf Steininger, *The German Question: The Stalin Note of 1952 and the Problem of Reunification* (New York: Columbia University Press, 1990).
8. Cf. Rolf Steininger, *Deutsche Geschichte*, vol. 3 (Frankfurt am Main: Fischer Taschenbuchverlag, 2001), 201f.
9. The so-called 'Morgenthau Plan', put forward in 1944 by US secretary of the treasury Henry Morgenthau, was aimed at converting Germany into a principally agricultural and pastoral country. See Michael Beschloss, *The Conquerors: Roosevelt, Truman and the Destruction of Hitler's Germany* (New York: Simon & Schuster, 2002).
10. 'Auftakt zu Verhandlungen Deutschland–Israel'. Josef Schöner (Bonn) to Karl Gruber (Vienna), 2 February 1952. *Israel 1952–1953*, Doc. 7.
11. Steininger, *Deutsche Geschichte*, vol. 3, 203.
12. Karl Hartl (Tel Aviv) to Erich Bielka-Bleibtreu (Vienna), 24 January 1952. *Israel 1952–1953*, Doc. 5. For more on Karl Hartl, see Rolf Steininger, 'Israel as Seen by Karl Hartl, the First Austrian Diplomat in Tel Aviv', *Quest. Issues in Contemporary Jewish History* 7 (July 2014), and www.rolfsteininger.at/.
13. Howard M. Sacher, *A History of Israel: From the Rise of Zionism to Our Time* (New York: Alfred Knopf, 2002), 466. See also Axel Frohn (ed.), *Holocaust and Shilumim: The Policy of Wiederguimachung in the Early 1950s* (Washington, DC: German Historical Institute, 1991); Occasional paper no 2.
14. 'Politische Lage in Israel nach Unterbrechung der deutschen Reparationsverhandlungen'. Karl Hartl (Tel Aviv) to Karl Gruber (Vienna), 10 May 1952. *Israel 1952–1953*, Doc. 19.
15. Sacher, *Israel*, 466.
16. Ibid.
17. Hans Peter Schwarz (ed.), *Konrad Adenauer. Reden. Eine Auswahl* (Stuttgart: Deutsche Verlags-Anstalt, 1975), 267.
18. *Bulletin der Bundesregierung*, 11 September 1952.
19. Steininger, *Deutsche Geschichte*, vol. 3, 201–9.
20. 'Wiedergutmachungsabkommen zwischen der Bundesrepublik Deutschland und Is-

rael'. Josef Schöner (Bonn) to Karl Gruber (Vienna), 16 September 1952. *Israel 1952–1953*, Doc. 51.

21. See Nahum Goldmann, *Mein Leben als deutscher Jude* (Frankfurt: Ullstein, 1983), 371–425.

22. Cf. Hansen, *Schatten*, 155–264.

23. Karl Hartl (Tel Aviv) to Adolf Schärf (Vienna), 7 December 1953. *Israel 1952–1953*, Doc. 182.

24. Karl Hartl (Tel Aviv) to Clemens Wildner (Vienna), 10 October 1952. Ibid., Doc. 57.

25. Minute by Hasso von Etzdorf, AA, 6 September 1952. *AAPD 1952*, Doc. 197.

26. Circular by Hasso von Etzdorf, AA, 16 September 1952. Ibid., Doc. 204.

27. 'Meinungsverschiedenheiten zwischen der westdeutschen Republik und den arabischen Staaten betreffend die Leistung einer Entschädigung an israelische Staatsbürger'. Robert Friedinger-Pranter (Cairo) to Karl Gruber (Vienna), 25 November 1952. *Israel 1952–1953*, Doc. 63.

28. 'Stellungnahme der Liga der Arabischen Staaten zum deutsch-israelischen Wiedergutmachungsabkommen. Vollständiger, aus dem Arabischen übersetzter Bericht über die Pressekonferenz'. 19 September 1952. Austrian Embassy Cairo to Foreign Office Vienna. Ibid., Doc. 55.

29. Cf. note 27.

30. 'Die arabische Reaktion auf das deutsch-israelische Wiedergutmachungsabkommen'. Circular by Hasso von Etzdorf, AA, 29 September 1952. *AAPD 1952*, Doc. 211.

31. 'Wiedergutmachungsabkommen zwischen der Bundesrepublik Deutschland und Israel'. Josef Schöner (Bonn) to Karl Gruber (Vienna), 25 October 1952. *Israel 1952–1953*, Doc. 59.

32. See note 27.

33. Günther Pawelke (Cairo) to AA, 14 October 1952. *AAPD 1952*, Doc. 216.

34. Conversation between Staatssekretär Walter Hallstein and Arab Delegation, 28 October 1952. Ibid., Doc. 222.

35. Günther Pawelke (Cairo) to AA, 31 October 1952. Ibid., Doc. 224.

36. Ibid., Doc. 234, note 4.

37. Karl Hartl (Tel Aviv) to Vizekanzler Adolf Schärf (Vienna), 25 November 1953. *Israel 1952–1953*, Doc. 175.

38. 'Ratifizierung des Israel-Abkommens'. Minute by Alexander Böker, AA, 4 November 1952. *AAPD 1952*, Doc. 226.

39. Günther Pawelke (Cairo) to AA, 7 November 1952. Ibid., Doc. 227.

40. 'Aufzeichnung über eine Besprechung betreffend die nächsten Maßnahmen der Bundesregierung in der Frage der arabischen Proteste', Helmut Sigrist, AA, 25 November 1952. Ibid., Doc. 234.

41. Minute by Alexander Böker, AA, 10 December 1952. Ibid., Doc. 244.

42. Berggötz, *Nahostpolitik*, 434.

43. Jelinek, *Moral*, Doc. 48.

44. Hansen, *Schatten*, 305, 320.

45. Cf. note 27.

46. Cited in Hans-Peter Schwarz, *Konrad Adenauer. Vol. II: The Statesman, 1952–1967* (Providence, RI and Oxford: Berghahn Books, 1997), 441.

47. See note 12.

48. Cf. Wolfgang G. Schwanitz, 'Adenauer in New York, Pawelke in Kairo', *Historisch-Politische Mitteilungen der Konrad-Adenauer-Stiftung* 10 (2003), 151–72.

49. Jelinek, *Moral*, Doc. 117.

50. Ibid., 51.

51. Herbert Blankenhorn, *Verständnis und Verständigung: Blätter eines politischen Tagebuchs 1949–1979* (Frankfurt: Propyläen, 1980), 365.

52. Cited in Berggötz, *Nahostpolitik*, 107.
53. Ibid.
54. Hansen, *Schatten*, 106.
55. Berggötz, *Nahostpolitik*, 101.
56. Hansen, *Schatten*, 402f.
57. *Wenn sie Vorurteile gegenüber Israel gehegt haben, so kommen diese jedenfalls in den Akten nicht zum Vorschein.* Berggötz, *Nahostpolitik*, 111.
58. Handwritten note of 5 June 1967. AAPD 1967, Doc. 200, note 1.
59. Berggötz, *Nahostpolitik*, 436.
60. Steininger, *Nahostkonflikt*, 84–88; Morris, *Victims*, 284–301. See also Keith Kyle, *Suez* (London: Weidenfeld & Nicolson, 1991); Wm. Roger Louis and Roger Owen (eds), *Suez 1956: The Crisis and its Consequences* (Oxford: Clarendon Press, 1989); W. Scott Lucas, *Divided We Stand: Britain, the US and the Suez Crisis* (London: Hodder & Stoughton, 1991).
61. Franz Josef Strauß, *Die Erinnerungen* (Berlin: Siedler, 1989), 342; Felix E. Shinnar, *Bericht eines Beauftragten: Die deutsch-israelischen Beziehungen 1951–1966* (Tübingen: Rainer Wunderlich, 1967), 143; Berggötz, *Nahostpolitik*, 374–402.
62. See 'Sonderprojekt der Ausrüstungshilfe "Frank./Kol."' Minute by Rolf Pauls, AA, 21 October 1964. AAPD 1964, Doc. 289; 'Waffenlieferungen an Israel'. Memorandum by the AA for the Cabinet, 4 January 1965. AAPD 1965, Doc. 1; Minute by Karl Carstens, AA, 4 January 1965. Ibid., Doc. 2.
63. 'Israel. Streng geheim'. Minute by Karl Carstens, AA, 23 February 1965. Ibid., Doc. 92.
64. Cited in Klaus Hildebrand, *Von Erhard zur Großen Koalition 1963–1969* (Stuttgart and Wiesbaden: Deutsche Verlags-Anstalt: 1984), 112.
65. Horst Osterheld, *Außenpolitik unter Ludwig Erhard 1963–1966: Ein dokumentarischer Bericht aus dem Kanzleramt* (Düsseldorf: Droste, 1992), 154. For Ulbricht's visit to Egypt, see Angelika Timm, *Hammer–Zirkel–Davidstern: Das gestörte Verhältnis der DDR zu Zionismus und Staat Israel* (Bonn: Bouvier, 1997), 184–91.
66. 'Waffenlieferungen an Israel'. Karl Heinrich Knappstein (Washington) to AA, 6 February 965. AAPD 1965, Doc. 58.
67. Ibid., Doc. 74, note 3.
68. *Die USA hätten uns in diese Sache hineingeritten und dass sie uns auch wieder heraushelfen sollten.* Osterheld, *Außenpolitik*, 154.
69. Karl Heinrich Knappstein (Washington) to Karl Carstens (Bonn), 12 February 1965. AAPD 1965, Doc. 74.
70. Ibid., Doc. 74, note 14.
71. 'Unterrichtung des Bundeskabinetts über den gegenwärtigen Stand der Nahostkrise durch den Herrn Bundesminister'. Minute by Hermann Meyer-Lindenberg, AA, 15 February 1965. Ibid., Doc. 77.
72. 'Waffenlieferungen. Gespräch mit Rusk'. Karl Heinrich Knappstein (Washington) to AA, 18 February 1965. Ibid., Doc. 85.
73. Cited in Osterheld, *Außenpolitik*, 158.
74. Record of conversation between Gerhard Schröder and George McGhee in Bonn, 22 February 1965. Ibid., Doc. 89.
75. Record of conversation between Ludwig Erhard and George McGhee in Bonn, 22 February 965. Ibid., Doc. 90.
76. Minute by Karl Carstens, AA, 22 February 1965. Ibid., Doc. 88.
77. Osterheld, *Außenpolitik*, 164.
78. Ibid., 166.
79. Record of conversation between Ludwig Erhard and the ambassadors of the three Western powers, 5 May 1965. AAPD 1965, Doc. 112.
80. Osterheld, *Außenpolitik*, 166.
81. In June 1967, a German officer told the German ambassador, Rolf Pauls, that they had

proved 'excellent' (*hervorragend bewährt*) in the Six-Day War. Rolf Pauls (Tel Aviv) to Willy Brandt (Bonn), 12 June 1967. *AAPD 1967*, Doc. 214.

82. See Kurt Birrenbach, *Meine Sondermissionen: Rückblick auf zwei Jahrzehnte bundesdeutscher Außenpolitik* (Düsseldorf and Vienna: Econ, 1984).

83. For the story of the Berlin Wall, see Rolf Steininger, *Berlinkrise und Mauerbau 1958 bis 1963* (Munich: Olzog, 2001/2009).

84. For the British EEC application see Rolf Steininger, 'Great Britain's First EEC Failure in January 1963', *Diplomacy & Statecraft* 7 (July 1996), 404–35.

85. Cf. Hans-Peter E. Hinrichsen, *Der Ratgeber: Kurt Birrenbach und die Außenpolitik der Bundesrepublik Deutschland* (Berlin: Wissenschaft und Forschung, 2002; see my review in *FAZ*, 20 September 2002).

86. Kurt Birrenbach (Tel Aviv) to Gerhard Schröder (AA), 18 May 1965. *AAPD 1965*, Doc. 132.

87. Birrenbach, *Sondermissionen*, 115; Shinnar, *Bericht*, 164. See also the reports Birrenbach sent to Chancellor Erhard, in *AAPD 1965*, Docs 167, 172, 173, 185.

Arieh Levavi was born in Vilnius, Lithuania, in 1912. His mother fled with him and his brother to Danzig on the eve of the Russian Revolution. He completed his studies at the universities of Heidelberg and Danzig in 1930; in 1932 he left Germany for Palestine. From 1936 to 1938 he was back in Germany on a special mission. After the formation of Israel he became the head of Eastern Europe in the Israeli Ministry of Foreign Affairs. He was the first secretary and then counsellor at the Israeli embassy in Moscow (1948–1950). In 1952 he became the director of Israeli diplomacy for Eastern Europe. From 1954 to 1957 he was the elected minister plenipotentiary of Israel to the Yugoslav government. In 1958 he was appointed ambassador to Argentina. He served as the ambassador during the capture of Adolf Eichmann (on 11 May 1960). Immediately after the capture, the Argentine foreign minister requested an unequivocal statement from him as to whether Eichmann had been arrested in Argentina. Levavi replied that he did not know the country in which Eichmann had been arrested, nor did he know whether Israeli citizens had been responsible for his capture. On 22 July 1960, the Argentinean government declared Levavi 'persona non grata'. Therefore, Levavi was expelled from Argentina. From 1964 to 1967, Levavi served as director of Israel's Ministry of Foreign Affairs and stood at the helm of the ministry during the delicate period around and including the Six-Day War. See the interesting Wikipedia article.

88. *AAPD 1965*, Doc. 119, note 4.

89. Cf. 'Reaktionen der arabischen Staaten auf die Aufnahme diplomatischer Beziehungen zu Israel'. Minute by Helmut Redies, AA, 16 March 1965. Ibid., Doc. 129.

90. Gordian Gudenus (Cairo) to Bruno Kreisky (Vienna), 15 May 1965. *Israel 1962–1965*, Doc. 96.

91. Minute by Franz Krapf, AA, 3 March 1965. *AAPD 1965*, Doc. 106.

92. Karl Hartl (Tel Aviv) to Adolf Schärf (Vienna), 13 January 1953. *Israel 1952–1953*, Doc. 80.

93. Golda Meir, *My Life* (London: Weidenfeld & Nicolson, 1975), 177.

94. Ibid.

95. Report by Rolf Pauls, 19 August 1965. *AAPD 1965*, Doc. 409, note 28.

96. Cited in Hansen, *Schatten*, 805.

97. Meir, *Life*, 177.

98. Ari Rath, *Ari heißt Löwe: Erinnerungen* (Vienna: Paul Zsolnay, 2012); see my review in *FAZ*, 3 December 2012.

99. Karl Hartl (Tel Aviv) to Foreign Minister Leopold Figl (Vienna), 4 August 1954. *Israel 1954–1955*, Doc. 110.

100. Karl Hartl (Tel Aviv) to Foreign Minister Leopold Figl (Vienna), 4 October 1954. Ibid., Doc. 126.

101. *Die Infragestellung Israels würde wohl schwere Störungen nach sich ziehen, wahrscheinlich*

aber keinen Weltkonflikt bedingen. Karl Hartl (Tel Aviv) to Adolf Schärf (Vienna), 7 December 1953. *Israel 1952–1953*, Doc. 182.

102. *Israel ist, ob es will oder nicht, doch ein Spritzer des von Hitler zertrümmerten Europas, der an den Küsten Kleinasiens kleben geblieben ist)(Es darf doch schon als erwiesen betrachtet werden, dass die Aufpfropfung Europas auf den uralt.en vorderasiatischen Ast misslungen ist – dieses Reis hat sich nie den Saft der Wurzel geholt und wird ohne raumfremde Hilfe verdorren.* Karl Hartl (Tel Aviv) to Foreign Minister Leopold Figl (Vienna), 28 April 1954. *Israel 1954–1955*, Doc. 53.

103. For the Moscow Declaration, see Rolf Steininger, *Austria, Germany and the Cold War: From the Anshluss to the State Treaty, 1938–1955* (New York and Oxford: Berghahn Books, 2008, 2012), 25–42; and Robert Keyserlingk, *Austria in World War II: An Anglo-American Dilemma* (Kingston, Montreal: McGill-Queen's University Press, 1988).

104. *Gnade Gott der Welt – in erster Linie den Arabern – die Israelen zählten anstelle von anderthalb 80 oder 200 Millionen. . . . Gar so koscher sind die Juden auch nicht, wenn sie glauben, dazu die Möglichkeit zu haben.* Karl Hartl (Tel Aviv) to Rosa Jochmann (Vienna), 7 August 1954. *Israel 1954–1955*, Doc. 111.

105. Karl Hartl (Tel Aviv) to Foreign Minister Leopold Figl (Vienna), 16 August 1954. Ibid., Doc. 112.

106. Karl Hartl (Tel Aviv) to Foreign Minister Leopold Figl (Vienna), 5 June 1954. Ibid., Doc. 78.

107. *Du weißt dabei gar nicht, wie gesund Antisemitismus ist: er ist es, der mich die letzten zwei Jahre hier aufrecht erhält.* Karl Hartl (Tel Aviv) to Karl Wolf (Vienna), 28 August 1954. Ibid., Doc. 120.

108. Asher Ben Natan in: Asher Ben Natan and Niels Hansen (eds), *Israel und Deutschland: Dorniger Weg zur Partnerschaft* (Cologne: Böhlau, 2005), 27.

109. For the *Bricha*, see Thomas Albrich, 'Waystation of Exodus: Jewish Displaced Persons and Refugees in Postwar Austria', in Michael Berenbaum and Abraham J. Peck (eds), *The Holocaust and History: The Known, the Unknown, the Disputed, and the Reexamined* (Bloomington, IN: University of Indiana, 1998), 716–32.

110. Josef Schöner (Bonn) to Bruno Kreisky (Vienna), 6 November 1965. *Israel 1962–1965*, Doc. 102.

111. Rolf Pauls (Tel Aviv) to AA, 17 November 1965. *AAPD 1965*, Doc. 420.

112. For the meeting in New York, see Rainer Blasius, 'Das Treffen Adenauer–Ben Gurion', in Ingrid Böhler, Eva Pfanzelter and Rolf Steininger (eds), *Stationen im 20. Jahrhundert* (Innsbruck, Vienna and Bozen: Studienverlag, 2011), 21–31.

113. 'Deutsch-israelische Wirtschaftsverhandlungen'. Minute by Rolf Lahr, AA, 4 October 1965. *AAPD 1965*, Doc. 380.

114. Cf. note 30.

115. 'Verhandlungen mit Israel über Wirtschaftshilfe'. Minute by Rolf Lahr, AA, 3 March 1966. *AAPD 1966*, Doc. 55.

116. Ibid., Doc. 439, note 2.

117. *Die Juden werden von Jerusalem über London bis New York alle Hunde von der Kette lassen.* Rolf Pauls (Tel Aviv) to Gerhard Schröder (Bonn), AA, 30 November 1965. Ibid., Doc 439.

118. Cf. note 30.

119. *AAPD 1965*, Doc. 439, note 13.

120. Rolf Pauls (Tel Aviv) to AA, 26 January 1966. *AAPD 1966*, Doc. 20.

121. 'Verhandlungen mit Israel über Wirtschaftshilfe'. Minute by Rolf Lahr, AA, 3 March 1966. Ibid., Doc. 55.

122. *AAPD 1966*, Doc. 157, note. 11.

123. Minute by Karl Carstens, AA, 27 January 1966. Ibid., Doc. 21.

124. Conversation between Alexander Böker with Foreign Minister Mahmoud Fawzi in Cairo, 9 October 1964. *AAPD 1964*, Doc. 280.

125. *AAPD 1966*, Doc. 157, note 12.
126. Ibid., Doc. 95, note 9.
127. 'Zusätzliche Hilfe für die Palästina-Flüchtlinge'. Minute by Alexander Böker, AA, 19 August 1966. Ibid., Doc. 264.
128. Ibid., Doc. 144, note 20.
129. *Das könnte sozusagen der Tropfen sein, der das arabische Fass zum Überlaufen bringen wird.* Gerhard Schröder to Ludwig Erhard, 10 May 1966. Ibid., Doc. 144.
130. Ibid., Doc. 191, note 16.
131. Ibid., Doc. 264, note 5.
132. See note 46.
133. Ibid.
134. *AAPD 1966*, Doc. 328, note 2.
135. *AAPD 1967*, Doc. 63, note. 7.
136. Conversation between Willy Brandt and Mohammed Hassouna, 21 April 1967. Ibid., Doc. 136.
137. Ibid., Doc. 169, note 10.
138. Handwritten note. Ibid., Doc. 200, note 1.

Chapter Six

FROM THE SIX-DAY WAR TO REUNIFICATION, 1967–1990

The Six-Day War and No Neutrality

On Monday, 5 June 1967, 183 Israeli fighter jets launched a pre-emptive strike against Egypt. The time, 7.45 a.m., was chosen with the expectation that the Egyptian pilots and commanders would be in their cars, coming in after breakfast. The plan worked – its timing and the surprise were perfect. Within seventy minutes the Israelis had destroyed 197 Egyptian aircraft and 16 radar stations. At 9.34 a.m. a second wave began, destroying 107 Egyptian aircraft and 14 air bases. Before the third Middle East war was even three hours old, Egypt had lost three-quarters of its air force. It was already clear that Israel had won.[1]

The war, which had begun months earlier, was basically a continuation of the wars of 1948/49 and 1956. The goal of Israel's Arab neighbours remained the same: the annihilation of the Jewish state. Since the Suez Crisis in 1956, there had been repeated incidents at the border. The most serious conflict occurred on 7 April 1967, when the Israelis used French Dassault Mirage fighter jets to shoot down six Syrian Russian-built MiGs.

On 13 May 1967, the Kremlin warned Cairo and Damascus that Israel was planning an attack on Syria. The prestige of Egypt's President Nasser was at stake in the Arab world. On 16 May, he called on UN Secretary General U Thant to withdraw the UN troops that had been stationed in the Sinai Peninsula and the Gaza Strip since 1957. U Thant readily and willingly complied by giving the order to withdraw. Going a step further, on 22 May Nasser announced a blockade of the Straits of Tiran for ships heading towards Eilat. At a press conference he clarified his decision: 'The Jews threaten with war. I answer: welcome. Well, we're ready for war. Our main objective in an all-out war is the destruction of Israel'.[2]

For Israel, the blockade was a *casus belli*. As usual, the position of the United States was decisive. When the Israelis asked President Lyndon B. Johnson (1908–1973) about his stance, he gave the famous answer: 'Israel will not be alone, unless it decides to go it alone'.[3] So for the time being there would be no war, and this time Israel would not go it alone. On 29 May, the Israeli Cabinet came to a stalemate: nine ministers were for and nine against a pre-emptive strike. This angered the Israeli generals, whose calls for a 'strong man' were growing ever louder. Finally, on 1 June, a 'Government of National Unity' was formed, with Moshe Dayan, the hero of the Suez Crisis of 1956, as defence minister. On 4 June, this government decided unanimously not to wait any longer, mainly because of a report from Meir Amit, head of the Israeli secret service Mossad, who had visited Washington incognito and returned with the impression that no one there was opposed to a pre-emptive strike.

On the morning of 5 June 1967, multiple strikes were carried out and the Israeli army advanced towards the Suez Canal. Recently accessed Soviet documents tell of the drama that took place in the Kremlin. At 6.00 p.m. on 6 June, Marshal Amer conveyed to the Soviet government an urgent message from Nasser stating that the situation was 'very dangerous and critical, and cannot remain so beyond tonight'. Six hours later, again at Nasser's behest, Amer told the Soviet ambassador that the situation was so grave that 'a ceasefire must be achieved by 5.00 p.m. the following morning'.[4]

Figure 6.1 5 June 1967: beginning of the Six-Day War. Two days later, the first Israeli soldiers are at the Suez Canal. Photo by Moshe Milner. Courtesy of Israel Government Press Office, Jerusalem.

Figure 6.2 7 June 1967: Israeli paratroopers with their commander Mordechai 'Motta' Gur (centre) overlooking the Old City and Temple Mount of Jerusalem. Photo by Eric Matzon. Courtesy of Israel Government Press Office, Jerusalem.

On 20 June 1967, Soviet leader Leonid Brezhnev (1906–1982) informed the Central Committee Plenum of the CPSU: 'For the UAR, this was the most critical point in the course of the fighting'. He continued:

> On receipt of Cairo's alarming report reflecting the dramatic nature of the situation on the Israeli–Egyptian front, we Politburo members met throughout the night. We contemplated possible scenarios for assisting the UAR forces that were experiencing defeat. Needless to say, in the given time frame it was impossible to transfer any significant quantity of weapons – tanks or planes – to reinforce Egypt's basically disintegrating front, halt the advance of the Israeli forces towards the Suez Canal zone, or provide air cover for the Egyptian capital and other cities. Nor was it possible to ignore the Egyptian command's loss of control over the army, which was in a state of chaos and confusion. Moreover, many of the airfields at which our planes could have landed had been destroyed. Under these circumstances, the only correct way to extract the UAR army from destruction was to make full use of political and diplomatic instruments.[5]

The situation of the Jordanian army was similarly catastrophic, despite the Israeli army's heavy losses in the fight for East Jerusalem. In the middle of the second day of the war, 6 June, King Hussein told the Soviet ambassador: 'This is the most difficult day of my life. Only an immediate ceasefire can save Jordan'.[6] At the same time, there was fierce fighting on every street and in every house in East Jerusalem. On Wednesday 7 June, Israeli troops led by Moshe Dayan reached the Wailing Wall, where he declared: 'We have reunited the divided Jerusalem, the divided capital of Israel; we have returned to our holy places, never to be separated from them again'.[7]

Figure 6.3 Overwhelmed by emotions: Israeli paratroopers beside the Wailing Wall in East Jerusalem for the first time in their lives. Photo by David Rubinger. Courtesy of Israel Government Press Office, Jerusalem.

Immediately after the Old City of Jerusalem was taken, scores of Arab families living close to the Wailing Wall were forcibly removed from their homes within thirty minutes so that bulldozers could level the entire area. On 14 June, the day of the Jewish Pentecost celebration of Shavuoth, about two hundred thousand Jews streamed to the Wailing Wall. The *Jerusalem Post* reported that Ben-Gurion, on his first visit to the Wailing Wall, demolished a street sign reading *El Buraq* – the name of the white horse upon which Mohammed rode to heaven – in a 'holy rage'.[8]

On 9 June, Israel concentrated its forces in the north and prepared for an attack on the Golan Heights. At the same time, two Egyptian tank divisions in the Sinai were wiped out. News of the loss of these two units ultimately forced Cairo to accept a ceasefire. As a consequence, representatives of Algeria, Syria and Iraq – states allied with Egypt that had been at war with Israel since 5 June – called Nasser the 'Arab destroyer of Arabian national pride'. They felt that the Soviet Union, having misled them with Soviet propaganda before the onset of the war, had now abandoned them.

On the evening of 9 June, Nasser announced his resignation:

> Regardless of the many factors upon which I based my position during the crisis, I am ready to assume full responsibility. I made a decision, and I ask you all to help me to carry it through. I have decided definitively to resign from every political office and to return to the ranks of the people, and with them fulfil my duty, just like any other citizen.

The Soviet Union did not want this to happen under any circumstances. The Politburo of the CPSU pledged immediate political and moral support to Nasser:

> You enjoy enormous authority in the Arab world. The Arab peoples believe in you, your friends trust you, and you alone, by not leaving your post as president, can and must do everything to preserve the achievements of the revolution and see them to their conclusion. The Arab world and all the progressive forces in the world neither understand nor approve of your departure from the leadership of the country at this critical moment.[9]

Nasser remained in office, and Moscow heaved a sigh of relief: an important goal had been achieved. Brezhnev later told the Central Committee of the CPSU:

> Our actions in this critical situation for the UAR were directed at stopping the aggressor while the Arab countries still retained a considerable part of their armed forces, preventing Israeli forces from occupying Cairo and Damascus, and averting the fall of the UAR's progressive regime – a fall that, we are convinced, would have set in motion a chain reaction in other Arab countries.[10]

Figure 6.4 7 June 1967: Major-General Uzi Narkiss (left), Defence Minister Moshe Dayan, and Chief of Staff Yitzhak Rabin entering the Old City of Jerusalem through the Lion's Gate. Photo by Ilan Bruner. Courtesy of Israel Government Press Office, Jerusalem.

Meanwhile, in a heated argument in the UN Security Council, the Soviet representative Nikolai Fedorenko directly attacked the United States, declaring Israel as its 'criminal henchman' and likening Israel's policy to Hitler's. The Israelis reacted by holding the Soviets' cooperation with Hitler from 1939 to 1941 against them – a charge that had not been heard in the United Nations for some years.

In the meantime, the Israeli army continued its successes in the north. The Syrian barriers were breached, and the Israelis took Quneitra at around noon on 10 June. The road to Damascus was open. In this dramatic situation, the desperate Syrian government asked the Soviet Union 'to undertake all possible action within the next 2–3 hours; otherwise it will be too late'. Brezhnev told the Central Committee: 'This was the second critical juncture in the Middle East crisis. We took appropriate new steps without delay'.[11]

Moscow severed diplomatic relations with Israel and, for the first time, used the 'hot line' – a telegraph connection set up between Moscow and Washington in 1963 after the Cuban Missile Crisis – to convey a personal message from Premier Kosygin to President Johnson: if Israel did not cease military actions 'in the next few hours', then the Soviet Union would be forced 'to adopt an independent decision'. The Kremlin was clearly threatening to intervene on behalf of the defeated Arab states – even at the risk of military conflict with the United States. Kosygin warned: 'We are ready to do this. However, these actions may bring us into a clash that could lead to a grave catastrophe'. He then proposed that Johnson demand that Israel cease military action unconditionally 'in the next few hours'. The Soviets, Kosygin stated, 'will do the same'; meanwhile, he warned Israel that 'if this [demand] is not fulfilled, then necessary actions will be taken, including military ones'.[12] At the same time, Soviet warships, comprising a missile cruiser in the Mediterranean accompanied by several submarines, were ordered to chart a course for the Syrian coast. The war threatened to get out of control. Washington was aware of the seriousness of the situation, and the tension in the White House was palpable. US defense minister, Robert McNamara, realized immediately what the Soviet message meant: 'Mr President, if you want war, you will get it'. Johnson did not want another war – he already had one in Vietnam.

On 10 June at 6.30 p.m., in the abandoned city of Quneitra, the Israelis stopped their advance and agreed to the UN's demands for a ceasefire. Between 5 and 10 June, the lives of the people in the states involved in the Six-Day War changed completely. Israel tripled its original territory by conquering the Sinai Peninsula, the West Bank, East Jerusalem and the Golan Heights. It won an overwhelming military victory over its Arab neighbours and almost overnight became the top military force in the Middle East. The mood in the country was generally euphoric.

Friedrich Bauer, second in command at the Austrian embassy in Tel Aviv, turned the spotlight on this situation by describing some almost anecdotal encounters: a nonconformist, independent deputy complained about the disease 'Annexionitis' (according to one opinion poll, over 40 per cent of the Israeli population supported annexing the occupied territories). Coming from Germany, he could only with great concern witness the euphoria of the German Jews who, after the victory, practically sang the German national anthem *Deutschland, Deutschland über alles*, but singing 'Zion' instead of Germany.

A Russian-born editor of an Israeli daily paper disgustedly told Bauer that the German press attaché had compared the Israelis' success to both the German Blitzkrieg of 1939–41 and Rommel's Western Desert campaign. His wife, a former Soviet partisan, said, 'God shall protect us from those'. Meanwhile, Jewish humour did not fall short: the term 'Middle East', it was said, 'became obsolete; it should now be called 'Jiddle East' (the Yiddish *Jidel* = small Jew). The joke expressed both legitimate pride and tentative doubt as to whether the 'little Jews' would be able to hold on to what they had conquered.[13]

Figure 6.5 Scores of Arab families living close to the Wailing Wall are forcibly removed from their homes so that bulldozers can level the entire area. Photo by Eric Matzon. Courtesy of Israel Government Press Office, Jerusalem.

On 10 June 1967, Kurt Waldheim, then Austria's representative to the United Nations (and from 1972 to 1981 its secretary general), said in an analysis of the Israeli victory that Israel had created 'military security in the long run. But a political solution to the question of its existence seems further away than ever'.[14] This was not a bad outlook. A few weeks later at a summit in Khartoum from 29 August to 1 September, Arab heads of state responded to the defeat with a threefold no: no peace with Israel, no recognition of Israel, and no negotiations with Israel. Their main decision read:

> [The conference has agreed on the need to consolidate all efforts to eliminate the effects of aggression, on the basis that the occupied lands are Arab lands and that the burden of regaining these lands falls on all the Arab states.
> The Arab heads of state have agreed to unite their international and diplomatic political efforts to eliminate the effects of the aggression and to ensure the aggressive Israeli forces' withdrawal from the Arab lands that have been occupied since the aggression of 5 June. This will be done within the framework of the main principles by which the Arab states abide: namely, no peace with Israel, no recognition of Israel, no negotiations with it, and insistence on the rights of the Palestinian people in their own country.

The triple 'no' of the 'Khartoum Formula' remained the framework for Arab states' future policies regarding Israel, boding ill for a peaceful solution to the Middle East conflict.

On 22 November 1967, the UN Security Council adopted Resolution 242, which has since remained the international basis of all peace efforts in the Middle East. It reaffirmed, as the framework of a just and lasting peace in the Middle East, the 'withdrawal of Israeli armed forces from areas occupied in the recent conflict' on the one side, and on the other side the 'termination of all claims or states of belligerency and respect for and acknowledgement of the sovereignty, territorial integrity, and political independence for all States in the area and their right to live in peace within secure and recognized boundaries, free from threats or acts of force'. However, Resolution 242 was controversial from the start: the official English version demanded Israel's withdrawal 'from territories', but not from all territories.[15] An attempt by the Soviet Union to insert the word 'all' failed during the negotiations.

The Six-Day War put an end to the traumatic threat of Israel's extermination by its Arab neighbours, and at the same time led West Germany to rethink its Middle East policies, especially given that the Federal Republic had not, as the Arabs saw it, been neutral – despite Chancellor Kurt Kiesinger's 7 June declaration before the German Bundestag:

> The Federal Government has decided on a policy of non-intervention in order to prevent an escalation of the conflict and to retain a basis for its participa-

tion in the establishment of peace and positive development in the Middle East. Despite the conflict, the government will try to maintain ties to the countries in that area. True to the principle of non-involvement, it will not deliver weapons to the warring parties, and will ensure that this decision is strictly observed.[16]

The Arabs were right: Germany had not really been neutral. On 29 May 1967, a week before the war began, the Israeli ambassador to Bonn, Ben Natan, had asked for political, military and financial support, in addition to two hundred thousand gas masks. Ben Natan also urged Bonn to consider 'whether any suspicious material could be delivered through third countries, e.g. France'. Overriding the vote of State Secretary Karl Carstens, Kiesinger had expressed his intention to provide gas masks without identification marks, to be taken from the Bundeswehr (German armed forces). However, the war ended before they could be delivered. On 6 June, the Cabinet approved the aforementioned 160 million Deutschmarks for Israel – but with the stipulation of 'total secrecy because of the foreign policy situation'.[17]

Two weeks after the war, Ministerial Director Hermann Meyer-Lindenberg, head of Political Department I at the Federal Foreign Office, prepared a document on German Middle East policy that remained valid for the following years. SPD foreign minister Willy Brandt (1913–1992) approved the document but made the noteworthy correction of replacing 'East Germany' with 'GDR' throughout the draft, foreshadowing a later development: his government's 1972 recognition of the GDR as a second German state, as part of its 'Ostpolitik'. Germany's interests in the Middle East were defined as follows:

1. Protecting Europe's south-east flank from increasing Soviet infiltration.
2. Resuming diplomatic relations with nine Arab countries (the UAR, Algeria, Iraq, Yemen, Kuwait, Lebanon, Saudi Arabia, Sudan and Syria).
3. Preventing international recognition of East Germany (GDR).
4. Safeguarding the nation's economic interests.
5. Maintaining a policy of non-interference in regional conflicts in the Middle East.

Pursuit of these interests was expected to be complicated by Germany's immense economic aid to Israel and the question of Israel's association with the EEC. Meyer-Lindenberg recommended that the Federal Government should 'immediately declare its willingness to generously help the Arab states with rebuilding'. Furthermore, an assessment should evaluate whether and how EEC involvement could strengthen relations between Europe and the entire Mediterranean region.

The Federal Government should specify 'which elements we consider to be part of a constructive peace settlement in the Middle East', namely:

1. Recognition of the State of Israel by the Arabs.
2. Free navigation in the Gulf of Aqaba and the Suez Canal.
3. Solution of the Arab refugee problem.
4. A peace agreement without annexation.
5. A solution for Jerusalem acceptable to all sides.

At the same time, humanitarian activities in the war-affected countries should continue: 'In this way, we show our interest in good relations with all states in the Middle East'.[18] Yet relations with the Arab states were not good. The signing of the 160 million Deutschmarks agreement with Israel, planned for early July, was postponed for fear of 'devastating effects', in particular suspension of oil deliveries to Germany or boycott of German goods by the Arab states.[19]

All this occurred at a time when Moscow and East Berlin, as well as several Arab states including the UAR, Syria and Iraq, were repeatedly claiming that the Federal Republic was worsening the crisis by supplying arms to Israel.[20] In a 3 July 1967 memorandum for the UN General Assembly, the West German government rejected these accusations as 'absurd. They are false and will not become true through constant repetition'. The war materials West Germany had supplied before spring 1965 to Israel (45 million US dollars) and to the Arab states (30 million US dollars) 'are less than 2 per cent of total arms supplied over the past twelve years to that region, which according to international estimates had a total value of 4 to 5 billion US dollars. Many states took part in that'.[21]

However, the anti-West German feelings on the Arab side remained unchanged. In Cairo on 27 July, embassy counsellor Lothar Lahn met with Arab League secretary general Mohammed Hassouna for the first time since the onset of the crisis to explain the policy of the Federal Government. Lahn headed the German staff at the Italian embassy in Cairo, which had represented German interests there since Egypt's termination of diplomatic relations. Hassouna was an expert on Germany: he had served as an embassy counsellor in Berlin in 1936, spoke German, and had had a German housekeeper for forty years. His position was clear. Lahn reported to Bonn:

> The Arab states are convinced, despite contradictory German assurances, that we are clearly on the side of Israel and that the part we played in the arms

deliveries along with the financial support only enabled Israel to prepare the aggression that led to military success. . . . He was sorry to tell me today that the German–Arab relations had reached a low point from which he currently did not see a way out.[22]

The grand coalition's policy of isolating the GDR had failed. It was now Bonn that was isolated from all Arab states in the Middle East, while the GDR clearly took their side and at the same time carried out massive propaganda attacks against Israel. East German deputy prime minister Gerhard Weiß, who visited Egypt and Syria in July 1967, explained when he arrived in Cairo on 6 July: 'The people of the GDR have followed the Arab people's heroic struggle against Israeli aggression with undivided sympathy. . . . The GDR condemns Israel's criminal invasion and stands firmly on the side of the progressive Arab states, demanding immediate and unconditional withdrawal of the aggressor's army to the line before the attack [i.e. the line of 1949]'.[23]

At the same time, the Soviet Union was ratcheting up the pressure on individual Arab states, especially the UAR, Libya and Syria, to recognize the GDR. After a conversation with UAR vice-minister for foreign affairs, Mohammed Murad Ghaleb, in November 1968, embassy counsellor Lahn reaffirmed 'the conviction that full diplomatic relations exclusively between the UAR and the Federal Republic will not be possible under the prevailing circumstances'.[24] The entire Arab world was disappointed by Bonn's Israel policy. Ministerial Director Paul Frank noted on 15 April 1969: 'For half a century the Arabs regarded Germany as their best friend, if not their only friend. Therefore, more than any other Western state we are now accused of having good relations with Israel'. Yet on 21 April 1969, Foreign Minister Willy Brandt stated unequivocally that good relations with Israel 'are an important goal of German foreign policy and cannot not be sacrificed on the altar of German–Arab friendship'.[25]

Bonn's policy of non-recognition was even further undermined in the following weeks, as the GDR was recognized by Iraq on 30 April 1969, by Cambodia on 8 May, by Sudan on 27 May, and by Syria on 6 June. Bonn feared other states would follow suit. The Foreign Office stated on 9 June that the government 'should not ignore this development. Efforts must be made, above all, to prevent full recognition of the GDR by means of a key country like the UAR. Otherwise, our position in the Middle East and the rest of the world threatens to erode further'.[26]

What could be done? First, Bonn made it clear to the Arab governments that the Iraqi government's decision to recognize the GDR was injurious to West Germany's vital interests and had put considerable strain on the German–Iraqi relationship – obviously with no effect. What else could be done? Generous economic deals for the Arab countries? This could easily increase the pressure on Bonn without resulting in political progress. Moreover, this could be the wrong message for those Arab states with a friendly attitude towards Bonn. Did Bonn have political leverage? So far, the neutral policy the Federal Government officially pursued in the Middle East included no arms supplies to the Arab states or to Israel. Should the government review this policy? State secretary Günther Harkort noted: 'I would have great concerns'.[27]

One of Willy Brandt's confidants, Egon Bahr, noted on 1 July 1969 that the states that had recognized the GDR were among the most politically unstable countries in the Arab world, so they were not 'necessarily exemplary. In the big picture, there is probably no immediate danger of the GDR's being recognized by many states all at once'.[28] Egypt's vice president, Hassan al-Kholy, had told Lahn on 4 June what the real problem was. He did not rule out a resumption of diplomatic relations with the Federal Republic, if it 'would permanently shelve the Hallstein Doctrine'. This meant that the Federal Republic 'should accept a GDR embassy in Cairo'.[29] On 11 July 1969, the UAR established diplomatic relations with the GDR.

On 2 August 1969, in view of the GDR's 'successes', Bonn's state secretary Georg Ferdinand Duckwitz, who was developing ideas for the future foreign policy of the new government (federal elections were scheduled for September 1969), stated in a paragraph about the GDR:

> We must free ourselves from the remnants of the Hallstein Doctrine. This does not necessarily mean that we recognize the GDR, but we should treat other countries' diplomatic relations with the GDR with complete equanimity. We cannot afford to give up our presence in those countries that acquire and maintain diplomatic relations with the GDR. Our economic strength, our political significance and our cultural achievements make it possible for us to compete successfully with the GDR in other countries where they and we are both represented.[30]

Egon Bahr agreed. If the Hallstein Doctrine were jettisoned, no state would be able to 'blackmail the Federal Republic with the threat of recognition any longer'.[31]

After the elections in September 1969, the Social Democratic Party and the Liberal Party formed a coalition government with Willy Brandt as chancellor and Walter Scheel as his foreign minister. This social-liberal coalition began its new *Ostpolitik* with a focus on Moscow, which US president Richard Nixon and his national security advisor Henry Kissinger were monitoring with suspicion.[32] In their view of the Middle East, the UAR was still the most important country. Signals from Cairo indicated that there was interest in improving German–Arab relations in general and German–

Egyptian relations in particular. The main question was whether the new German government was prepared to accept the presence of two German embassies in a Third World country.

The Federal Government, Duckwitz opined on 1 December 1969, 'will not be able to avoid the answer to this question. . . . The Egyptian side is waiting for a reaction from us. . . . Cairo is still the key to the Arab world, whether it suits us or not'. If Bonn should say no, he feared the consequences. Politically, disappointment and resentment on Egypt's side would cause the Egyptian propaganda apparatus, which operated far beyond Egypt, to characterize the Federal Republic as an enemy. Economically, Egypt's debt service and German–Egyptian economic relations would end, and an interesting future market would be lost. And culturally, continuing the Hallstein Doctrine would further diminish Germany's still important but vulnerable cultural position in Egypt, which was predominantly in Bonn's interest.[33]

On 10 February 1970, Willy Brandt and several of his Cabinet members attended a high-level meeting to decide Bonn's future Middle East policy and prepare for talks with Israel's foreign minister, Abba Eban, in Bonn on 22 February. Attendees included the ministers Walter Scheel (FDP, foreign), Helmut Schmidt (SPD, defence), Hans-Dietrich Genscher (FDP, interior), Erhard Eppler (SPD, developing aid) and Horst Ehmke (SPD, chancellery), as well as several state secretaries. Brandt opened the meeting by stating that Bonn's Middle East policy should be balanced, but by no means indifferent to the fate of Israel; and that the proclaimed 'normalization' of relations with Israel did not signify a devaluation of these relations, but rather a goal to be achieved. These two points should be clear. He then mentioned UN Resolution 242 of November 1967, which Bonn had so far regarded as the best basis for a peace settlement in the Middle East, despite the unforeseen developments in the situation since 1967. According to Brandt: 'With regard to Israel, we must pursue a policy without any complexes'.

Walter Scheel agreed, stressing Bonn's desire for a balanced policy in the Arab world and good relations with all states in the Middle East: 'In keeping with our principle of not sending weapons to areas of tension, we want to normalize our relations with the Arab countries, though certainly not at the expense of Israel. Diplomatic relations with five out of fourteen Arab states is not enough. However, our policy towards the Arab countries must be seen in the context of our *Ostpolitik*'. Scheel then turned to Israel, a 'difficult factor'. In contrast to the Arabs, the Israelis had 'very concrete and precise wishes'. If even more loans were extended to Israel, the whole world would consider them just another form of arms delivery. Therefore, 'it is clear that Israel will receive no Deutschmark that cannot be represented openly'.[34]

Helmut Schmidt then presented an overview of the military situation in the Middle East. He thought another war was possible, and pointed out that Israel was on the brink of becoming a nuclear power, 'if it has not already crossed this threshold'.[35] SPD federal secretary Hans-Jürgen Wischnewski, a Bundestag member who was so well versed in the Arab world that he was nicknamed Ben Wisch, spoke of Germany's policy, which 'in these days and hours' was facing a particularly complicated situation in at least three Arab places – namely Algiers, Beirut and Tripoli. In this context, Abba Eban's visit should not be connected with anything spectacular. He recommended a truly generous debt settlement, ongoing economic aid of 140 million Deutschmarks for 1970, and generosity with respect to the 'humanitarian' issue.

Brandt agreed that the talk with Abba Eban should undoubtedly be matter of fact, but he added: 'There are also difficult customers on the Israeli side. . . . One thing needs to be clear: I don't like blackmail, even if it comes from friends'. Scheel agreed: 'I too am no friend of blackmail'. Scheel then stated three future principles for Germany's Middle East policy:

1. It should strike the right balance, which also meant preserving or restoring ties with the Arab side with an eye to future developments.
2. It should be better conceived and conveyed politically, compared to prior policy; that is: 'We must have a clear political position and issue statements'.
3. The policy 'must be open and not get lost in secrecy'.

After two and a half hours it was decided: (1) to give 140 million Deutschmarks in economic aid to Israel; (2) to supply no weapons to the Middle East; and (3) to refrain from any military cooperation with Middle East states.[36] In anticipation of the meeting with the Israeli foreign minister, ministerial director Paul Frank laid out some fundamental aspects of the German–Israeli relationship in a memorandum. These are so interesting that they are quoted here in detail. As Frank saw it:

> The Israelis see the relationship between the Federal Republic of Germany and Israel mostly from the perspective of the German people's collective liability for the crimes of the Third Reich. In the wake of the division of Germany, Israel's interest in this has been concentrated unilaterally on the Federal Republic. Israel has assumed the place of Judaism, against which the crimes were committed. In dealings with the Federal Republic, the Israeli government assumes that the crimes of the past create a special relationship between Israel and the Federal Republic. As an act of reparation, the Federal Republic must contribute to the existence of Israel and not allow the other side to do anything to oppose the existence of Israel.

To this we must say: the Federal Republic cannot make the past the only basis for its relations with Israel. Otherwise it will be impossible to eliminate the past from the relationship with Israel, even if the German people want to. In any case, the history books will testify to the crimes of the Third Reich.

Anyone who wants to avoid serious misunderstandings in German–Israeli relations must also recognize and take into account that the majority of people living in Germany today were not conscious participants in the time between 1933 and 1945. The majority of the German people today, therefore, will not tend to see relations with Israel primarily from the perspective of the past.

Both governments must help to ensure that Germany and Israel do not tragically go in opposite directions. Just when the Israelis are beginning to move towards the Federal Republic, the young people of Germany, detached from the past, are distancing themselves from Israel because of the Middle East conflict and the associated problems. In my opinion, we should draw the Israeli foreign minister's attention to this threat.

Discussion of German–Israeli relations is too often defined by considerations of German–Arab relations. The desired 'balance' of our Middle East policy is not the decisive criterion. The overriding concern in our foreign relations, and with respect to Israel as well, is keeping the peace, or rather restoring peace where it has been disturbed. This overriding concern, which corresponds to the genuine wishes of the majority of the German people, is now more important for the development of German–Israeli relations than are complexes about the past, or the Federal Republic's relations with Arab states. In so far as the Middle East conflict continues and intensifies, German–Israeli relations will be increasingly burdened. On the one hand, Israel's desire for economic support and supply of weapons will intensify, while on the other hand, the German public's aversion to this conflict will likewise grow. Escalation of the conflict will also foster polarized opinions in Germany, with some taking sides for Israel, and others for the Arabs. Precisely this would be fatal for the development of prosperous German–Israeli relations and a genuine overcoming of the past. There is a real danger to world peace in the Middle East.[37]

Three years later, the Yom Kippur War would seem to prove this last statement true.

On 18 February 1971, Paul Frank, promoted to state secretary in the German Foreign Office, asked Germany's representative in Cairo to inform the Egyptian government of Bonn's readiness to 'arrange to resume diplomatic relations with all the Arab states that wished to do so, to be carried out without preconditions by either side',[38] and thereby raised the issue of such a resumption in the Arab world. To counter the 'danger of a landslide' in this development, it was initially thought the resumption process should be carried out gradually and extended over a long period. This met with criticism from the Foreign Office, where in April 1971 Helmut Redies, who headed the Middle East and North Africa desk in the political department, spoke of an 'increasingly unpleasant affair' for the Federal Government, and warned against stalling too long: 'Because the first resumption (Algeria) was delayed, the resumption with other individual countries, in terms of time, is condensed and the risk of a landslide is thus increased. . . . It is incomprehensible that we take one defeat after another with further recognitions [of the GDR], instead of taking responsibility for the inevitable revision of our policy and acting accordingly'.[39]

Nevertheless, the Federal Government did not decide to start talks about resuming relations with Algeria and Sudan until November 1971. A month later Frank pointed out in a circular: 'The Federal Government cannot escape the Arabs' initiatives if it wants to regain the lost political terrain in the Arab world. . . . Since the majority of Arab states want to resume diplomatic relations, it can be expected that other Arab states will step up. For us this means recovery of political terrain'.[40]

Diplomatic relations were resumed with Algeria on 21 December 1971 and with Sudan two days later. On 14 March 1972, the Council of the Arab League decided: 'Any member state that has not yet entered into diplomatic relations with the Federal Republic of Germany shall be free to act at its discretion'. That same year the following countries did just that: Lebanon on 30 March; Oman, Bahrain and the United Arab Emirates on 17 May; Egypt on 8 June; and Kuwait on 22 December. This was followed in 1973 with Qatar on 15 January, and Saudi Arabia on 18 September; and in 1974 with Iraq on 23 February, and Syria on 7 August.[41] Now there were two German ambassadors in each of the most important capitals of the Middle East and an Arab ambassador in both Bonn and East Berlin.

The extent of Bonn's involvement in the Middle East conflict became clear in September 1972. Ten days after the opening ceremonies of the Munich Olympic Games, in the early hours of 5 September, eight Palestinian terrorists calling themselves members of the organization Black September attacked the Israeli Olympic team. They invaded the athletes' quarters, killed two Israelis, took nine as hostages, and demanded both the release of two hundred Arabs imprisoned in Israel and the transfer to Egypt of the hostages and their captors.

The Israeli government immediately rejected the release of the imprisoned Arabs. Chancellor Brandt tried urgently to reach Egypt's President Sadat by telephone at 6.30 p.m. When he was told around 8.00 p.m. that the president was not in Cairo, but that he could speak to Prime Minister Aziz Sidky in about an hour, Brandt asked to speak to a 'responsible' member of the government 'immediately'. At 8.40 p.m. he spoke to Sidky and proposed that the terrorists be flown to Cairo with the hostages, who should be given the opportunity to leave Egypt again. This proposal was, in Brandt's opinion, 'in the interest of the Federal Republic and Egypt'. Sidky saw it differently and rejected the proposal on the grounds that 'Egypt did not want to get involved in this affair at all'.[42]

What happened next is well known. The terrorists extended their ultimatum several times, and an attempt to free the hostages ended in a bloodbath on the Fürstenfeldbruck Air Base: all nine Israelis and one police officer were killed by the eight terrorists, three of whom survived. Officially, Israel refrained from criticism, while Cairo stressed that the permission to land was denied because Egypt could 'come under suspicion of complicity to some extent'.[43]

A crisis in German–Israeli relations arose on 29 October, when a Lufthansa plane travelling from Damascus to Munich via Zagreb with thirteen passengers and a crew of seven was hijacked by two Arab terrorists who demanded the release of the three surviving terrorists of the Olympic attack. The Federal Government acceded to their demands. The three survivors were flown to Zagreb, boarded the Lufthansa plane and flew to Tripoli, where the hostages were released. Israel was outraged at the 'surrender to the terrorists'. Abba Eban accused the Federal Government of releasing murderers 'who now have the chance to kill again'.[44]

On 1 November, German ambassador Jesco von Puttkamer reported from Tel Aviv on the debate in the Knesset:

> It was the harshest and strongest anti-German debate since the reparations confrontation in 1952. Nevertheless, the Israeli government is trying to mitigate damages. The public sees [Israel's ambassador in Bonn, Eliashiv] Ben-Horin's being ordered to come to Israel to report mostly as a diplomatic demonstration.

Figure 6.6 7 June 1973: Israel's prime minister, Golda Meir, welcomes West German chancellor, Willy Brandt, at Lod Airport. Photo by Moshe Pridan and Moshe Milner. Courtesy of Israel Government Press Office, Jerusalem.

I remain of the opinion that as long as the situation is under control, the Israeli government is not really interested in aggravating the crisis.[45]

That was probably true, yet the Middle East conflict undoubtedly took on a new dimension after the Munich assassinations. Paul Frank made this clear in a talk with Tunisia's president Bourguiba and foreign minister Masmoudi in December 1972. According to Frank, the Federal Government was concerned about the future development of German–Arab relations – fresh attacks would surely have very negative effects. Bourguiba called the attack in Munich 'a fooly' (*eine Narrheit*), but stressed that the background of the events should not be overlooked. It was unfortunate that the world, and especially the great powers, had not yet begun a serious effort to reach a fair solution to the Middle East conflict, especially for the Palestinian refugees. Bourguiba continued: 'The Middle East is increasingly a politically decaying area, and the spread of anarchist thinking among the Palestinians is the result'.[46]

Willy Brandt visited Israel from 7 to 11 June 1973. The talks there were friendly, however, they point to why the Israelis were so surprised by what happened later. Secretary of State Mordecai Gazit said there was 'stability' in the region: the ceasefire had lasted three years, and Israel did not think the situation in the Middle East was dangerous. 'One has to accept that the present state will continue for years', he stated.[47] Gazit was wrong. Four months later Israel had a rude awakening.

Figure 6.7 Israelis protesting Willy Brandt's visit to Israel in June 1973.
Photo by Moshe Pridan and Moshe Milner. Courtesy of Israel Government Press Office, Jerusalem.

The Yom Kippur War and No Solidarity[48]

On 28 September 1970, Egypt's Gamal Abdel Nasser died. His successor was Anwar Sadat (1918–1981), whom neither Israel nor Washington took seriously. Henry Kissinger, then President Nixon's national security advisor, said: 'Who is Sadat? We all thought he was a fool, a clown'.[49] No actions had followed Sadat's numerous announcements about recapturing occupied territories, and his threats of war were not taken seriously – until Saturday, 6 October 1973. At 2.00 p.m. on Yom Kippur, the highest Jewish holiday, Egyptian and Syrian troops simultaneously attacked Israeli positions in a coordinated action on two fronts: the Suez Canal and the Golan Heights. In Bonn, Israeli ambassador Eliashiv Ben-Horin complained to foreign minister Walter Scheel that it was 'Arab malice (*Niedertracht*) to attack on Yom Kippur – worse than on Christmas Eve for Christians'.[50]

Still feeling the emotions of its 1967 victory over the Arabs, Israel was completely surprised by the attack. Zvi Zamir, the director of the Israeli foreign intelligence agency Mossad, later explained: 'We simply did not believe that the Arabs were capable of this. We scorned them'.[51] Neither Mossad nor AMAN, the more important military intelligence agency, had foreseen this danger, and all warnings had been ignored[52] – until midnight on 6 October, when an Egyptian Mossad agent passed on secret information that the attack would begin on 6 October at 6.00 p.m.

The attack actually started at 2.00 p.m., four hours before the IDF was expecting it. AMAN's director, General Eli Zeira, considered the midnight message to be deliberate misinformation conveyed by a double agent. On the morning of 6 October, the Israeli military had not been able to agree on a course of action: chief of staff David Elazar demanded a general mobilization (two hundred thousand men), while defence minister Moshe Dayan wanted to mobilize only two divisions and refused to comply with Elazar's demand, arguing that if the Arabs felt threatened by a general mobilization they might execute a pre-emptive strike. Elazar demanded a pre-emptive strike against the Syrian air force, and again Dayan refused, saying Israel should not become an aggressor. He and the other ministers remembered 1967 and were convinced that an attack by Egypt and Syria could easily be repelled. Prime Minister Golda Meir also opposed a pre-emptive strike, but she approved a mobilization of up to one thousand men, beginning at 10.00 a.m. Meir justified her refusal of a pre-emptive strike to US ambassador Kenneth Keating by stating that she wanted to 'avoid bloodshed'.[53]

When the Egyptians and Syrians began their attack at 2.00 p.m., the Syrians had 930 tanks, 930 guns, and thirty SA-6 anti-tank missile batteries at their disposal, as well as two tank divisions with 460 tanks in reserve. On the Israeli side, there were just 177 tanks. An Israeli commander later

Figure 6.8 October 1973: Yom Kippur War. The beginning of the war caught thousands of Israeli soldiers in the Sinai and the Golan Heights unprepared. They suffered heavy losses; Israel was on the brink of final disaster. Only after the United States started airlifting massive quantities of weapons, ammunition, fighter planes and tanks did Israel regain control.
Courtesy of Israel Government Press Office, Jerusalem.

said that it felt like another holocaust was about to happen. On the morning of 7 October, the Syrian units broke through the defensive line on the Golan Heights and pushed into the Jordan Valley. Dayan later said of the Syrian and Egyptian soldiers: 'They fought better than in 1967'; in particular the Syrians were 'determined, fanatic. It was a sort of jihad'.[54]

Israel lost 100 tanks on the Golan front, and the rest ran out of ammunition. 'The Third Temple [the State of Israel] is in danger', Dayan told General Benny Peled, the commander of the Israeli air force, which was supposed to stop the Syrians: 'The Sinai is sand. Here [the Golan and Jordan Valley] are our houses'.[55] The situation was serious. Just how serious became clear when Golda Meir gave the order to arm thirteen Jericho nuclear missiles, each with a range of 500 km and an explosive power of 20 kilotons of TNT.[56] Despite the catastrophic situation on the Sinai front, Peled withdrew several aircraft from there and deployed them against the Syrians.[57]

Meanwhile, the situation worsened on the Suez front. In the first minutes of their attack the Egyptians had fired 10,500 shells on Israel's Bar-Lev defence line while using German and British water cannons to clear passages through ramparts of sand ten metres high; then they crossed the canal on eleven floating bridges. On 7 October, 100,000 soldiers, 1,020 tanks, and 13,500 military vehicles located on the east bank advanced 20 km under the protection of SA-6 missiles. On Monday 8 October, a failed Israeli counteroffensive turned into 'a tankman's nightmare', as General Ariel Sharon described the disaster. Thousands of Israeli soldiers were killed, and many were taken prisoner. The Israelis lost 400 tanks and 49 aircraft, including fourteen F-4 Phantoms. In Washington on 9 October, Kissinger, who had become secretary of state on 21 September, asked the Israeli ambassador Simcha Dinitz in disbelief: 'Explain to me how 400 tanks could be lost to the Egyptians?'[58] (as well as 100 tanks to the Syrians). Dinitz put in an urgent request for American weapons.

The Israeli air force bombed Damascus on 10 October. With new weapons from the United States, the army launched its attack on Damascus on 11 October; three days later it was only 30 km from Syria's capital. The air force was unhindered, as the Syrians had no more SA-6 missiles and the Soviet supply flights had only just started. Syrian president Hafez al-Assad now wanted to stop the Israelis' advance with a ceasefire. At this point Moscow, convinced that the Egyptians would not have any more victories, proposed a ceasefire to Washington.[59] Kissinger remained cautious, referring to domestic issues (i.e. the resignation of Vice President Agnew), but advised Israel's ambassador that 'everything depended on the Israelis pushing back to the pre-war lines as quickly as possible. We could not stall a ceasefire proposal forever'.[60]

On 13 October, in view of the shipments of Soviet supplies – primarily SA-6 missiles and tanks for Syria – President Nixon gave the order for a massive airlift: every day for the next two weeks, twenty-five widebodied aircraft flew 1,000 tons of war materiel to Israel, providing 'invaluable help', as Golda Meir noted retrospectively. 'Not only did this give us new courage, but it also made the position of the US clear to the Soviets. This undoubtedly contributed to making our victory even possible'.[61] When the first US plane landed, Meir had tears in her eyes.

Kissinger thought it necessary to prolong the fighting, to create 'a situation in which [the Arabs] would have to ask for a ceasefire rather than we'.[62] Sadat, however, opposed a ceasefire – and made a fatal mistake by allowing his tanks to push further east, outside of the 30-km protective shield of the SA-6 missiles. The consequences were catastrophic. Sadat's 1,000 Egyptian tanks were met by 750 Israeli tanks, and on 14 October 1973 the largest tank battle since the Second World War ended in the resounding defeat of the Egyptians, who lost 250 tanks compared to only 20 on the Israeli side. Hundreds of Egyptian soldiers were dead. As Israel's former chief of general staff Chaim Bar-Lev put it: 'The Egyptians are acting again in their traditional way, and we are resuming our old ways. It was like in the old days'.[63] On 16 October, the Israelis under Ariel Sharon crossed the Suez Canal, and a few days later, to the horrified surprise of the Egyptians, Israeli troops were just 64 km from Cairo while Egypt's 20,000-man Third Army was being encircled on the east bank of the canal.

Meanwhile, political developments overall were intensifying because, for the first time in history, the Arab countries were using oil as a weapon by proclaiming an oil embargo against the United States and the Netherlands. In addition, Saudi Arabia's King Faisal called for a jihad against Israel, which in turn led to far-reaching decisions in Washington. To secure US oil supplies, plans were drawn to occupy the oilfields of Saudi Arabia, Kuwait and Abu Dhabi, if necessary. It never came to that: by 18 October Sadat also wanted a ceasefire. Kissinger stated internally: 'The Arabs may despise us, or hate us, or loathe us, but they have learned that if they want a settlement, they have to come to us. No one else can deliver. Everyone in the Middle East knows that if they want peace they have to come through us'.[64]

In an urgent letter to Nixon, Soviet leader Leonid Brezhnev stressed the two superpowers' responsibility 'not to let things go unchecked', and asked him to send Kissinger to Moscow to work out an armistice.[65]

While Kissinger was still in Moscow, Sadat was 'begging' [Kissinger] for an immediate truce. Kissinger, however, wanted to win time for the Israelis. Although he had agreed with Brezhnev that a UN resolution should be passed by midnight of 22 October, he sent UN ambassador John Scali a cable advising him to 'proceed at a deliberate pace in the Security Council. We do not have the same interest [as the Soviets] in such speed'.[66] At 12.52 a.m. on 22 October, the United Nations Security Council adopted the Moscow agreement as Resolution 338, and the warring parties were asked to begin negotiations for a 'just and lasting peace' in the Middle East, based on Resolution 242. But the ceasefire, which was to go into effect twelve hours later, was violated before it had even begun. Israeli troops on the west side of the canal received massive reinforcement, while at the same time Egypt's Third Army was completely surrounded. Kissinger advised Meir in Tel Aviv: 'You won't get violent protests from Washington if something happens during the night, while I'm flying'. His strategy was 'to keep the Arabs down and the Russians down'.[67]

Moscow saw it differently. 'Kissinger took us for fools and negotiated a deal with Tel Aviv', Brezhnev fumed.[68] Using the 'hotline' for the first time since 1967, he spoke of 'betrayal', and demanded that Nixon act immediately to counter Israel. Kissinger now called on Tel Aviv to comply with the armistice confirmed by the new UN Resolution 339 on 23 October, to go into effect the next day – but then broken again. According to Kissinger, this time Moscow decided 'to take a chance with a decisive showdown'[69] like the one in 1967 during the Six-Day War, when the Soviets used the 'hotline' for the first time and announced there would be military action if Washington did not stop Israel. This time Brezhnev said it 'straight' – as Kissinger understood it, 'in effect an ultimatum' –[70] that both Soviet and American troops should uphold the ceasefire. Brezhnev threatened that if Washington refused, Moscow 'would be faced with the necessity to consider urgently the question of taking appropriate steps unilaterally' and intervening with troops in the Middle East.[71] Soviet airborne divisions comprising fifty thousand men were already on alert. When Washington learned that Soviet ships carrying nuclear weapons had set course for the Egyptian coast, Kissinger decided it was necessary 'to go to the mat'.[72] US military commands were ordered to raise their alert levels to DEFCON (defense condition) 3, which meant putting nuclear-armed units on the 'highest state of peacetime alert' (DEFCON 2 would mean that nuclear forces were ready for imminent use). When Washington became aware that eight Soviet transports with soldiers on board were prepared to embark from Budapest to Egypt, and that some units of the People's Army of the GDR had been placed on alert, it reinforced DEFCON 3 by recalling B-52s stationed on Guam back to the US mainland, alerting the 82nd Airborne Division and ordering aircraft carriers to the Eastern Mediterranean.[73]

In a letter to Brezhnev, Nixon rejected the Soviet 'ultimatum' and instead proposed a multilateral UN peacekeeping force to oversee the ceasefire. Its composition should be left to the discretion of Secretary General Kurt Waldheim. Brezhnev agreed to this,[74] and the result was UN Resolution 340, adopted by the Security Council on 25 October. It called for an immediate and complete ceasefire, and created a United Nations Security Force for the Middle East to secure its implementation. The Yom Kippur War was officially over.

But Egypt's Third Army was still entirely cut off and in danger of being destroyed by the Israelis. This was unacceptable to the Americans, who did not want to lose Sadat as their new partner in the Middle East. Kissinger warned ambassador Dinitz: 'You will not be permitted to destroy the army', describing it as 'inconceivable that the Soviets' would allow that to happen.[75] That had an effect. On 28 October, direct Egyptian–Israeli talks occurred for the first time since 1948. Egyptian general Mohamad el-Gamasy and Israeli general Aharon Yariv met for the famous Kilometre 101 talks on the Cairo–Suez road.

In his memoirs, published in 1982, Kissinger devotes almost 250 pages to this war, which occupied him day and night only a few days after his appointment as secretary of state. His conclusion was that the United States 'had emerged as the pivotal factor in the diplomacy'.[76] Kissinger is hard on the European allies who disappointed him. During the airlift, the airbase at Lajes (the Azores) was 'overtaxed', which signalled another diplomatic problem: no other bases in Spain or in the United Kingdom were available for refuelling empty aircraft returning from Israel. It took severe diplomatic pressure to secure Portuguese cooperation, but ultimately Kissinger was highly pleased with the Portuguese, whereas his anger with other Europeans steadily grew.[77]

This dissatisfaction began as early as 16 October 1973, when the American NATO ambassador Donald Rumsfeld informed his colleagues at the meeting of the NATO Joint Council in Brussels about the US airlift to Israel, and stated that the United States could not stand idly by in the face of the Soviet 'adventurism' (*Abenteuerei*). The US expected 'understanding and support' from its allies, as Germany's NATO ambassador Franz Krapf reported to Bonn. According to Rumsfeld: 'The current stance of the allies in this crisis will affect the future mutual relationship. . . . The alliance must now develop a common policy that would make clear to the Soviets that their interests would be harmed, should they impair the interests of the alliance'.[78] But although he proposed a number of measures, including the slowing or even suspension of deliberations by the Conference on Security and Cooperation in Europe (CSCE), export controls, credit restrictions, and so forth, not one was implemented. The alliance did not develop a common policy.

Kissinger, who had drafted Rumsfeld's speech, was incensed. He expressed his contempt for the European allies to former West German defence minister Franz Josef Strauß: 'One must doubt that Europe is even capable of a partnership'.[79] And these doubts primarily concerned a highly trusted US ally, the Federal Republic of Germany. What had happened? On 16 October, the American ambassador in Bonn, Martin Hillenbrand, spoke to Foreign Minister Scheel about the US position on the Middle East, especially regarding the decision to set up the airlift to Israel. This decision, Hillenbrand said, 'was forced by the massive delivery of Soviet supplies', the atmosphere in Washington was 'very tense', and a lack of understanding on the part of individual allies could harm bilateral relations with the US. Then he disclosed that the United States was supplying Israel from US bases in Germany in an operation that had already begun. Scheel confirmed the ambassador's expectation, noting that he was right to assume that the Federal Republic had a special understanding for the special role of its main ally. Bonn had proved this during the Vietnam War, when West German relations with the United States were not strained, 'but rather deepened the understanding for each other. The United States could expect the same from us today'. However, it would be preferable, 'as an ally of the United States, to know more about the extent of the deliveries, for the sake of clarity'.[80]

On 17 October, US embassy first secretary David Anderson told the Foreign Office what should be transported to Israel from the Federal Republic: sixty-five M-60 tanks of the latest design, twenty-three 155-mm howitzers, and 75,000 rounds of 105-mm ammunition. This materiel was to be transported to Bremerhaven and from there loaded onto an Israeli ship to Israel. On 18 October, Egypt lodged a protest with the German government against the movement of military supplies from US bases in Germany to Israel. The next day, the German embassies in London, Paris and Washington, as well as the permanent representations at NATO in Brussels and the United Nations in New York, were instructed to issue the following press release: 'This is an American operation. The US government informed the Federal Republic of their request. It is up to the American side to provide information. All questions should be answered with "no comment"'.

State Secretary Paul Frank told Ambassador Hillenbrand on 23 October:

> The Federal Republic assumed that with the ceasefire the American supplies from the Federal Republic of Germany, the use of facilities in the Federal Republic of Germany, and finally flights over the territory of the Federal Republic of Germany has ended. ... We did not hesitate for a second, at a moment of tension, to defer the central and legitimate interests of the Federal Republic of Germany to the legitimate interest of maintaining balance in the Middle East. Now, since the ceasefire, we have assumed that this 'servitude' was no longer necessary.

Frank was referring to the unrest the arms delivery had provoked in the Arab states and the subsequent threat of an oil embargo, which, if followed through, would be a visceral hit to the Federal Republic.[81] At the time West Germany depended on oil for up to 55 per cent of its power supply, and about 71 per cent of its oil imports – 103 million tons in 1972 – came from oil-producing Arab countries that were parties in the conflict.

Two days earlier, Ambassador Hans-Georg Steltzer had reported from Cairo about the acting Egyptian foreign minister, Fahmi:

> Fahmi expressed his deepest concern about the continuation of the American deliveries to Israel from bases in West Germany. ... He must point out that Greece, Cyprus, Turkey and Spain rigorously refused to cooperate with the Americans, not to mention Great Britain, Italy and France. West Germany would be the only country, except for the USA, to support the Israeli war effort.

Should this continue, he, Fahmi, had to 'fear the worst' for relations between the Federal Republic and the Arab states. Steltzer reported further that Fahmi had mentioned that actions would be taken against us very soon'.[82]

On 24 October, a representative of the West German Foreign Office was informed by the inspector general of the Bundeswehr, Admiral Armin Zimmermann, that the ministry had had news 'early today, absolutely surprising', that two Israeli freight ships had arrived at the port of Nordenham near Bremerhaven and another Israeli ship was expected 'tomorrow'. Further:

> The port of Nordenham is the only port specifically designed for loading war materiel. A company under the Federal Ministry of Transport performs this type of loading. The American headquarters contacted the Bundeswehr's Territorial Command South and requested that the Federal Ministry of Transport intervene to have the Israeli ships loaded without delay. The reason for this was that the loading company refused to load the ships because of other contractual obligations. The Ministry of Defence informed the Ministry of Transport that it was absolutely opposed to loading the ships. At that moment, the minister of defence Georg Leber [SPD] and foreign minister Walter Scheel [FDP] were with the chancellor [Willy Brandt] to discuss the issue.[83]

This was probably too much for Paul Frank. That evening he asked the American envoy Frank E. Cash to see him. Cash was accompanied by his colleague David Anderson. Frank explained the matter, referring to his conversation with ambassador Hillenbrand the day before, and to the new state of affairs, about which the Federal Republic had 'learned more or less by chance'. The Federal Republic was 'extremely concerned. This is either political insensitivity . . . or the United States intends to get the Federal Republic involved in this conflict, despite its declared neutrality'. He brought up the conversation between Scheel and ambassador Hillenbrand on 16 October, noting how, in a 'dramatic moment', Bonn had shown understanding of the American position and turned a blind eye because of the 'emergency situation'. But now 'the operation must end; the Israeli ship, already loaded, must disappear immediately, tonight if possible. The ship still in Nordenham will not be loaded'.[84]

The next day, Hillenbrand saw Frank at the Foreign Office. He was instructed to deliver 'a strong demarche', as he told Frank. And then he made clear: 'The emotions in Washington are running very high'. His government was disappointed and very much concerned about Germany's attitude. Frank referred to Arab threats, stressing that an oil embargo against the Federal Republic 'will lead to chaotic situations'. The ambassador could at least, Frank reasoned, clarify that it was the chiefs of staff in Washington that had approved the action.[85]

This talk was particularly delicate, as the Foreign Office had already informed the diplomatic missions of the Arab states on 23 October 'that such an American action, if it had taken place, was now complete'. It was too late. Muhammad Khatib, the head of the Office of the Arab League, explicitly informed the German Foreign Office: 'The Arab states can no longer trust the Federal Republic, since the statements and explanations from the German side do not correspond to its actions and are cause for serious concern'.[86]

Looking back, Kissinger had harsh criticism for the European allies, especially Bonn. On 25 October, the day the Nixon administration put its nuclear forces on DEFCON 3, the West German government had issued a peremptory statement to publicize what it had already told Washington privately: 'Weapons deliveries using West German territory or installations from American depots in West Germany to one of the warring parties cannot be allowed. The West German Government is relying on America to permanently halt deliveries from and over Germany'. Kissinger later recalled: 'Since we were already carrying out the Federal Republic's private request, the purpose of the public statement could only be to distance Bonn from Washington for the benefit of a presumed Arab constituency in the midst of an acute crisis'. On 25 October, Washington sent a sharp note to Bonn: 'The US G[overnment] believes that for the West to display weakness and disunity in face of a Soviet-supported military action against Israel could have disastrous consequences'. Earlier that day Kissinger had made the following argument to Ambassador Berndt von Staden:

> We recognize that the Europeans are more dependent upon Arab oil than us, but we disagree that your vulnerability is decreased by disassociating yourselves from us on a matter of this importance. Such disassociation will not help the Europeans in the Arab world. The Arabs know that only the US can provide the help to get a political settlement. Not only will European capitulation to the Arabs not result in ensuring their oil supply, but it can have disastrous consequences vis-à-vis the Soviet Union who, if allowed to succeed in the Near East, can be expected to mount ever more aggressive policies elsewhere. To the degree that Soviet influence can be reduced, we will gain a long-term advantage, even if we pay a short-term price.[87]

Von Staden reported on a talk he had with Kissinger on 26 October, in which Kissinger clarified that Washington viewed the Federal Republic's attitude as 'very astonishing'. He, Kissinger, was even more astonished that the Federal Republic 'had touched on fundamental alliance questions in this situation'. The disagreement could have catastrophic consequences for the security of the alliance. It was even possible that the West would follow the route of ancient Greece. As a historian, he (Kissinger) could only regard this development with melancholy. Kissinger then explained what was really at stake for the United States, namely, preventing the spread of Soviet influence in the Middle East. Yet the allies did not want to pay even a temporary price. He could only repeat that he was deeply concerned, for too much had happened and the incidents were too numerous.

Under these circumstances, he did not see how the West could survive fifty or even just five years. The difficulties were symptomatic of the alliance. At no time had the founding fathers of European unification assumed that 'Europe' could ever be in opposition to the United States. He, Kissinger, had foreseen this.

He continued that the Nixon administration was the last one with an emotional attachment to Europe. Future administrations would treat Europe with cool political calculation. Von Staden ended his report by stressing that the talk was free of any aggression: 'It transpired in a very quiet, friendly atmosphere. Kissinger was reserved in his criticism. It was obviously important to him, at a very late and urgent stage, to present in detail the American position and the danger threatening the alliance'.[88]

Two days later, Ambassador von Staden reported from Washington: 'The wave of resentment over the behaviour of the allies – including the Federal Republic – is currently high'. The Federal Republic was singled out for reproach owing to two circumstances:

> One, we saw ourselves as the only allied country compelled by circumstances to take a public stand in a form that surprised the political public of this country. On the other hand, the deployment of a considerable part of the conventional American forces on our soil makes the USA particularly sensitive to German behaviour. This is all the more so since the stationing of troops abroad is met with growing resistance in this country. . . . The allies deeply upset the president.[89]

Kissinger felt that the United States' NATO allies were by no means prepared to pay even a short-term price to reduce Soviet influence. His memoirs mention a letter written to him by Willy Brandt on 28 October:

> We have proven more than once that we are not indifferent and that we know who our ally is. But it is another matter, when from German soil – without the German government even being fully informed, much less asked in advance – American equipment is used for purposes that are not the responsibility of the German government. . . . I reject strongly any suspicion that the Federal Republic of Germany lacks solidarity with the Western Alliance.[90]

Brandt's letter was received ungraciously in Washington. Kissinger wrote: 'This letter was immediately leaked to the press by the Germans – suggesting that its line of argument was thought to have a certain popular appeal in Germany. . . . He [Brandt] thought it necessary to add the wounding point that he made this judgement without knowing details of the actions or reasons that had caused us to act as we did', although 'he had been given a very full account'. The major purpose of the letter, according to Kissinger, was to explain the German ban on US resupply of Israel from German depots: Germany had acted as it did because the common NATO responsibilities did not extend to the Middle East. Neither Nixon nor Kissinger accepted this interpretation, as Nixon made clear in his reply to Brandt on 30 October:

> You note that this crisis was not a case of common responsibility for the alliance, and that military supplies for Israel were for purposes that are not part of the alliance responsibility. I do not believe we can draw such a fine line when the USSR was and is so deeply involved, and when the crisis threatened to spread to the whole gamut of East–West relations. It seems to me that the alliance cannot operate on a double standard, in which US relations with the USSR are separated from the policies that our Allies conduct towards the Soviet Union. By disassociating themselves from the US in the Middle East, our Allies may think they protect their immediate economic interests, but only at great long-term cost. A differentiated détente in which the Allies hope to insulate their relations with the USSR can only divide the alliance and ultimately produce disastrous consequences for Europe.[91]

It was clear to Kissinger that Europe 'wanted the option to conduct a policy separate from the United States and in the case of the Middle East objectively in conflict with us'.[92]

Bonn was at least trying to calm things down. On 29 October, Frank told Hillenbrand that 'we should absolutely avoid making this isolated case into an issue for the alliance'.[93]

Washington shared that view. On 2 November, Kissinger informed the NATO ambassadors about the situation in the Middle East. The conversation was 'without discord', as von Staden reported to Bonn. Kissinger expressed his criticism 'in a grave but generally conciliatory manner' and emphasized that Washington's disappointment with the allies had not resulted from a single action or from the European response to the US decisions. It was rather a disappointment that had grown over many months for several reasons, and was, 'as a whole, the result of a European attitude that was perceived in Washington as hardly comprehensible and accommodating'.[94]

At the end of the traditional NATO meeting on 11 December 1973 in Brussels, Kissinger met the foreign ministers of the nine members of the European Community for the first time. 'The meeting did help to heal the wounds', Kissinger acknowledged.[95] Ambassador Franz Krapf reported to Bonn that the nine EEC members had decided not to dwell on the recent misunderstandings and difficulties, but to work together'.[96]

Meanwhile, Bonn's reaction became a polemical topic in domestic politics. Karl Carstens, the chairman of the CDU/CSU parliamentary caucus, stated on 28 October: 'The government has done a disservice to the cause of peace and to our country'. Franz Josef Strauß observed that 'Brandt's beautiful speeches in the Bundestag and the frivolity of Scheel reinforced the USA's impression that these Germans cannot be taken seriously'. CDU chairman Helmut Kohl said on 29 October that 'the government placed itself outside the Western community with its policy; any policy that would bring the German–American alliance into dubious light is dangerous to the Federal Republic'.[97] Paul Frank had to put up with being insulted as the 'heating oil diplomat' (*Heizöldiplomat*) of the Foreign Office.[98]

From Chancellor Helmut Schmidt to Reunification

The military successes of the Egyptians and Syrians at the beginning of the Yom Kippur War had restored the 'Arab honour' lost during the Six-Day War. But by the end of the war they had realized that they would have to negotiate to recover occupied territories, and that only with the help of the United States would successful negotiations be possible. To that end Kissinger started his 'shuttle diplomacy': travelling continuously between Cairo, Jerusalem and Damascus, he sought 'to prove to the Arabs that they are better off dealing with us on a moderate program than dealing with the Russians on a radical program'.[99] To the NATO partners, he explained the basic objective of American policy as twofold: to make clear to the Israelis that their security could no longer be guaranteed by military superiority; and to convince the Arabs that they had no chance of enforcing extreme demands by force.[100]

Two 'important problems' remained unresolved for the Arabs: the liberation of the occupied territories, and the rights of the Palestinians. The Saudi oil minister Ahmed Yamani stressed this to Willy Brandt at the beginning of 1974: 'Israel does not intend to withdraw from these areas. But the Arabs want their territory back. The world must condemn the occupation and demand complete withdrawal. Certain countries have not yet clearly supported this demand'.[101] Yamani evidently meant the Brandt/Scheel government, which had repeatedly stressed the 'absolute balance' of its Middle East policy since its conception in 1969, but which now took a different tone as the Bonn government referred again and again to resolutions of the European Community (EC).

On 6 November 1974, the EC foreign ministers rolled out a five-point resolution addressing the Middle East conflict. A peace agreement should necessarily be based on the following principles:

1. Inadmissibility of territorial acquisition by violence.
2. Israel's agreement to end the territorial occupation.
3. Respect for the sovereignty, territorial integrity, and independence of each state in the territory, as well as its citizens' right to live in peace within secure and recognized borders.

4. Acknowledgment of the legitimate rights of the Palestinians.
5. Application of international guarantees in accordance with UN Resolution 242.

These remained the principles of Germany's Middle East policy, as was repeatedly and clearly conveyed to the Israelis.[102] Many people thought Bonn was hiding behind Europe. State secretary Frank described the resolution as being held up 'like a protective shield'.[103]

Then, as today, oil was another problem. The German Foreign Office, having noted that the Arabs had first used oil as a political weapon during the Yom Kippur War, further commented: 'The connection between the price of oil and the Middle East conflict is obvious. Without peace or at least progress towards a peaceful solution of the Israeli–Arab conflict, oil will retain its character as a potential political weapon. Everything that serves to solve the Middle East conflict also serves to solve the oil problem'.[104] Therefore, the government was clear that 'our interest is stable peace and cooperation in this area. Israel would be best served by this, too'.[105] However, 'a lasting peace settlement for the Middle East is impossible without a solution for the Palestinians',[106] whose problem had been regarded as a mere refugee problem since 1948.

That had now changed. In October 1974, the Arab League emphasized the Palestinians' right to self-determination and right of return to their home country. These rights were also invoked in the EC Foreign Ministers' Resolution, which had been accepted by the European heads of state and governments. The Germans supported the Palestinians' right of self-determination in the UN's Palestine debate on 19 November 1974. However, in an interview with the French daily *Le Figaro* on 3 February 1975, Helmut Schmidt, West Germany's chancellor since May 1974, pointed out another problem: 'As long as the PLO does not clearly state two things, namely that Israel has a right to exist within secure borders and that the PLO will abstain from terrorist acts, I cannot seriously raise the question. This does not mean that we do not fully understand the hardships and needs of the Palestinians. But these are two separate issues'.[107]

The Arab League and the overwhelming majority of the UN General Assembly accepted the PLO as the sole representative of the Palestinian people. The question in Bonn was how to deal with the PLO, which sooner or later would form a Palestinian government. The answer was: 'We have to live with the PLO, and the PLO has to live with us; otherwise there will be a risk of lagging behind inevitable political developments and losing the connection with the present and the future'.[108] In every decision, though, one had to take account of Israel, which saw the PLO as a terrorist organization. What Bonn wanted was to adapt gradually to a changing situation:

Figure 6.9 8 July 1975: Honour guard for Israel's prime minister Yitzhak Rabin in Bonn, the first visit of an Israeli prime minister to Germany.
Courtesy of Israel Government Press Office, Jerusalem.

'This could be achieved with moderate, but not too timid, increased contact with PLO representatives . . . but without crossing the "recognition threshold"'.[109]

Egypt's president Nasser had died in 1970, and his successor, Anwar Sadat, was now a new player in the Middle East. Sadat had clear ideas about the PLO. He regarded it with reserve and kept a 'cool distance' from it, but included it as a necessary evil in his political calculations. Although the United States and Israel faced challenges in dealing with the PLO, they had to accept two 'indispensable facts': that 'there is no getting around the PLO' and its readiness to accept Israel as a negotiating partner, and that 'a Palestinian state will emerge on the territory of the West Bank and the Gaza Strip', as Sadat told Willy Brandt in April 1974.[110]

Sadat considered the right-wing Likud government in Israel under Menachem Begin a 'strong' partner with which to seal a deal. To the surprise of many observers, Sadat started his peace initiative with a visit to Jerusalem. In a speech before the Knesset on 20 November 1977, he recognized Israel's right to exist.[111] Towards the end of 1977, Chancellor Helmut Schmidt visited Egypt, where he praised Sadat at a dinner on 27 December:

> You, Mr President, took a path with a statesmanlike vision that can bring about a definitive solution to the long-standing conflict that weighs heavily on all people of this region. . . . I share with you the hope that the strong impulse

emanating from your unprecedented initiative will meet with the necessary response and lead to a comprehensive peace settlement.[112]

Following Sadat's trip to Jerusalem, Begin became a 'hindrance to any progress', as US secretary of state Cyrus Vance told German foreign minister Hans-Dietrich Genscher in April 1978.[113] Nevertheless, in the end there was progress. The talks between Israel and Egypt reached a climax at the Camp David summit in September 1978 with Begin, Sadat and US President Carter. After thirteen days they reached an agreement recorded in history as the Camp David Accords: Israel returned the Sinai Peninsula to Egypt, and Egypt became the first Arab state to recognize Israel.[114] Sadat would pay for it with his life. On 6 October 1981, the eighth anniversary of the start of the Yom Kippur War, he was assassinated by Islamic fanatics. Thus began a new chapter in the bloody history of the Middle East.

The relationship between Bonn and Jerusalem deteriorated extensively after Menachem Begin's election victory in May 1977. Begin accused Schmidt of having attended and applauded the execution of Hitler's would-be-assassins of 20 July 1944, and of 'never having broken his allegiance to Hitler'.[115] Begin's predecessor, Rabin, had invited Schmidt to visit Israel, but no such visit was made. Schmidt, who had 'political doubts' about whether a visit in 1978 was 'politically useful', told the Israeli ambassador in Bonn that 'he would openly express criticism of the settlement policy in Israel'.[116] Schmidt viewed the Camp David agreement critically, since only the United States, Egypt and Israel were involved. He told Jordan's King Hussein: 'Without the Palestinians, a solution is unthinkable . . . Because of a conversation between some gentlemen at Camp David, they cannot effectively be ignored!'[117] However, he also stressed to the secretary general of the Arab League: 'Resolution of the Middle East conflict also requires the PLO's goodwill recognition of Israel's right to exist'.[118]

From then on, Bonn was even more strongly involved in the European Community and was decisive in its Resolution of Venice in June 1980, which again called for the right of the Palestinians to self-determination and their participation in a peace settlement. Nonetheless, Schmidt emphasized to King Hussein of Jordan: 'Europe cannot permanently take the place of the US in the Middle East or anywhere else'. To Hussein's question of whether pressure from America would help a peace settlement in the Middle East, Schmidt replied: 'With six million Jewish voters it is indeed difficult for any American government to be objective'.[119]

Schmidt even played the Middle East card to defend the NATO double-track decision of December 1979. On 1 September 1980, he pointed out the Soviet SS-20 nuclear missiles to Egypt's vice-president Mohammed Mubarak in Bonn, emphasizing that the situation was extremely dangerous, not just for Europe but for the entire Mediterranean region, the Near East, the Middle East, and South Asia. The great danger was that the Soviet Union would have extraordinary military superiority in this area for years to come; Schmidt continued that the prospect of nuclear blackmail, which could result in an attack on the Aswan Dam and subsequent disaster for Egypt, could not be dismissed. Mubarak thanked the chancellor for these 'extremely important statements', assuring Schmidt that Egypt would discuss this with the United States.[120] Speaking to Saudi Crown Prince Fahd in April 1981, Schmidt reiterated the main objectives of Europe's position on the Middle East: (1) self-determination of the Palestinians and the participation of the PLO; (2) the right of all people in the region to live within safe and recognized borders; and (3) Israel's withdrawal from occupied areas in accordance with UN Resolution 242. Crown Prince Fahd responded: 'These are clear words. Camp David is a waste of time'.[121] A year later, the Israelis stated their position unequivocally. In conversation with Hans-Dietrich Genscher, Prime Minister Begin demanded: (1) annulment of the Venice Declaration of 1980; (2) no participation by the PLO in a peace settlement; and (3) no right of self-determination for Palestinians.

Regarding Israel's third demand, Begin argued that 'this expression [self-determination] must not be used; it would lead inevitably to a Palestinian state. I understand that you as Germans, as a divided country, plead for the right of self-determination for the population of the GDR. However, this is a very different matter for the Palestinians. There are already twenty-two Arab states. A Palestinian state is a deadly threat to Israel'.[122] President of the Knesset, Menachem Savidor, claimed in November 1982 that the establishment of a Palestinian state would enable the PLO to bring another million Palestinians to the occupied territories. Israel, Savidor warned, would have to reckon with a march à la Khomeini (the revolutionary leader of Iran) because of the population pressure.[123]

In a conversation with state secretary Berndt von Staden in Bonn, secretary general of the Israeli foreign ministry David Kimche was even more direct: 'Israel can never agree to include the PLO in the negotiation process. If the West strengthens the PLO, there is no hope for other Palestinians; the PLO will block the peace process. A stronger PLO is an obstacle to peace'. At that point ministerial director Otto von der Gablenz remarked: 'The Germans also have some experience in ignoring realities'. Kimche responded: 'The silent majority of Palestinians rejects the PLO, who have terrorized the population of the West Bank. The Arabs have done little or nothing for the Palestinians', going on to note, accurately, that 'in one night at a casino, wealthy oil Arabs spend large sums on tips alone, while Palestinians who have lived in camps for thirty-four years survive on the same amount for an entire year'.[124]

Kimche then explained that the settlement policy was grounded in religion and history. In contrast to Christianity and other religions, the Jewish religion had been territorially bound to Eretz Israel for three thousand years. It was a national religion. The complete separation of the country, such as existed until 1967, must not be repeated: 'Israel has a right to settle anywhere in this country. Settlements are part of the philosophy of Israel. Since undeveloped public land is being settled, nobody is harmed'. Addressing UN Resolution 242, Kimche said that withdrawal from the occupied territories would defeat the purpose of the settlement policy, and in any case, 'the settlement policy does not predetermine the negotiations'. Then, he argued further, Israel's security was at stake: 'In the entire world, no other country's existence is as threatened as Israel's'.

Staden countered that the world community did not agree with this reasoning. Objectively, Israel was isolated; he doubted it could maintain its position in the long term. Kimche acknowledged the risk of isolation, but at the same time pointed out that Jews and Israelis had defied the entire British Empire; moreover, he claimed, logic was foreign to the Arabs: 'They are guided by emotions, hatred and distrust. A Palestinian state leads to Khomeini'.[125]

German arms exports were a particularly delicate issue in the Middle East. In April 1983 the new German chancellor Helmut Kohl told the British prime minister Margaret Thatcher that whereas Bonn did not intend to be a 'weapons supplier for the whole world', it did not 'want to be absent either'.[126] This issue impacted Saudi Arabia particularly. The Saudis had first expressed their wishes in 1979, and the Schmidt government had consoled them (*waren vertröstet worden*). In 1983 their wish list included 300 of the most recent Leopard 2 tanks, 150 helicopters, 150 Gepard anti-aircraft systems, armoured personnel carriers and other materiel, altogether valued at 12 billion Deutschmarks. A decision on whether to allow this order to proceed was necessary, as the companies Krauss-Maffei and Krupp had enquired about approval.

Various responses were discussed in the German Foreign Office. Undersecretary Per Fischer (ambassador to Israel, 1974–77) spoke of 'political arguments against the delivery of heavy weapons'. To meet the Saudis' demands would be to signal a 'radical change in our arms export policy'. Fischer's colleague Walter Gorenflos was more flexible: from a domestic and foreign policy perspective he would not consider supplying the Leopard 2, 'but we should seriously check whether we can supply other materiel to the Saudis'. Fischer mentioned that Israel could be expected to react by stressing the 'heavy burden' on Israeli–German relations and lamenting 'extraordinarily sharp criticism' and 'one-sided partisanship in the Middle East conflict'.[127] The German ambassador to Israel at that time, Niels

Figure 6.10 West German chancellor Helmut Kohl with the Grand Mufti of Jerusalem in front of the Dome of the Rock. Photo by Harnik Nati.
Courtesy of Israel Government Press Office, Jerusalem.

Hasen, underscored Fischer's position: a delivery of Leopard 2 tanks would mean a 'very heavy, long-term burden' on the two countries' mutual relations, and the destruction of a large part of the goodwill that had been built up in Israel in recent decades.[128]

In October 1983, Chancellor Kohl visited Saudi Arabia and arranged with King Fahd 'to include matters of defence in our cooperation'.[129] Three months later Kohl was in Israel, where prime minister Yitzhak Shamir spoke of dramatic consequences of German arms sales to Saudi Arabia: they would have a 'terrible impact on the Israeli mood and cause deep despair'.[130] This outcome, Kohl added later, must be taken into account when making the decision on whether to supply arms to the Saudis. In October 1984, two German state secretaries, Jürgen Ruhfus and Andreas Meyer-Landrut, attempted to find a solution by positing an 'essential' basis for the negotiations: 'In a fair resolution of the Middle East conflict, all states must be assured of the rights of secure existence and self-determination'. The Saudi defence minister rejected this,[131] so no Leopard 2 tanks were delivered. However, the Saudis still wanted them, and in 2014–15 there was even talk of eight hundred Leopard 2s.

In 1990, the Israelis adamantly opposed the impending German reunification. There was still a great deal of unease and distrust of the Germans. The newspaper *Maariv* printed such lines as: 'The Israeli people have six million reasons to resist a reunification'. Prime minister Shamir stated that 'a united Germany would once again bring mortal danger to the Jews'. On 3 October 1990, the day of Germany's reunification, Knesset speaker Dov Shilansky said: 'If the Germans celebrate today, the Jewish people should wear sackcloth, scatter ashes, sit on the ground, and recite funeral songs. Jews and Germans are still separated by mountains of ashes and bones, and the world must be on its guard against Germany'.[132] Such rhetoric was not well received in Bonn.

Notes

1. See Michael B. Oren, *Six Days of War: June 1967 and the Making of the Modern Middle East* (Oxford: Oxford University Press, 2002); 'Foreign Relations of the United States 1964–1968, Vol. XIX: Arab–Israeli Crisis and War, 1967' (Washington, DC: United States Government Printing Office, 2004); Tom Segev, *1967: Israel, the War, and the Year that Transformed the Middle East* (New York: Metropolitan, 2007). See also Rolf Steininger, "Der Sechstagekrieg", *Aus Politik und Zeitgeschichte* 19 (7 May 2007). The controversial question of why the Soviet Union falsely informed Egypt and Syria is discussed in Isabella Ginor and Gideon Remez, *Foxbats over Dimona: The Soviets' Nuclear Gamble in the Six-Day War* (New Haven, CT: Yale University Press, 2008). Their thesis is that the Soviet Union sparked the war. For a different view, see Yaacov Ro'i and Boris Morozov (eds), *The Soviet Union and the June 1967 Six-Day War* (Washington, DC: Woodrow Wilson Center Press, 2008).
2. 'Pressekonferenz Präsident Nasser'. Gordon Gudenius (Cairo) to Lujo Tončić-Sorinj (Vienna), 29 May 1967. *Israel 1966–1968*, Doc. 50.
3. Memorandum of Conversation, 26 May 1967. *FRUS 1964–1968*, XIX, Doc. 77.
4. 'The Soviet Union's Policy Regarding Israel's Aggression in the Middle East'. Report by Brezhnev to the CPSU Central Committee Plenum, 20 June 1967. Translation of the Russian original in: Ro'i and Morozov, *Soviet Union*, 302–36, here 313. For the SED's German translation of 1967, see *Vertraulich. Rede des Genossen L. I. Breschnew auf dem Juniplenum (1967) des ZK der KPdSU: 'Über die Politik der Sowjetunion im Zusammenhang mit der Aggression Israels im Nahen Osten'*, 20 June 1967, 65 pages, in: Stiftung Archiv der Parteien und Massenorganisationen im Bundesarchiv, Berlin.
5. Ro'i and Morozov, *Soviet Union*, 313.
6. Ibid., 314.
7. Moshe Dayan, *Story of My Life* (London: Weidenfeld & Nicolson, 1976), 260.
8. 'Bazar der Gerüchte'. Friedrich Bauer (Tel Aviv) to Lujo Tončić-Sorinj (Vienna), 16 June 1967. *Israel 1966–1968*, Doc. 61.
9. Ro'i and Morozov, *Soviet Union*, 319.
10. Ibid., 315.
11. Ibid., 317.
12. The Kosygin message is taken from *FRUS 1964–1968*, XIX, Doc. 243.
13. 'Bestandsaufnahme und Stimmungsbericht'. Friedrich Bauer (Tel Aviv) to Lujo Tončić-Sorinj (Vienna), 25 July 1967. *Israel 1966–1968*, Doc. 74.
14. 'Der israelische Sieg und seine Konsequenzen'. Kurt Waldheim (New York) to Lujo Tončić-Sorinj (Vienna), 10 June 1967. Ibid., Doc. 59. For East Berlin's reaction, see Timm, *Hammer–Zirkel–Davidstern*, 206–29.
15. Ambassador Meir Rosenne: 'The UN Security Council Resolution 242 has been the pivotal point of reference in all Arab–Israeli diplomacy since 1967'. See his article at jcpa.org; see also United Nations Security Council Resolution 242 in: en.wikipedia.org.

16. *AAPD 1967*, Doc. 217, Anm. 7.
17. Ibid., Doc. 200, Anm. 7.
18. 'Deutsche Nahostpolitik'. Minute by Hermann Meyer-Lindenberg, AA, 23 June 1967. Ibid., Doc. 232.
19. 'Abschluß des deutsch-israelischen Kapitalhilfeabkommens'. Minute by Günther Harkort, AA, 4 July 1967. Ibid., Doc. 245.
20. Ibid., Doc. 242, note 6.
21. Ibid., Doc. 257, note 7.
22. 'Deutsch-arabische Beziehungen'. Lothar Lahn (Cairo) to AA, 27 July 1967. Ibid., Doc. 285.
23. Ibid., Doc. 283, note 5.
24. 'Deutsch-ägyptische Beziehungen'. Lothar Lahn (Cairo) to AA, 16 November 1968. *AAPD 1968*, Doc. 379.
25. 'Die deutsche Nahost-Politik'. Minute by Paul Frank, AA, 15 April 1969. *AAPD 1969*, Doc. 123.
26. 'Deutsch-arabische Beziehungen'. Minute AA, 9 June 1969. Ibid., Doc. 193.
27. Ibid., Doc. 148, note 24.
28. 'Haltung der Bundesregierung zur Frage der Anerkennung der DDR durch Staaten der Dritten Welt'. Minute by Egon Bahr, AA, 1 July 1969. Ibid., Doc. 217.
29. Ibid., Doc. 189, note 10.
30. Memorandum by Karl Ferdinand Duckwitz, AA, 2 August 1969. Ibid., Doc. 254.
31. 'Rahmenvertrag mit der DDR'. Minute by Egon Bahr, AA, 18 September 1969. Ibid., Doc. 295.
32. Cf. Steininger, *Deutschland und die USA*, 448–74.
33. 'Deutsch-ägyptisches Verhältnis'. Minute by Georg Ferdinand Duckwitz, AA, 1 December 1969. *AAPD 1969*, Doc. 384.
34. This was exactly the course Scheel had supported in a cabinet meeting on 22 February 1965, when he demanded: 'Not another screw should be sent' (see Chapter 5).
35. A year later, Helmut Schmidt was even clearer. In a cabinet meeting of 9 June 1971, he emphasized that for Germany, 'Israel is also an important state in the line of defence in an otherwise Soviet-oriented part of the world. It plays an important role in the defence of the Mediterranean Sea and thus in the defence of all of Europe – Israel is the only clear-cut Western-oriented state. In addition to all special obligations that Israel imposes on us, this is a central, practical-political point of view'. Minute by Freiherr von Braun, 11 June 1971. *AAPD 1971*, Doc. 205.
36. 'Koalitionsgespräch über die Nahostpolitik'. Minute by Walter Gehlhoff, AA, 11 February 1970. *AAPD 1970*, Doc. 48.
37. 'Besuch des israelischen Außenministers Abba Eban in Bonn (22. bis 24.2.1970)'. Minute by Paul Frank, AA, 18 February 1970. Ibid., Doc. 65.
38. *AAPD 1971*, Doc. 45, note 15.
39. 'Wiederaufnahme der Beziehungen zu den arabischen Staaten'. Minute by Helmut Redies, AA, 19 April 1971. Ibid., Doc. 134.
40. 'Wiederaufnahme diplomatischer Beziehungen zu den arabischen Staaten; hier: Wahrung unserer deutschlandpolitischen Belange'. Circular by Paul Frank, AA, 8 December 1971. Ibid., Doc. 435.
41. Cf. *AAPD 1972*, Doc. 257, notes 4–8.
42. 'Zwischenfälle in München am 5./6. September 1972; hier: Kontakte des Bundeskanzlers mit der ägyptischen Führung'. Minute by Wolf-Dietrich Schilling, Chancellery, 5 September 1972. Ibid., Doc. 256.
43. 'Anschlag auf israelische Olympiamannschaft; hier: Haltung der ägyptischen Regierung'. Hans Georg Steltzer (Cairo) to AA, 7 November 1972. Ibid., Doc. 259.
44. Jesco von Puttkamer (Tel Aviv) to Paul Frank, AA, 30 October 1972. Ibid., Doc. 352.

45. Ibid., Doc. 352, note 11.
46. 'Gespräche von StS. Frank in Tunesien und Libyen am 20. und 21. Dezember 1972; hier: Palästinenser-Frage'. Minute by Helmut Redies, AA, 22 December 1972. Ibid., Doc. 422.
47. 'Besuch des Herrn Bundeskanzlers in Israel; hier: Delegationsgespräche'. Minute by Helmut Redies, AA, 13 June 1973. AAPD 1973, Doc. 184.
48. Important: FRUS 1969–1976, Vol. XXV; Burr, *October War*; Kissinger, *Crisis*; William B. Quandt, *Peace Process: American Diplomacy and the Arab–Israeli Conflict since 1967* (Washington DC: Brookings Institution, 1993); Richard Parker (ed.), *The October War: A Retrospective* (Gainesville: University of Florida Press, 2001); Abraham Rabinovich, *The Yom Kippur War: The Epic Encounter that Transformed the Middle East* (New York: Schocken Books, 2004); Henry A. Kissinger, *Years of Upheaval* (Boston and Toronto: Little, Brown and Company, 1982), 450–666. See also, Rolf Steininger, 'Bittere Lektion: Der Jom Kippur-Krieg im Herbst 1973 brachte Israel für einen Moment an den Rand des Untergangs', *Die Zeit* 37 (5 September 2013).
49. Cited in: Morris, *Victims*, 395.
50. Conversation between Walter Scheel and Eliashiv Ben-Horin, 8 November 1973. AAPD 1973, Doc. 314.
51. Cited in: Morris, *Victims*, 394.
52. Burr, *October War*, Doc. 7; and FRUS 1969–1976, Vol. XXV, Doc. 97.
53. Burr, *October War*, Doc. 9.
54. Ibid., Doc. 55.
55. Cited in: Morris, *Victims*, 394.
56. Burr, *October War*, Doc. 55, note 30. By comparison, the bomb dropped on Hiroshima had an explosive force of 13 kilotons. See Rolf Steininger, 'Tod im Feuersturm: Vor 70 Jahren zerstörten amerikanische Atombomben die japanischen Städte Hiroshima und Nagasaki', in Rolf Steininger, *'Faszinierende Lektüre' II: Rezensionen, Vorträge und Beiträge 2015–2017* (Innsbruck: Innsbruck University Press, 2017), 99–109.
57. Morris, *Victims*, 419.
58. Kissinger, *Years of Upheaval*, 496; FRUS 1969–1976, Vol. XXV, Doc. 134.
59. Ibid., Doc. 149. For Moscow's direct involvement in the Middle East conflict, see Isabella Ginor and Gideon Remez, *The Soviet–Israeli War 1967–1973: The USSR Military Intervention in the Egyptian–Israeli Conflict* (Oxford: Oxford University Press, 2017).
60. Burr, *October War*, Doc. 25.
61. Meir, *Life*, 458.
62. Burr, *October War*, Doc. 27.
63. Morris, *Victims*, 432.
64. Kissinger, *Years of Upheaval*, 578.
65. FRUS 1969–1976, Vol. XXV, Doc. 202.
66. Burr, *October War*, Doc. 49.
67. FRUS 1969–1976, Vol. XXV, Doc. 230.
68. Burr, *October War*, Doc. 60.
69. Kissinger, *Years of Upheaval*, 581.
70. Ibid., 583.
71. FRUS 1969–1976, Vol. XXV, Doc. 267.
72. Burr, *October War*, Doc. 72.
73. Ibid.
74. FRUS 1969–1976, Vol. XXV, Doc. 273.
75. Burr, *October War*, Doc. 83.
76. Kissinger, *Years of Upheaval*, 612.
77. Burr, *October War*, Doc. 31.
78. Franz Krapf an AA, 17 October 1973. AAPD 1973, Doc. 324.

79. Berndt von Staden (Washington) to Paul Frank, AA, 20 October 1973. Ibid., Doc. 332.
80. Conversation between Walter Scheel and Martin J. Hillenbrand, 16 October 1973. Ibid., Doc. 322.
81. Ibid., Doc. 335, note 2.
82. Ibid., Doc. 337, note 6.
83. Ibid., Doc. 335, note 6.
84. Conversation between Paul Frank and Frank E. Cash, 24 October 1973. Ibid., Doc. 335.
85. Conversation between Paul Frank and Martin J. Hillenbrand, 25 October 1973. Ibid., Doc. 337.
86. 'Besuch des Leiters des Büros der Arabischen Liga, Herr Khatib'. Minute by Lothar Lahn, AA, 25 October 1973. AAPD 1973, Doc. 339.
87. Kissinger, *Years of Upheaval*, 714.
88. Berndt von Staden (Washington) to Walter Scheel, AA, 26 October 1973. AAPD 1973, Doc. 341.
89. Ibid., note 22.
90. Willy Brandt to Richard Nixon, 28 October 1973. Ibid., Doc. 342; also in: Helga Grebing, Gregor Schöllgen and Heinrich. A. Winkler (eds), *Willy Brandt: Berliner Ausgabe*, Bd. 6: *Ein Volk der guten Nachbarn: Außen- und Deutschlandpolitik 1966–1974* (Bonn: J.H.W. Dietz, 2005), Doc. 81.
91. Kissinger, *Years of Upheaval*, 714; Grebing, Schöllgen and Winkler, *Willy Brandt: Berliner Ausgabe*, Bd. 6, Doc. 82.
92. Kissinger, *Years of Upheaval*, 715.
93. Conversation between Paul Frank and Martin J. Hillenbrand, 29 October 1973. AAPD 1973, Doc. 343.
94. 'Unterrichtung der NATO-Botschafter durch Außenminister Kissinger über Entwicklung und Stand des Nahost-Konflikts'. Berndt von Staden (Washington) to AA, 2 November 1973. Ibid., Doc. 356.
95. Kissinger, *Years of Upheaval*, 722.
96. 'Zusammenkunft der Außenminister der Neun mit Außenminister Kissinger'. Franz Krapf (Brussels) to AA, 11 December 1973. AAPD 1973, Doc. 414.
97. Ibid., Doc. 343, note 9.
98. Paul Frank, *Entschlüsselte Botschaft: Ein Diplomat macht Inventur* (Stuttgart: Deutsche Verlags-Anstalt, 1981), 366.
99. Kissinger, *Years of Upheaval*, 616.
100. 'Nahost-Krise. Unterrichtung der NATO-Botschafter durch Außenminister Kissinger am 25.1.1974'. Berndt von Staden (Washington) to AA, 25 January 1974. AAPD 1974, Doc. 24.
101. Conversation between Willy Brandt, Algerian minister for industry and energy, Abdessalam, and the Saudi minister for oil, Yamani, 16 January 1974. Ibid., Doc. 10.
102. As did foreign minister Hans Dietrich Genscher in November 1975 and the president of the Bundestag, Annemarie Renger, in August 1976. Cf. *AAPD 1976*, Doc. 360, and Ambassador Per Fischer (Tel Aviv) to AA, 2 December 1975 and 2 August 1976, in Ben Natan and Hansen, *Israel*, 109–117; for the three points, see *AAPD 1974*, Doc. 10, note 6.
103. Cited in Schumann, *Nahostpolitik*, 110.
104. Minute by Peter Hermes, AA, 5 October 1974. *AAPD 1974*, Doc. 292.
105. Paul Frank, AA, to Berndt von Staden (Washington), 31 January 1974. Ibid., Doc. 30.
106. 'Die deutsche Haltung gegenüber der Palästinenserfrage'. Minute by Walter Jesser, AA, 17 February 1975. *AAPD 1975*, Doc. 29.
107. Cited in ibid. Doc. 28, note 14.

108. See note 8.
109. Minute by Lothar Lahn, AA, 26 March 1975. *AAPD 1975*, Doc. 62.
110. Conversation between Willy Brandt and Anwar Sadat in Cairo, 21 April 1974. *AAPD 1974*, Doc. 124.
111. For Sadat's trip to Jerusalem, see Agstner and Steininger, *Israel*, 2016, 46 and 117–19. For his speech before the Knesset, see Laqueur and Rubin, *Israel–Arab Reader*, 207–15.
112. *AAPD 1977*, Doc. 379, note 9.
113. Minute by Fredo Dannenbring, AA, 5 April 1978. Ibid., Doc. 101.
114. Cf. Lawrence Wright, *Thirteen Days in September: Carter, Begin, and Sadat at Camp David* (New York: Alfred Knopf, 2014); see my review in MGZ 75, 2017.
115. *Frankfurter Allgemeine Zeitung*, 5 May 1981.
116. Conversation between Helmut Schmidt and ambassador Yohanan Meroz, 26 September 1978. *AAPD 1978*, Doc. 278.
117. Helmut Schmidt to King Hussein of Jordan, 30 July 1980. Minute by Klaus Max Franke, German Chancellery, 31 July 1980. *AAPD 1980*, Doc. 223; see my review in *FAZ*, 6 June 2011.
118. Helmut Schmidt to the secretary general of the Arab League, Chedli Klibi, 22 July 1980. Minute by Heinz Wilhelm Fiedler, AA, 23 July 1980. Ibid., Doc. 219.
119. See note 19.
120. Conversation between Helmut Schmidt and Mohammed Mubarak, 1 January 1980. Ibid., Doc. 97. When the Geneva disarmament talks between the United States and the Soviet Union failed at the end of 1983, 108 Pershing II missiles were deployed in the Federal Republic. For the double-track-decision, see Steininger, *Deutschland und die USA*, 610–22.
121. Meeting between the German and Saudi-Arab delegations at the King's Palace in Riyadh, 28 April 1981. *AAPD 1981*, Doc. 118.
122. Ambassador Niels Hansen (Tel Aviv) to AA, 4 June 1982. *AAPD 1982*, Doc. 174.
123. Conversation between Hans-Dietrich Genscher and Menachem Savidor in Bonn, 9 November 1982. Ibid., Doc. 296.
124. For this problem, see Efraim Karsh, *Palestine Betrayed* (New Haven, CT and London: Yale University Press, 2010); see my review in *Das Historisch-Politische Buch*, 2010.
125. Conversation between Berndt von Staden and David Kimche in Bonn, 14 September 1982. *AAPD 1982*, Doc. 239.
126. Conversation on 22 April 1983. *AAPD 1983*, Doc. 111; see my review of the *AAPD* volumes 1983 and 1984 in *FAZ*, 7 March 2015.
127. Minute by Per Fischer, 27 May 1983. Ibid., Doc. 159.
128. Minute by ambassador Niels Hansen (Bonn), 8 July 1983. Ibid., Doc. 209.
129. Ambassador Freiherr von Stein (Djidda) to AA. Ibid., Doc. 299.
130. Conversation between Helmut Kohl and Yitzhak Shamir in Jerusalem, 24 January 1984. *AAPD 1984*, Doc. 18.
131. Minute by Jürgen Ruhfus and Andreas Meyer-Landrut, 4 October 1984. Ibid., Doc. 263.
132. Mentioned in: Weingardt, *Israel- und Nahostpolitik*, 334.

Chapter Seven

FROM REUNIFICATION TO THE PRESENT

The Gulf War and Chequebook Diplomacy

While the Germans were preparing for their reunification, a new conflict developed in the Middle East. Iraqi troops under Saddam Hussein invaded Kuwait on 2 August 1990. On 29 November the UN Security Council issued Iraq an ultimatum to withdraw from the small emirate by 15 January 1991. At the same time, US president George H.W. Bush organized an international military alliance for a possible war against Iraq. All this gave Bonn a taste of the fact that united Germany would face new challenges in several ways. In 1989 Bush had declared the Federal Republic to be a 'partner in leadership'; now, on 13 September 1990, he told chancellor Helmut Kohl that 'Germany must assume its fair share of responsibility in the efforts to resolve the Gulf Crisis'. Kohl offered to provide sixty Fuchs ABC armoured reconnaissance vehicles, wheeled vehicles, mobile cranes and ABC defence equipment from the former national army of the GDR, amounting to a total contribution of 3.3 billion Deutschmarks for the year 1990. US secretary of state James Baker said these figures were larger than the American side had suggested and expected, but 'unfortunately nothing could change the fact that no German troops were in the Gulf'. Kohl replied that Germany was doing more than the others but 'getting a beating' for it; it would be easier and cheaper to send a parachute brigade, but for constitutional reasons this was not possible. Baker conceded that the amount offered by Kohl was substantially higher than 'what the Americans would have demanded'.[1]

Ultimately, on 6 January 1991, eighteen of the Bundeswehr's Alpha jets were deployed to southern Turkey, and on 8 February – after the start of the Gulf War on 17 January – forty-nine soldiers of the 36th Tactical Fighter Wing, equipped with Hawk missiles, were sent to East Turkey. For the first time since the Second World War, German soldiers were in an area threatened by war. The decision triggered heated discussions in Germany and led to a rapid increase in the number of conscientious objectors. NATO and the Federal Republic assumed that Iraq might attack Turkey, leading to a situation in which every NATO member was obliged to assist under Article 5 of the treaty. But not only did the SPD see this differently; it also felt that participation of the Bundeswehr would only be permissible under a UN Security Council resolution. (That opinion changed at the beginning of 1999, when a new government was formed by the SPD, with Gerhard Schröder as chancellor, and the Green Party, with Joschka Fischer as foreign minister. The Bundeswehr then supported NATO against Yugoslavia during the Kosovo War.)

During the Gulf War it became known that the Federal Republic had supported Iraq in its war efforts. German companies helped to increase the range of Iraqi Scud missiles from 280 to 600 km so that they could reach Israeli territory – and earned good money doing so. Allegedly, Germans were also involved in the set-up of poison gas production. For purposes of damage control, foreign minister Genscher visited Israel at the end of January 1991 with an offer of money that Israel could use to buy US Patriot anti-rocket missiles. Ultimately the Federal Republic contributed approximately 18 billion Deutschmarks – about one-third of the Federal defence budget – to supporting the Gulf War, and still had to put up with the accusation of chequebook diplomacy. Meanwhile, Israelis in Tel Aviv donned German gas masks and sat in their basements to protect themselves from Iraqi missiles.[2]

To improve its tarnished image in Israel, in December 1991 Bonn again involved itself in secret arms deliveries, this time of Soviet-style tanks and tank vehicles as well as other equipment from the former national army of the GDR. Although the undertaking was a secret operation, the materiel was discovered in Hamburg, and the Chancellery's minister of state Lutz Stavenhagen had to resign. Even so, a short time later Bonn delivered two Dolphin class submarines free of charge to Israel, and a third one at a 50 per cent discount.[3]

A year later, the Oslo Peace Accords set in motion a peace process negotiated by Israel's recently elected prime minister, Yitzhak Rabin, and his foreign minister, Shimon Peres. (As mentioned earlier, it ended with Rabin's assassination on 4 November 1995.) Europe welcomed Oslo, which basically was the old 1980 Venice Declaration. In 1993, Palestinian leader Yasser Arafat was received in Bonn. The EU–Israel Association Agreement was reached in 1995. By 1998 the Federal Republic had invested 350 million dollars in the Palestinian territories (more than the United States).

Figure 7.1 One of the many development projects in Palestine financed by Germany. Photo courtesy of Clemens Strickner, Vienna.

The Schröder/Fischer government in Bonn supported the peace process unconditionally, in line with the EU policy of that time. In 1999 the Venice Declaration was broadened when the EU reaffirmed the Palestinians' lasting and unrestricted right of self-determination, including the option of a state, and agreed to consider recognition of a Palestinian state in due time.

The Iraq War and Chancellor Gerhard Schröder's 'Betrayal'

The day after the devastating terrorist attacks in New York and Washington on 11 September 2001, as the White House discussed targets of US retaliatory actions, Defense Secretary Donald Rumsfeld mentioned Iraq. Secretary of State Colin Powell opposed this idea, believing the focus should be on al-Qaeda. Although relieved to hear Powell's objection, Richard A. Clarke, the national coordinator for security, infrastructure protection, and counter-terrorism, vented his anger at the same time: 'I thought I was missing something here. Having been attacked by al-Qaeda, for us now to go bombing Iraq in response would be like our invading Mexico after the Japanese attacked us at Pearl Harbor'. Powell shook his head: 'It's not over yet'.[4]

The United States opened fire on Iraq on 20 March 2003,⁵ fulfilling the wishes of the 'neocons' in Washington: vice-president Dick Cheney, Pentagon chief Donald Rumsfeld, his deputy Paul Wolfowitz, undersecretary of defense for policy Douglas Feith, Pentagon consultant Richard Perle, undersecretary of state for arms control and international security affairs John Bolton, Cheney's chief of staff Lewis 'Scooter' Libby, and Bush advisor Karl Rove were all behind the action. Hussein's Iraq had been on their minds long before 9/11. Now they were just waiting for the opportunity to finish the 'job' left undone by George W. Bush's father in 1991. They were motivated not only by the oil, but also by the idea of introducing democracy to the Middle East – 'like after the war in Germany', as national security adviser Condoleezza Rice put it – by eliminating the tyrant Saddam Hussein.

For the public, the 'good selling argument' (Wolfowitz's term) would be to link the terrorist attacks to Iraq. The neocons placed Saddam Hussein at the centre of world terrorism and asserted that he would soon have weapons of mass destruction. Where there was no evidence, they were invented, and the warmongers met with inordinately strong support in the White House. According to the well-known US historian George Herring,

> Bush combined the Old West mentality of his native Texas with the missionary spirit of evangelical Christianity. He saw the world in terms of good and evil, and was certain he had been 'called' to defend his country and extend 'God's gift of liberty' to 'every human being in the world'. His faith helped him to choose a course. Once he had decided, there was no second-guessing. A war with Iraq would protect the security of the United States and eliminate a force of evil.⁶

In the following weeks and months, the neocons wove an amazing net of lies to justify the war against Iraq to the public. The 'axis of evil' and the 'Bush doctrine', invented for the 'War on Terror', gave the global public a plausible reason for a pre-emptive strike. The unforgettable images of 10 May 2003 depict Bush, dressed in a pilot's uniform, landing on the aircraft carrier USS *Abraham Lincoln* in San Diego Bay, where beneath a banner proclaiming 'Mission Accomplished' he then hailed the victory of the US forces in Iraq. This proved a gigantic miscalculation, as the war lasted eight more years. Only in 2011 did Bush's successor, Barack Obama, end the war – in a way. It had caused endless suffering at enormous cost. Hundreds of thousands of Iraqis had been killed or had left the country. Meanwhile the total neglect of Afghanistan had furthered the war that prevailed there then, and still prevails now. The Iraq War was, echoing the famous sentence by the chairman of the joint chiefs of staff, Omar Bradley, during the Korean War, 'The wrong war, at the wrong place, at the wrong time, and with the wrong enemy'.⁷ George Herring called the Iraq War the 'wrong war, in the wrong place, with the wrong methods'.[8] It accomplished nothing.

Meanwhile, 'old Europe' – as Donald Rumsfeld termed the European countries that refused to participate in the Iraq War – was still critical of American policy regarding Iraq. More interesting and more meaningful is the critique Richard Clarke laid out in his book *Against All Enemies*, which became a bestseller immediately after its publication in New York in 2004. The title comes from the official oath, taken by Clarke himself, to defend the US Constitution 'against all enemies'. From his point of view, Iraq was not a threat to the United States and had nothing to do with the terror attacks in New York or Washington – the majority of the terrorists came from Saudi Arabia. When Iraq had invaded Kuwait in 1990, Clarke was one of the first to recommend military action against the aggressor. Later he also favoured regime change in Iraq, 'but not the way it was done, not at the cost we have paid and will pay for it, not by diverting us from eliminating our vulnerabilities to terrorism at home; not at the incredibly high price of increasing Muslim hatred of America and strengthening al-Qaeda. ... Al-Qaeda has metastasized. It was like a Hydra, growing new heads'.[9]

After 11 September, Clarke wrote, there was an opportunity to unite people around the world with a set of shared values – religious tolerance, diversity, freedom and security – but 'we squandered the opportunity. ... We did in fact lash out in a largely unilateral and entirely irrelevant military adventure against a Muslim nation. ... We will pay the price for a long time'.[10]

France and above all Germany did not belong to the 'coalition of the willing' fighting in Iraq. Before the autumn of 2002 Bundestag election, chancellor Gerhard Schröder publicly stated that Germany would in no way participate in the Iraq War. As a 'peace chancellor' he was able to win an election long thought lost. Yet Schröder's anti-war policy led to a low point in the history of German–American relations. There was no love lost between the two; he and Bush had nothing to say to each other. This ice age lasted until Schröder was voted out in 2005. George W. Bush explains why in *Decision Points*, a memoir published five years later in which Schröder was sharply criticized and accused of insult and deceit. For Bush, Schröder was 'one of the toughest leaders to figure out'.[11]

This episode goes back to 31 January 2002, when a secret meeting at the White House was held between just six people: Schröder, German ambassador Wolfgang Ischinger, and the Chancellery's foreign policy head Dieter Kastrop on the German side; and Bush, Condoleeza Rice, and chief of staff Andy Card on the American side. Bush writes in his memoir that Schröder fully supported his Iraq policy. Bush explained to the chancellor that he was determined to make diplomacy work, but that although the military option was his last choice, he 'would use it if necessary'.[12] According to Bush, Schröder answered: 'What is true of Afghanistan is true for Iraq. Nations that sponsor terror face consequences. If you make it fast and make it decisive I will be with you'. Bush continues in his memoirs: 'I took this as a statement of support'.[13]

Bush, therefore, thought Schröder was on his side. Assuming the chancellor would have to devote attention to the 2002 German election campaign, Bush, still in a good mood, asked foreign minister Joschka Fischer at the UN General Assembly in mid-September: 'When is this damn election over?' Bush says in his memoirs: 'But when the German elections arrived later that year, Schröder had a different take. He denounced the possibility of using force against Iraq'.[14] 'That guy has been cheating on me', Bush complained to Dan Coats, the then US ambassador in Berlin.[15] His memoirs state: 'As someone who valued personal diplomacy, I put a high premium on trust. Once that trust was violated, it was hard to have a constructive relationship again'.[16] Schröder replied publicly:

> Former US president Bush is not telling the truth. The conversation [on 31 January 2002] concerned the question of whether the terrorists responsible for the 11 September attacks in the US were supported by Saddam Hussein. As was the case with my later meeting with the US president, I made it clear that if Iraq were to provide shelter and sanctuary for al-Qaeda fighters, as Afghanistan did previously, Germany would reliably stand by the US. This connection [between Iraq and al-Qaeda], however, was false and fabricated, as it turned out in the course of 2002. . . . As we know today, the Bush administration's justification for the Iraqi war was based on lies.[17]

Schröder's account was backed by former top German officials, namely, the two other participants in said conversation. Wolfgang Ischinger assured the *Tagesspiegel*: 'Nobody could interpret the conversation as a blank German cheque for a military action against Iraq'.[18] Dieter Kastrop also supported the chancellor's statement: 'Schröder expressed himself in such a way that Bush could not have understand it to be a carte blanche to start a war against Iraq with German help'.[19]

The government spokesperson at that time, Uwe-Karsten Heye, delivered an assessment that raised serious doubts about the ex-president's field of vision: 'We have noticed that the intellectual level of the former president of the most important nation has an extremely low threshold,' he told the television news station N24, 'and that's why it was difficult to communicate with him'. In Heye's recollection of President Bush, 'he had no idea what was going on in the world. He was so keen to be a Texan. I think he knew every longhorn in Texas'.[20]

The Federal Republic did not participate in the Iraq War, but since 2006 it has been involved in maritime surveillance off the coast of Lebanon in

Figure 7.2 Israel's prime minister, Benjamin Netanjahu, welcomes Chancellor Angela Merkel in Jerusalem. Merkel: 'Israel's security was and is a very important matter for every German chancellor'. Photo by Amos Ben Gershon. Courtesy of Israel Government Press Office, Jerusalem.

the context of a UN mission – carried out with NATO partners of Germany who are involved in Afghanistan – to prevent arms deliveries to Hezbollah in Lebanon, a declared enemy of Israel. Even though the allied troops were officially withdrawn in 2011, a thousand German soldiers are still engaged.

Notes

1. See Steininger, *Deutschland und die USA*, 737.
2. Heribert Schwan and Rolf Steininger, *Helmut Kohl: Virtuose der Macht* (Mannheim: Artemis & Winkler, 2010), 272f.; cf. the report 'Im vereinten Deutschland' by the former Israeli ambassador in Bonn, Benjamin Navon, in: Ben Natan and Hansen, *Israel*, 192f.
3. Navon, 'Im vereinten Deutschland', 193, cf. note 1.
4. Richard Clarke, *Against All Enemies: Inside America's War on Terror* (New York: Free Press, 2004), 31; see my review in *FAZ*, 24 September 2004.
5. Thomas E. Ricks, *Fiasco: The American Military Adventure in Iraq* (New York: Penguin, 2006).
6. George C. Herring, *From Colony to Superpower: U.S. Foreign Relations since 1776* (Oxford: Oxford University Press, 2008), 946.
7. Cf. Rolf Steininger, *Der vergessene Krieg: Korea 1950–1953* (Olzog: Munich, 2006, 2007), 176.
8. Herring, *Colony*, 960.
9. Clarke, *Enemies*, 264, 287.
10. Ibid., 285.
11. George W. Bush, *Decision Points* (New York: Crown Publishers, 2010), 233.
12. Ibid., 234.
13. Ibid.
14. Ibid.

15. www.spiegel.de, 14 November 2010.
16. Bush, *Decision Points,* 233.
17. www.spiegel.de, 9 September 2010.
18. Ibid., 9 November 2010.
19. www.derwesten.de, 10 November 2010.
20. Ibid. The records of the famous conversation between Bush and Schröder might clarify the details of what was discussed. In 2013 I submitted a FOIA request for the release of the American record, but in early 2018 the request was still 'under senior review'. The Federal Chancellery twice rejected my request for the release of the German record.

Conclusion

For over a century, Germany has played a central role in the region of the Middle East, where crises abound and one of world's most attention-grabbing and impassioned conflicts persists. The German state first became involved there in 1898, when Kaiser Wilhelm II lent support to the Zionist Theodor Herzl's project to found a Jewish state in Palestine.

The Middle East was the site of major combat operations during the First World War. Germany, then an ally of the Ottomans, was a crucial player in Middle Eastern affairs. In this period the Kaiser, who had pronounced himself the protector of the region's 300 million Muslims in 1898, in fact became the protector of the Jews in Palestine during the war.

Germany's role in the Middle East was much reduced in the interwar period, but Hitler's 1933 rise to power raised the Germans' profile there. Even as the Nazis worked to exterminate Europe's Jews during the Second World War, Germany pursued its interests in the Middle East, devoting considerable attention to Iraq – and to the Grand Mufti of Jerusalem, whom Hitler received in Berlin on 28 November 1941.

A new phase of Germany's Middle East policy began under completely altered conditions with the establishment of the Federal Republic and the GDR in 1949. For the next forty years, there were two Germanys coping with the Cold War and a heavy dependence on oil. Israel might not have survived the 1950s and early 1960s had West Germany not supplied it with money and arms. In 1952 Bonn launched an official Middle East policy that included a reparation agreement with Israel, which Chancellor Konrad Adenauer implemented over the protests of the Arab states. Bonn started supplying Israel with weaponry in 1957, further increasing the discontent of Israel's neighbours. By the mid-1960s this approach was sparking further conflict with the Arab states. The prospect of Arab states extending diplomatic recognition to the GDR provoked the greatest crisis to date in the Federal Republic's young life. The *Ostpolitik* of the Brandt/

Scheel government put an end to the issue of recognition of the GDR and the claim to sole representation of Germany.

Things have changed since 1990/91. The Cold War is over, and there is only one Germany, with no room for blackmail. Nevertheless, three of the points mentioned in Chapter 5 are still valid, namely: (1) Germany's historical responsibility towards Israel after the Holocaust, (2) the interests of Germany's European partners and the United States in the region, and (3) the interests of the Arab states.

Germany today has excellent relations with both the Arab states and Israel, but it no longer plays a decisive role in the Middle East. Nor does the EU. And although the United States decides in the Middle East, it is no longer 'the pivotal factor in the diplomacy', as Kissinger had described it at the end of the Yom Kippur War in 1973.[1] In those days, the Russians were definitely out, but that has changed: the Russians are back, and under president Vladimir Putin they have become key players in the region, especially in Syria. The Middle East has changed. The much-cited Arab Spring now feels more like winter, with states falling apart.

And then there is still Iraq and the fight against the so-called Islamic State (IS). US troops withdrew from Iraq in 2011, but in 2014 the Americans were back to conduct air raids targeting the Islamic terrorists of the IS. This time Germany was involved in delivering weapons to a war zone for the first time in German postwar history, assisting the Kurds in their struggle against the IS. In addition, German jet fighters were stationed in Turkey (now in Jordan) to support the alliance against the IS, and a German cruiser protects the French aircraft carrier *Charles de Gaulle* in the Eastern Mediterranean as it fights the IS.

Things are obviously changing again under the administration of President Donald Trump.[2] In February 2017, Trump put Iraq 'on notice' and introduced new sanctions. He ordered his chiefs of staff to come up with a plan to destroy the IS, and signed executive orders banning citizens of seven predominantly Muslim countries – Libya, Sudan, Somalia, Syria, Iraq, Iran and Yemen – as well as all refugees from Syria, from entering the United States. Furthermore, US policy towards the Middle East conflict is undergoing a major shift: Trump has recognized Jerusalem as the capital of Israel, the US embassy in Israel was moved from Tel Aviv to Jerusalem. At the same time, and in spite of Trump's criticism of Israel's settlement policy (there now being 600,000 settlers in the West Bank and East Jerusalem), the Knesset has passed a controversial law legalizing 3,800 settler homes built on private Palestinian land in the occupied West Bank.

Regarding the Israeli–Palestinian conflict, Germany keeps to the 'road map for peace', a plan to resolve this conflict worked out in April 2003 by the Quartet – a group comprising the United States, European Union, Russian Federation and United Nations. The road map calls for a two-state solution in which citizens of an independent Palestinian state live side by side with Israelis in peace. So far, the road is blocked. Trump no longer seems committed to this solution. At a joint White House press conference with Israel's prime minister Netanyahu on 8 February 2017, Trump said he was looking at two states or one state: 'I could live with either one'.[3] The BBC aptly described this enduring, intractable diplomatic impasse as 'blame and bitterness keeping peace at bay'.[4]

Notes

1. Kissinger, *Years of Upheaval*, 612.
2. For more on Trump, see Michael D'Antonio, *Never Enough: Donald Trump and the Pursuit of Success* (New York: St. Martin's Press, 2015; see my review in *FAZ*, 30 August 2016); David Johnston, *The Making of Donald Trump* (New York: Melville House Publishing, 2016; see my review in *FAZ*, 15 October 2016).
3. Ibid.
4. www.bbc.com, 7 January 2017.

Epilogue to the English Edition

This translation is a slightly abridged text of the original German edition *Deutschland und der Nahe Osten: Von Kaiser Wilhelms Orientreise 1898 bis zur Gegenwart* (Reinbek and Munich: Lau, 2015, 259 pp.). A few new sources have been added and a few alterations made in line with the latest research.

I thank all who have been involved in this edition: Professor Dr Sabine Schindler, the vice-rector of the Leopold Franzens University of Innsbruck, for some of the funding for the translation; Dr Margaret Davidson and Hanna Witt for the translation; Jaime Taber for editing; my son Axel for the technical work on the photos; and archive specialist Holly Reed of the National Archives II, College Park, Maryland, and Sharon Revach of the Israel Government Press Office in Jerusalem, for their assistance in obtaining the photos. For the photos from Jerusalem, the respective photographers – if known – are also credited.

I am grateful to publisher Willi J. Lau from Lau-Verlag, Reinbek and Munich, for charging only a modest licence fee; I am particularly grateful to the senior editor of Berghahn Books, Chris Chappell, for overseeing the whole project. Last but not least, my thanks go to Marion Berghahn, PhD, the publisher of Berghahn Books, Oxford and New York. Upon publication of the German version, Dr Berghahn decided almost immediately, before the first reviews were out, that there would be an English version. In 2018 there will also be an Arabic version, published by the National Council for Culture, Arts and Letters in Kuwait.

Rolf Steininger
November 2018

Selected Bibliography

I. Documents

English
Burr, William (ed.). *The October War and U.S. Policy* (Washington, DC: National Security Archive, 2003).
Department of State (ed.). *Foreign Relations of the United States, 1964–1968: Volume XIX: Arab–Israel Crisis and War, 1967* (Washington, DC: United States Government Printing Office, 2004); *1969–1976, Volume XXV: Arab–Israel Crisis and War, 1973* (Washington, DC: United States Government Printing Office, 2011).
Gust, Wolfgang (ed.). *The Armenian Genocide: Evidence from the German Foreign Office Archives 1915–1916* (New York and Oxford: Berghahn Books, 2014).
Kissinger, Henry A. *Crisis: The Anatomy of Two Major Policy Crises* (New York: Simon & Schuster, 2003).
Laqueur, Walter, and Barry Rubin (eds). *The Israel–Arab Reader: A Documentary History of the Middle East Conflict* (New York: Penguin, 1984).

German
Agstner, Rudolf, and Rolf Steininger (eds). *Israel und der Nahostkonflikt 1976–1981* (Innsbruck: Innsbruck University Press, 2016).
Gust, Wolfgang (ed.). *Der Völkermord an den Armeniern 1915/16: Dokumente aus dem Politischen Archiv des Auswärtigen Amts* (Springe: Klampen, 2005).
Institut für Zeitgeschichte (ed.), on behalf of the Auswärtiges Amt. *Akten zur Auswärtigen Politik der Bundesrepublik Deutschland* (Munich: Oldenbourg, 1994–2014).
Jelinek, Yeshayahu A. (ed.). *Zwischen Moral und Realpolitik: Deutsch-israelische Beziehungen 1945–1965. Eine Dokumentensammlung* (Gerlingen: Bleicher, 1997).
Steininger, Rolf (ed.). *Berichte aus Israel 1946–1972: Die Berichte der diplomatischen Vertreter Österreichs*, 12 volumes (Munich: Olzog, 2004).
——— (ed.). *Der Kampf um Palästina 1924–1939: Berichte der deutschen Generalkonsuln in Jerusalem* (Munich: Olzog, 2007).

Steininger, Rolf, and Rudolf Agstner (eds). *Berichte aus Jerusalem 1924–1938: Die Berichte der österreichischen Generalkonsuln* (Munich: Olzog, 2004).
——— (eds). *Israel und der Nahostkonflikt 1972–1976* (Munich: Olzog, 2006).
Vogel, Rolf (ed.). *Der deutsch-israelische Dialog: Dokumentation eines erregenden Kapitels deutscher Außenpolitik*, 8 volumes (Munich: K.G. Saur, 1987).

II. Memoirs

English
Burns, E.L.M. *Between Arab and Israeli* (London: George G. Harrap, 1962).
Bush, George W. *Decision Points* (New York: Crown Publishers, 2010).
Churchill, Winston. *The Second World War*, Vol. III: *The Grand Alliance* (London: Houghton Mifflin, 1950).
Clarke, Richard A. *Against All Enemies: Inside America's War on Terror* (New York: Free Press, 2004).
Dayan, Moshe. *Story of My Life* (London: Weidenfeld & Nicolson, 1976).
Felmy, Hellmuth, and Walter Warlimont. *German Exploitation of Arab Nationalist Movements in World War II* (Heidelberg: United States Army, 1952).
Kissinger, Henry A. *Years of Upheaval* (Boston and Toronto: Little, Brown and Company, 1982).
Meir, Golda. *My Life* (London: Weidenfeld & Nicolson, 1975).
Townshend, Charles. *My Campaign in Mesopotamia* (London: Butterworth, 1920).

German
Ben Natan, Asher, and Niels Hansen (eds). *Israel und Deutschland: Dorniger Weg zur Partnerschaft* (Cologne: Böhlau, 2005).
Birrenbach, Kurt. *Meine Sondermissionen: Rückblick auf zwei Jahrzehnte bundesdeutscher Außenpolitik* (Düsseldorf and Vienna: Econ, 1984).
Blankenhorn, Herbert. *Verständnis und Verständigung: Blätter eines politischen Tagebuchs 1949–1979* (Frankfurt: Propyläen, 1980).
Carmel, Alex, and Ejal Jakob Eisler. *Der Kaiser reist ins Heilige Land: Die Palästinareise Wilhelms II 1898. Eine illustrierte Dokumentation* (Cologne: Kohlhammer, 1999).
Frank, Paul. *Entschlüsselte Botschaft: Ein Diplomat macht Inventur* (Stuttgart: Deutsche Verlags-Anstalt, 1981).
Goldmann, Nahum. *Mein Leben als deutscher Jude* (Frankfurt: Ullstein, 1983).
Grobba, Fritz. *Männer und Mächte im Orient: 25 Jahre diplomatischer Tätigkeit im Orient* (Göttingen: Musterschmidt, 1967).
Lichtheim, Richard. *Rückkehr: Erinnerungen aus der Frühzeit des deutschen Zionismus* (Stuttgart: Deutsche Verlags-Anstalt, 1970).
German edition:
Osterheld, Horst. *Außenpolitik unter Ludwig Erhard 1963–1966: Ein dokumentarischer Bericht aus dem Kanzleramt* (Düsseldorf: Droste, 1992).

Rath, Ari. *Ari heißt Löwe. Erinnerungen* (Vienna: Paul Zsolnay, 2011).
Shinnar, Felix E. *Bericht eines Beauftragten: Die deutsch-israelischen Beziehungen 1951–1966* (Tübingen: Rainer Wunderlich, 1967).

III. Monographs/Articles

English

Barr, James. *A Line in the Sand: Britain, France and the Struggle for the Mastery of the Middle East* (New York: Simon & Schuster, 2012).
Chubin, Shahram (ed.). *Germany and the Middle East: Patterns and Prospects* (New York: Continuum International, 1992).
Fromkin, David. *A Peace to End All Peace: The Fall of the Ottoman Empire and the Creation of the Modern Middle East* (New York: Avon, 1989).
Gensicke, Klaus. *The Mufti of Jerusalem and the Nazis: The Berlin Years* (London: Mitchell, 2007).
Gossman, Lionel. *The Passion of Max von Oppenheim: Archaeology and Intrigue in the Middle East from Wilhelm II to Hitler* (Cambridge: Cambridge University Press, 2013).
Herring, George C. *From Colony to Superpower: U.S. Foreign Relations since 1776* (Oxford: Oxford University Press, 2008).
Krämer, Gudrun. *A History of Palestine: From the Ottoman Conquest to the Founding of the State of Israel* (Princeton, NJ: Princeton University Press, 2008).
Lebel, Jennie. *The Mufti of Jerusalem: Haj-Amin el Husseini and National-Socialism* (Belgrade: Čigoja štampa, 2007).
Lesch, David W., and Mark L. Haas (eds). *The Middle East and the United States: History, Politics, and Ideologies* (Boulder, CO: Westview Press, 2014).
Little, Douglas. *American Orientalism: The United States and the Middle East since 1945* (London: I.B. Tauris, 2003).
Lüdke, Tilman. *Jihad Made in Germany: Ottoman and German Propaganda and Intelligence Operations in the First World War* (Münster: Lit, 2005).
Mallmann, Klaus-Michael, and Martin Cüppers. *Nazi Palestine: The Plans for the Extermination of the Jews in Palestine* (New York: Enigma, 2010).
McKale, Donald M. '"The Kaiser's Spy": Max von Oppenheim and the Anglo–German Rivalry before and during the First World War', *European History Quarterly* 27 (1997), 199–220.
———. *War by Revolution: Germany and Great Britain in the Middle East in the Era of World War I* (Kent: Kent State University Press, 1998).
McMeekin, Sean. *The Berlin–Baghdad Express: The Ottoman Empire and Germany's Bid for World Power 1898–1918* (London: Penguin, 2010).
Morris, Benny. *Righteous Victims: A History of the Zionist–Arab Conflict, 1881–2001* (New York: Vintage Books, 2001).
Nicosia, Francis. *The Third Reich and the Palestine Question* (New Brunswick, NJ and London: Transaction Publishers, 2000).

Oren, Michael B. *Six Days of War: June 1967 and the Making of the Modern Middle East* (Oxford: Oxford University Press, 2002).
———. *Power, Faith, and Fantasy: America in the Middle East, 1776 to the Present* (New York: W.W. Norton & Company, 2007).
Parker, Richard (ed.). *The October War: A Retrospective* (Gainesville: University of Florida Press, 2001).
Quandt, William P. *Peace Process: American Diplomacy and the Arab–Israeli Conflict since 1967* (Washington, DC: Brookings Institution, 1993).
Rabinovich, Abraham. *The Yom Kippur War: The Epic Encounter that Transformed the Middle East* (New York: Schocken, 2004).
Rogan, Eugene. *The Fall of the Ottomans: The Great War in the Middle East, 1914–1920* (New York: Basic, 2016).
Rubin, Barry, and Wolfgang G. Schwanitz. *Nazis, Islamists and the Making of the Middle East* (New Haven, CT: Yale University Press, 2014).
Schwanitz, Wolfgang G. (ed.). *Germany and the Middle East, 1871–1945* (Princeton, NJ: Wiener Publishers, 2004).
Segev, Tom. *One Palestine, Complete: Jews and Arabs Under the British Mandate* (London: Abacus, 2001).
———. *1967: Israel, the War, and the Year that Transformed the Middle East* (New York: Metropolitan, 2007).
Steininger, Rolf. 'Israel as Seen by Karl Hartl, the First Austrian Diplomat in Tel Aviv'. *Quest: Issues in Contemporary Jewish History* 7 (July 2014).
———. *The German Question: The Stalin Note of 1952 and the Problem of Reunification* (New York: Columbia University Press, 1990).
———. *Austria, Germany and the Cold War: From the Anschluss to the State Treaty, 1938–1955* (New York and Oxford: Berghahn Books, 2008, 2012).
Trumpener, Ulrich. *Germany and the Ottoman Empire, 1914–1918* (Princeton, NJ: Princeton University Press, 1968).
Wright, Lawrence. *Thirteen Days in September: Carter, Begin, and Sadat at Camp David* (New York: Alfred A. Knopf, 2014).
Yaqub, Salim. *Imperfect Strangers: Americans, Arabs, and US–Middle East Relations in the 1970s* (Ithaka, NY and London: Cornell University Press, 2016).

German

Balke, Ralf. *Hakenkreuz im Heiligen Land: Die NSDAP-Landesgruppe Palästina* (Erfurt: Sutton, 2001).
Berggötz, Sven Olaf. *Nahostpolitik in der Ära Adenauer: Möglichkeiten und Grenzen 1949–1963* (Düsseldorf: Droste, 1998).
Bodenheimer, Max, and Henrietta Hannah Bodenheimer. *Die Zionisten und das kaiserliche Deutschland* (Bensberg: Schäuble, 1972).
Eiff, Hansjörg. 'Die jüdische Heimstätte in Palästina in der deutschen Außenpolitik 1914–1918', *Zeitschrift für Geschichtswissenschaft* 60 (2012), 3, 202–27.
———. 'Die jüdische Heimstätte in Palästina in der Außenpolitik der Weimarer Republik', *Zeitschrift für Geschichtswissenschaft* 61 (2013), 12, 1005–28.
Fürtig, Henner. *Kleine Geschichte des Irak* (Munich: C.H. Beck, 2004).

Gensicke, Klaus. *Der Mufti von Jerusalem und die Nationalsozialisten: Eine politische Biographie Amin el-Husseinis* (Darmstadt: Wissenschaftliche Buchgesellschaft, 2007); see also English edition.

Hansen, Niels. *Aus dem Schatten der Katastrophe: Die deutsch-israelischen Beziehungen in der Ära Konrad Adenauer und David Ben Gurion* (Düsseldorf: Droste, 2002).

Hinrichsen, Hans-Peter E. *Der Ratgeber: Kurt Birrenbach und die Außenpolitik der Bundesrepublik Deutschland* (Berlin: Wissenschaft und Forschung, 2002).

Jaschinski, Klaus, and Julius Waldschmidt (eds). *Des Kaisers Reise in den Orient 1898* (Berlin: Weist, 2002).

Koop, Volker. *Hitlers Muslime: Die Geschichte einer unheiligen Allianz* (Berlin: BeBra, 2012).

Kreutzer, Stefan M. *Dschihad für den deutschen Kaiser: Max von Oppenheim und die Neuordnung des Orients (1914–1918)* (Graz: Ares, 2012).

Lawrence von Arabien. *Genese eines Mythos: Begleitband zur Sonderausstellung 'Lawrence von Arabien'* (Mainz: Zabern, 2010).

Loth, Wilfried, and Marc Hanisch (eds). *Erster Weltkrieg und Dschihad: Die Deutschen und die Revolutionierung des Orients* (Munich: Oldenbourg, 2014).

Mallmann, Klaus-Michael, and Martin Cüppers. *Halbmond und Hakenkreuz: Das Dritte Reich, die Araber und Palästina* (Darmstadt: Wissenschaftliche Buchgesellschaft, 2006); see also English edition.

Richter, Jan Stefan. *Die Orientreise Kaiser Wilhelms II. 1898. Eine Studie zur deutschen Außenpolitik* (Hamburg: Dr. Kovac, 1997).

Röhl, John C.G. 'Wilhelms seltsamer Kreuzzug', *DIE ZEIT*, Nr. 42 (8 October 1998), 30–36.

Schölch, Alexander. 'Das Dritte Reich, die zionistische Bewegung und der Palästina-Konflikt', *Vierteljahrshefte für Zeitgeschichte* 30 (1982), 646–74.

Schumann, Frederik. *Die deutsche Nahostpolitik 1969–1973: Die sozial-liberale Koalition zwischen Interessenpolitik und moralischer Verpflichtung* (Saarbrücken: Akademikerverlag, 2012).

Schwan, Heribert, and Rolf Steininger. *Helmut Kohl: Virtuose der Macht* (Mannheim: Artemis & Winkler, 2010).

Schwanitz, Wolfgang G. *Islam in Europa, Revolten in Mittelost: Islamisten und Genozid von Wilhelm II und Enver Pascha übe Hitler und al-Husaini bis Arafat, Usama Bin Laden und Ahmadinejad sowie Gespräche mit Bernard Lewis* (Berlin: trafo, 2013).

———. 'Adenauer in New York, Pawelke in Kairo', *Historisch-Politische Mitteilungen der Konrad-Adenauer-Stiftung* 10 (2003), 151–72.

——— (ed.). *Deutschland und der Mittlere Osten im Kalten Krieg* (Leipzig: Universitätsverlag, 2004).

Segev, Tom. *Es war einmal ein Palästina* (Berlin: Siedler, 1999).

———. *1967: Israels zweite Geburt* (Munich: Siedler, 2007).

Steininger, Rolf. *Der Große Krieg 1914–1918 in 92 Kapiteln* (Reinbek and Munich: Lau, 2016).

———. *Der Nahostkonflikt* (Frankfurt am Main: Fischer Taschenbuch Verlag, 2005; revised edition 2012).

———. 'Der Sechstagekrieg', *Aus Politik und Zeitgeschichte* 19 (7 May 2007).

———. *Deutschland und die USA: Vom Zweiten Weltkrieg bis zur Gegenwart* (Reinbek and Munich: Lau, 2014).

———. 'Bittere Lektion: Der Jom-Kippur-Krieg im Herbst 1973 brachte Israel für einen Moment an den Rand des Untergangs', *Die Zeit* 37 (5 September 2013), 19.

Thurau, Peter. *Lawrence von Arabien: Ein Mann und seine Zeit* (Munich: C.H. Beck, 2010).

Timm, Angelika. *Hammer–Zirkel–Davidstern: Das gestörte Verhältnis der DDR zu Zionismus und Staat Israel* (Bonn: Bouvier, 1997).

Weingardt, Markus A. *Deutsche Israel- und Nahostpolitik: Die Geschichte einer Gratwanderung seit 1949* (Frankfurt and New York: Campus, 2002).

Wildangel, René. *Zwischen Achse und Mandatsmacht: Palästina und der Nationalsozialismus* (Berlin: Klaus Schwarz, 2007).

Will, Alexander. *Kein Griff nach der Weltmacht: Geheime Dienste und Propaganda im deutsch-österreichisch-türkischen Bündnis 1914–1918* (Cologne, Weimar and Vienna: Böhlau, 2012).

Zechlin, Egmont. *Die deutsche Politik und die Juden im Ersten Weltkrieg* (Göttingen: Vandenhoek & Ruprecht, 1969).

INDEX

Note: Page numbers in *italics* indicate illustrations.

A

Abdul Hamid II, 1, 6
Abdul Rahman Azzam, Hassan, 60, 62
Abdullah I, 22, 30, 56
Adenauer, Konrad (1876–1967), 65, 158; *Aktion Geschäftsfreund*, 95; Berlin crisis and EEC, 89; Luxembourg Agreement, 67–74, 76, 158; meeting with Ben-Gurion in New York, 95, 98; reparations, 65; Suez War, 79; trip to US, 76; weapons for Israel, 81
Agnew, Spiro Theodore, 129
al-Gailani, Raschid Ali, 48, 50, 55
al-Haschimi, Taha, 48
al-Husseini, Mohammed Amin (1895–1974), 1–2, 32, *51*, 60, 70–71, 158; in Berlin, 55–56; fight against the Jews, 36, 55–56; in Iraq, 49; meeting with Hitler, 51–53; Muslim SS division, 55; and Oppenheim, 28; relations with Germany, 43, 48–49
al-Kholy, Hassan, 120
Allenby, Sir Edmund H., x, 21, *22*, 23
al-Said, Nuri, 48
Amerungen, Otto Wolff von, 60
Amer, Abd al-Hakim, 109
Amit, Meir, 109
Anderson, David, 133–134
Arab League, xi; founding of Israel, 60, 62; Palestine, 139; PLO, 139–140, 142; Six-Day War, 116
Arafat, Yasser, 56, 151
Armenian genocide, x, 16, 17–20
Assad, Hafez al-, 129
Austrian Consulate General, 3

B

Baden, Friedrich von (Grand Duke), 24
Bahr, Egon, 120
Baker, James, 150
Balfour, Lord Arthur James, 26
Balfour Declaration, x, 30, 33, 55
Bar-Lev, Chaim, 129
Barzel, Rainer, 95–96, *96*
Basler Kongress, 7
Bauer, Fiedrich, 115
Becker, Julius, 127
Begin, Menachem (1913–1992): accusing Ben-Gurion, 64; accusing German chancellor Helmut Schmidt, 141; Camp David Agreement, 141; against negotiations with Germany, 66; Palestine, 142; Sadat, 140
Ben-Gurion, David (1886–1973), 60, 62, 66, 68, 78, 86, 95; Israel 1948/49, 60; meeting with Adenauer, 81, 98; restitution agreement with Germany, 64–65; Six-Day War, 112
Ben Gurion, Paula, 98
Ben-Horin, Eliashiv, 125, 127
Ben Natan, Asher (1921–2014), 91, 94–96, 117
Berggötz, Sven Olaf, 2, 78
Bernstorff, Johann Heinrich von, 26–27
Bethmann Hollweg, Theobald, 14, 18–19
Bevin, Ernest, 60
Bey, Talaat, 18–19
Birrenbach, Kurt, 87–90
Bismarck, Otto von, 11
Blankenhorn, Herbert, 75
Blomberg, Axel von, 49
Blomberg, Werner von, 49
Bodenheimer, Max, 8
Böhm, Franz, 67
Böker, Alexander, 74, 78, 98–100
Bolton, John, 153

Index

Bosse, Robert, 10–11
Bourguiba, Habib, 126
Bradley, Omar, 153
Brandt, Willy (1913–1992), 101, 117, *125*, 140; Middle East policy 1967, 117–122; Olympic games massacre 1972, 124; visit to Israel, 125–126; Yom Kippur War and letter to Nixon, 136
Brentano, Heinrich von, 77, 88
Brezhnev, Leonid Iljitsch (1906–1982): Six-Day War, 110, 112, 114; Yom Kippur War, 130–131
Brode, Heinrich, 24
Burr, William, 3
Bush, George H.W., 150
Bush, George W., 153–154

C

Camp David Agreement, xiii, 141
Card, Andy, 154
Carter, James Earl, 141
Carstens, Karl, 81, 83, 98, 117, 137
Cash, Frank E., 134
Cheney, Dick, 153
Churchill, Winston, 2, 30, 47, 49–50
Clarke, Richard A., 152, 153
Claims Conference, 67
Cüppers, Martin, 2

D

Damascus, 8
Davis, Leslie, 18
Dayan, Moshe (1915–1981): Suez War, 80, 109; Six-Day War, 111, *113*; Yom Kipur War, 127–128
Dehler, Thomas, 65–66
Deliverance Day, 31
Dinitz, Simcha, 129, 131
Dirks, Walter, 66
Döhle, Walter, 3, 31, 40, 42–44
Duckwitz, Georg Ferdinand: on GDR, 120–121
Durra, Abu, 45

E

Eban, Abba, 121–122
Eckardt, Felix von, 67
Ehmke, Horst, 121
Eichmann, Adolf, 105
Eiff, Hansjörg, 2
Eisenhower, Dwight D., 76
Elazar, David, 127
el-Gamasy, Mohamad, 131
el-Shukeri, Ahmed, 71
Enkelman, Kurt, 76
Eppler, Erhard, 121

Erhard, Ludwig (1897–1977): diplomatic relations with Israel, 91–92; tanks for Israel, 83–87, 99
Esch, Hansjoachim von der, 72
Eshkol, Levi, 89
Etzdorf, Hasso von, 69–72
Europe and Middle East Policy, 138–139

F

Fahd ibn Abdul, 142, 144
Fahmi, Nabil, 133
Faisal (Syria, Iraq), 20, 47
Faisal (Saudi-Arabia), 130
Farrag Tajeh, Ahmed, 73
Fawzi, Mahmoud, 98–99
Feith, Douglas, 153
Felmy, Hellmuth, 50, 54
Fischer, Fritz, 15
Fischer, Joschka, 151
Fischer, Per, 143–144
First World War: alliance between Germany and the Ottoman Empire, 13; Armenian genocide, 17–20; cease-fire, 23; disaster of Kut-al-Amara, 21; General Allenby's actions, 23; German revolutionary efforts, 14–17; Jews in Palestine, 24–28; jihad, 13; the Kaiser's spy; Lawrence of Arabia, 20, *22*; McMahon and Hussein, 20, *22*; military operations, 13–14; Sykes-Picot agreement, 21
Fjodorenko, Nikolaj, 114
Frangi, Abdalla, 51
Frank, Paul, 119; German-Israeli relations, 122–123, 126; Yom Kippur War, 133–134, 137–138, 139
Frederick II of Hohenstaufen, 9
Friedinger-Pranter, Robert, 71, 76

G

Gaulle, Charles de, 89
Gazit, Mordecai, 126
GDR. *See* German Democratic Republic
Genscher, Hans-Dietrich, 121, 141–142, 151
Gensicke, Klaus, 2
Georges-Picot, François, 21
German Consular General in Jerusalem (1924–1939), xi, 3, 30
German Democratic Republic: diplomatic relations with Arab states, 98–99, 101, 119–120; trade agreement with Egypt 1952, 76; Ulbricht's visit to Egypt 1964, 84–86, 90, 98
German policy towards Palestine 1937, 40
German Templars, xi, 31, *37*, 40, 45
Germany 1945–2018: diplomatic relations with Israel, 77, 89–90, 102; Middle East policy 1965, 90–91; Middle East policy 1967, 117, 120–122, 138–139; relations with Israel, xii, 122–123; reparation policy toward Israel, 65,

Index

67–74; weapons for Israel, 81, 83–87; weapons for Saudi Arabia, 143–144; with Arab states, 123–124
Goebbels, Joseph, 55
Goldmann, Nahum, 65, 65–66, 68, 77
Goltz, Colmar Freiherr von der, 16, 21
Gorenflos, Walter, 143
Grobba, Fritz, 43–44, 49–50, 52, 54, 57
Grotewohl, Otto, 99
Gruber, Karl, 71
Gudenus, Gordion, 90
Gumbel, Karl, 83
Gur, Mordechai 'Motta', *110*

H

Haas, Walter, 31
Haddad, Ottman Kamal, 48
Haifa, 9, 10, 37, 39
Hallstein, Walter, 73, 77–78
Hallstein Doctrine, 77; 'Cairo model', 98–99, 120
Hanisch, Marc, 2
Hansen, Niels, 78, 144
Hantke, Arthur, 27
Harriman, Averell, 84–85
Hartl, Karl (1909–1979): anti-Semitism, 91; Begin 'fascist', 66; Israel a 'premature birth', 93; Luxembourg Agreement, 68, 76; payments to Israel, 74
Hase, Karl-Günther von, 85, 97
Hassan, Ahmet, 73
Hassouna, Mohammed, 101, 118
Haavara, 67
Hebron, 32
Herring, George, 153
Herzl, Theodor (1860–1904), x; Basler Kongress, 7, 54; *Der Judenstaat*, 7–8; Kaiser Wilhelm 8, 10, 61–64, 158; Zionism, 6–7
Heuss, Theodor, 86
Heye, Uwe-Karsten, 155
Hillenbrand, Martin, 132, 134, 137
Himmler, Heinrich, 56
Hitler, Adolf (1889–1945): admiration for Hitler in Palestine, 34–36, 38, 40–41, 44–45, 47; attitude towards the Arabs, 54; and Iraq, 49–50; meeting with Husseini, 51–53; Muslim SS division, 55
Hohenlohe-Langenburg, Ernst II, Count zu, 18–19
Holocaust, 55–56, 159
Hussein bin Talal (King of Jordan), 101, 110, 141
Hussein ibn Ali (Sherif of Mecca), 20
Hussein, Saddam, 150, 153
Husseini. *See* al-Husseini

I

Iraq, 47; British-Iraqi war, 49; coup d'etat, 48–50
Ischinger, Wolfgang, 154–155

Israel: founding, 62; diplomatic relations with Germany, 77, 88–91, 94–98; embassy in Tel Aviv, 91; Hartl, 92; Luxembourg Agreement, 67–76; restitution policy, 65; right to exist, 139; PLO, 142; settlement policy, 141–143; *Shilumin*, 67

J

Jaffa, 32, 42, 44
Jelinek, Yeahayahu, 78
Jerusalem, x, *3*, 33, 42, 144, 156; Allenby, *22*, 23; British troops, 33; Kaiser Wilhelm, 10; Six-Day War, 110, *111*, *113*, *115*; US embassy, 159; Wailing Wall, 9, *11*, 111, 115
Jews, in Palestine, 24–28, 32, 34–36, 39; in Iraq, 50, 55; Second World War, 55–56; West Germany, 65, 68, 97, 102
Jihad, 13–14, 32, *42*, 49
Johnson, Lyndon B., 83, 109, 114
Junck, Werner, 49
Jürgens, Curt, 94

K

Kapp, Karl, 30
Kastrop, Dieter, 154–155
Keating, Kenneth, 127
Khomeini, Ruhollah Musavi, 142
Kiesinger, Kurt Georg, 89, 116–117
Kimche, David, 142–143
Kissinger, Henry (1923–), *3*, 120; Germany, 135–138; Yom Kippur War, 127, 129–132, 159
Klein, Fritz, 16–17
Knappstein, Karl Heinrich, 84–85
Kohl, Helmut (1930–2017), 138, 143–*144*, 150
Kollek, Teddy, 86
Kosygin, Alexei N., 114
Krapf, Franz (1911–2004), 90, 132, 137
Kressenstein, Friedrich Kreß, 26
Kreutzer, Stefan M., 1, 16
Krone, Heinrich, 88
Kühlmann, Richard von, 16
Kut-al-Amara, 21

L

Lahn, Lothar, 118
Lahr, Rolf (1908–1985), 95, 97, 101
Lansing, Robert, 18
Lawrence, Thomas Edward, of Arabia (1888–1935), 17, 20–21
Lean, David, 20
Lebel, Jennie, 2
Leber, Georg, 134
Levavi, Arieh, 89, 105
Libby, Lewis, 153

Lichtheim, Richard, 25, 28
Loth, Wilfried, 2
Luxembourg Agreement, xii, 67–74, 158
Lübke, Heinrich, 94

M

Mallmann, Klaus-Michael, 2
Maude, Frederick, 21
McGhee, George, 85–87
McMahon, Henry, 20
McNamara, Robert, 83, 114
Mehmed V, Sultan, 14
Meir, Golda (1898–1978): German ambassador, 91, 93; German reparations, 95–96; welcomes Willy Brandt, *125*; Yom Kippur War, 127–130
Mende, Erich, 83
Merkel, Angela, *156*
Meroz, Yohanan, 78
Metternich, Paul Graf Wolff, 19
Meyer-Landrut, Andreas, 144
Meyer-Lindenberg, Hermann, 100, 117
Mikle Israel, 10
Moltke, Helmuth von, 13
Mordtmann, Johann Heinrich, 18
Morgenthau, Henry Sr, 18
Morgenthau, Henry Jr, 66, 102
Moscow Declaration, 93
Mubarak, Mohammed, 141–142
Munir, Ahned, 25
Murad Ghalib, Mohammed, 119
Mussolini, Benito, 54

N

Nachrichtenstelle für den Orient, 15
Nadolny, Rudolf, 16
Naguib, Mohammed, 75, 79
Narkiss, Uzi, 113
Nasser, Gamal Abdel (1918–1970), 81, 99, 127, 140; invitation to Walter Ulbricht, 84; reaction to establishment of diplomatic relations between Germany and Israel, 90; Suez War, 79, *79*; Six-Day War, 108–109, 112
NATO double-track decision, 141–142, 149, 151
Nazareth, 42
Nazis in Palestine, 40
Netanjahu, Benjamin, 156, 160
Nixon, Richard (1913–1994), 120, 129–131, 135–137
Nord, Erich, 31, 33–34

O

Obama, Barack, 153
Oil, 57, 135
Olympic games 1972, 124–126

Oppenheim, Max von, x, 14–16
Osterheld, Horst, 86–87
Ostpolitik, 120, 159
O'Toole, Peter, 20
Ottoman Empire, 10–13, 17–18, 20, 27

P

Palestine, Kaiser Wilhelm, 11; Balfour Declaration, 30; clashes between Jews and Arabs, 32–34; division 1937, 42–43; division 1947, 53–54; German policy, 40; Nazis in Palestine, 40; Palestinian state 'deadly threat to Israel', 142
Pascha, Djemal, 24–26
Pascha, Enver, 12
Pascha, Talaat, 26–27
Pasha, Abdel Rahman Azzam, 62
Pasha, Abdul, 75
Pauls, Rolf (1915–2002), 91–93, 98
Pawelke, Günther (1900—1976), 49, 72–73, 75–76
Peel, William Robert Wellesley (1867–1937), 42
Peel Plan, 42–43
Peled, Benny, 128
Peres, Shimon (1923–2016), 81, 87, 92, 151
Perle, Richard, 153
Pfeiffer, Gerhard, 99–100
Pferdmenges, Robert, 88
Pinkas, David Z., 68
PLO (Palestine Liberation Organization), 139–140, 142
Pomiankowski, Josef, 17
Pourtalès, Friedrich, 13
Powell, Colin, 152
Putin, Vladimir, 159
Puttkamer, Jesco von, 125

R

Rabin, Yitzhak (1922–1995), 113, *140*–141, 151
Rahn, Rudolf, 49
Rath, Ari, 93, 97
Redies, Helmut, 99, 113
Reparations. *See* restitution
Restitution, 65, 67–74, 94–98, 102
Ribbentrop, Joachim von (1893–1945), 49, 52, 55–56
Rice, Condoleezza, 153–154
Riesser, Hans, 72
Roberts, Frank, 86
Rommel, Erwin, 48, 115
Röhl, John, 9
Rove, Carl, 153
Ruhfus, Jürgen, 144
Rumsfeld, Donald, 132, 152–154
Ruppin, Arthur, 25
Rusk, Dean, 85

S

Sadat, Anwar (1918–1981): PLO, 140; terror attack in Munich 1972, 124; trip to Jerusalem, 140; Yom Kippur War, 127, 130
Sanders, Liman von, 23
Savidor, Menachem, 142
Scali, John, 130
Schabinger, Emil, 25–26
Schärf, Adolf, 91
Scheel, Walter (1919–2016), German minister, 86, 94, 120–122, 127, 132, 134, 137
Schmid, Heinrich, 60
Schmidt, Helmut (1918–2015), 2, 121–122, 139, 141, 146
Schöner, Josef, 68, 94
Schnirer, Tobias, 8
Schröder, Gerhard (CDU, 1910–1989), Foreign minister, 81, 84–86, 94, 101
Schröder, Gerhard (SPD, 1944–), German chancellor, 151, 154–155
Schumann, Frederik, 2
Schwanitz, Wolfgang G. (German historian), 2, 16, 27, 52
Second World War: Barbarossa, 50; Directive No. 30, 50; Directive No. 32, 50; Husseini's anti-Semitism, 48, 55; Holocaust, 56; Iraq, coup d'etat, 48–50; meeting between Hitler and Hussdini, 51–53; meeting between Hitler and Mussolini, 54; Muslim SS division, 55; Red Cross, 56; Special Force Junck, 49; Special Staff F, 51, 55
Seidener, Josef, 8
Seydoux, Roger, 86
Shamir, Yitzchak, 144–145
Sharett, Moshe, 77
Sharif, Omar, 20
Sharon, Ariel, 129
Shazar, Zalman, 92
Shilansky, Dov, 145
Shilumin, 67
Shinnar, Felix, 86
Shukeiry, Ahmed, 60
Sidky, Aziz, 124
Simhoni, Assaf, 80
Six-Day War: Nasser, 108–109, 112; Arab League, 116; Austrian embassy, 115; Brezhnev, 110, 112; Dayan, 111; GDR-reaction, 119; Johnson, 109; Kosygin, 114; UNO resolution 242, 116; West-German reaction, 116–117
Soviet Union: NATO double-track decision, 141–142, 149; Suez War, 79; Six-Day War, 110, 112, 114, 145; Yom Kippur War, 130–131
Staden, von Berndt (1919–2014, German ambassador in Washington, State Secretary), 135–137, 142–143
Stavenhagen, Lutz, 151
Steltzer, Hans-Georg, 133
Strauß, Franz Josef (1915–1988, German minister of defence), 81, 87, 132, 137

Suez War, xii, 79
Sykes-Picot agreement, 21

T

Templars. *See* German Templars
Thatcher, Margaret, 143
Tiberias, 42
Townsend, Charles, 21
Tributzahlungen, 102
Trump, Donald, 159–160
Tyler, William, 84

U

UAR: United Arab Republic=Egypt, recognition of GDR, 101, 119–120
Ulbricht, Walter: visit to Egypt, 84–86, 99
UNO: division of Palestine 1947, 53, 61, 181; Six-Day War, Resolution 242, 116; Yom Kippur War, Resolutions 338 and 340, 130–131
US policy: Adenauer in Washington, 76; Armenian genocide, 18; German arms sales to Israel, 84–87; Suez War, 79; Six-Day War, 109, 114; US embassy in Jerusalem, 160; War against Iraq, 150, 152–156; Yom Kippur War, 127, 129–137, 159
U Thant, 108

V

Vance, Cyrus, 141
Vogel, Rolf, 3
Voigt, Hermann, 78

W

Wailing Wall, 11, 111, 115
Waldheim, Kurt, 116, 131
Wangenheim, Hans Freiherr von, 24
Warburg, Otto, 27
Waßmuß, Wilhelm, 16–17
Weingart, Markus A., 2
Weiß, Gerhard, 113
Weizsäcker, Ernst von, 48
Wilhelm II (1859–1941, King of Prussia and German Emperor), x, 1–2, 8, 23–24, 40, 49; Jewish state, 6–8; Jews, 25; jihad, 13; meeting with Herzl, 8, 10; Muslims, 10; Palestine, 10–12; protection of Jews, 27–28
Will, Alexander, 1
Wilson, Woodrow, 27
Winzer, Otto, 99
Wischnewski, Hans-Jürgen, 122
Wolff, Heinrich (1881–1946, German Consul general in Jerusalem), 31, 35–36, 38

Wolff-Metternich, Paul Graf, 19
Wolffsohn, David, 8
Wolfowitz, Paul, 153
World War I. *See* First World War
World War II. *See* Second World War

Y

Yamani, Ahmed, 138
Yariv, Aharon, 80, 131
Yom Kippur War: DEFCON 3, 130; Egypt's Third army, 130–131; Germany and Kissinger, 135; Golan front, 128; jihad against Israel, 130; Kissinger, 127, 129–131, 159; and Nixon, 138; Suez front, 128; US air lift, 129; West-Germany, 132–135

Z

Zamir, Zvi, 138
Zionism, 6–7, 54, 60
Zimmermann, Armin, 134
Zinn, Georg August, 94

www.ingramcontent.com/pod-product-compliance
Lightning Source LLC
Chambersburg PA
CBHW071203070526
44584CB00019B/2894